W9-BGT-912

BLACK WRITERS AND THE AMERICAN CIVIL WAR

To my nieces and nephews.

BLACK WRITERS AND THE AMERICAN CIVIL WAR

Edited, with an Introduction,
by
Richard A. Long

THE
BLUE & GREY
PRESS

I wish to express my deep appreciation to Carolyn Clarke
for her help with this project and to
Sara Hollis for her assistance with a preparatory project.

Copyright © 1988 by The Blue & Grey Press,
a division of Book Sales, Inc.
110 Enterprise Avenue
Secaucus, NJ 07094

All Rights Reserved.

Manufactured in the United States of America.
ISBN: 1-55521-248-4

CONTENTS

INTRODUCTION

While there is a general awareness of the fact that the slavery question was central to the causes of the Civil War, many historians, amateur and professional, have sought more elevated, more nuanced reasons for the conflict, or have sought villians in a relatively powerless group of people, the Abolitionists. A parallel to this attitude has been a tendency to neglect the Black presence in the Civil War and the resulting perception that Blacks were almost wholly passive. That there is a body of highly literate description of and reaction to the war by Blacks who were active in the war period is unknown outside of a small circle of scholars and Black history enthusiasts.

In this collection we present selections from eight Black men and women, all of whom were directly involved in the war, to demonstrate the form and content of a larger body of writing.

The neglect of these writers, despite the great fame of one of them, Frederick Douglass, both in his time and among later generations, reflects a general cultural disposition to neglect Black contributions to and participation in the stream of American life. The historiography of the Civil War, which has both its amateur and professional wings, is no exception, especially enhanced in this case by a kind of pathological solicitude for the war as a crime engineered by alien forces against a primordial innocence.

Black participation in the war, whether or not the devil theory requires such neglect, has generally been given minimal attention. In the introduction to his important *The Negro's Civil War*, James M. McPherson quotes from W.E. Woodward who, in a 1928 biography of General Grant, states "The American negroes are the only people in the history of the world, so far as I know, that ever became free without any effort of their own...." Mr. Woodward went on to remark that Blacks strummed banjoes and sang "melodious spirituals." There are perhaps no more W.E. Woodwards who take pen in hand with so little knowledge of the period on which they would write, but his legacy has not yet been dissipated.

In the bibliography of sources used for Bruce Catton's *Centennial History of the Civil War* (1961, 1963, 1965), published in E.B. Long's *The Civil War Day by Day* (1971), a listing numbering over 2,200 items, none of the authors in this collection is cited directly. Certain works by contemporary Black scholars treating the Civil War are listed including Benjamin Quarles's *The Negro and the Civil War* (1953) and *Lincoln and the Negro* (1962), as well as John Hope Franklin's *From Slavery to Freedom* (1952) and the *Emancipation Proclamation* (1963). Quarles and Franklin, of course, take account of the writers in this collection.

The absence of such names as Frederick Douglass and George Washington Williams from the bibliography is all the more glaring since, in its comprehensiveness, the bibliography includes works as disparate as Carl W. Brechan's *The Complete and Authentic Life of Jesse James* (1953) and James Freeman Clark's *A Discourse on Christian Politics* (1854).

The impressive Civil War documentary selection by Henry Steele Commager, *The Blue and the Gray* (1950), which excerpts hundreds of sources including Higginson's *Army Life in A Black Regiment*, is equally reticent concerning all of the eight authors included in this collection. Seven do appear, though some only very briefly, in McPherson's *The Negro's Civil War* (1965) which weaves testimony of all kinds from a mass of sources in order to present a comprehensive view of the participation of Blacks in the war on the Union side.

Four of our authors, Douglass, Brown, Wilson, and Taylor were born into Southern slavery, but each had made an escape from that institution. Two, Rollin and Langston, were born free in the slaveholding South. Langston was taken as a child to free soil to assure his enjoyment of freedom. George Washington Williams and Charlotte Forten were both born in Pennsylvania but in radically different circumstances, he to an illiterate or semi-literate ex-slave father in the Western part of the state, she into a family in Philadelphia well-known in the Black Citadin society there.

One of our authors was a medical practitioner (Brown);

two practiced law (Langston and Williams). Brown wrote extensively in several genres, Williams became an historian; both Langston and Douglass served as U.S. Ministers to Haiti. Forten translated at least one popular novel from the French. Frances Ann Rollins was a young schoolteacher with literary aspirations. All-in-all the eight authors represent a remarkable range of talent and achievement.

The participation of our eldest authors in the war was various. Douglass, of course, as the pre-eminent spokesman for Blacks, commented in his periodical, *Douglass' Monthly*, and in frequent speeches and letters on all aspects of the war and its meaning for Blacks. When the Union finally gave its consent to the recruitment of Black soldiers, Douglass actively recruited for the army, as did William Wells Brown and James Mercer Langston: the two younger men, Wilson and Williams, the latter underage, served in the Union Army. Both Charlotte Forten and Susie King Taylor served behind the federal lines in the Port Royal area of South Carolina, Forten as a teacher in the schools conducted by the Federal government and private associations; Taylor as a laundress and as a teacher to men of the Thirty-Third United States Colored Troops. Frances Anne Rollin, a school girl during the war, returned to her native Charleston as a teacher immediately after the war.

Two of the authors are represented by writings contemporary with the war; Douglass by periodical pieces and speeches, Charlotte Forten by entries from her journal for the years 1862 and 1863. Immediately after the war William Wells Brown wrote *The Negro in the American Rebellion*, an overall history, and shortly after Francis Anne Rollin completed her biographical enterprise, *Life and Public Services of Martin R. Delany*, published in 1868 and republished with some additions in 1883. In the 1880's two large-scale histories of the war, both by the former soldiers, both based on archival research, newspaper accounts, and oral testimony appear: George Washington Williams' *A History of the Negro Troops in the War of the Rebellion* and Joseph T. Wilson's *The Black Phalanx*. In 1894, John Mercer Langston published his interesting, if stilted, *From the Virginia Plantation to the National Capitol*, with chapters devoted to the

Civil War and Reconstruction.   At the dawn of the century Susie King Taylor's slim book, apparently long in gestation, *Reminiscences of My Life in Camp* ,appeared.

All of these writers were engaged, as have been most Black writers in American history, in redressment, in placing the story of Black men and women in its fullness on view against a chorus of disparagement and calumny. Individually and as members of a despised and victimized group, theirs is a considerable achievement despite the obstacles which they surmount with grace and faith. The interplay of their varied testimony in a single volume will, I hope, serve to advance their collective, but yet unattained, aspirations.

WILLIAM WELLS BROWN

WILLIAM WELLS BROWN
(1815-1884)

William Wells Brown was born in Lexington, Kentucky. After being taken to St. Louis as a boy, he spent a year working on a steamboat. Later, he had the good fortune to work in the printing establishment of Elijah Lovejoy, known as the first Abolitionist martyr. Lovejoy, after his press was destroyed in St. Louis, moved to Alton, Illinois where he died defending his new press against a mob. Though the teenage Brown returned to steamboating, where he aided in the escape of several slaves, his intellectual development was such that by 1843 he began to lecture for the Anti-Slavery society, having one of the most brilliant careers on the Abolitionist lecture platform. He went to England in 1849 where he continued his labors and lived for several years.

Brown also found the means to study medicine and began to practice as a physician, but his primary focus until the outbreak of the Civil War was the anti-slavery cause. To this end he brought literary as well as oratorical skills. He had first written *The Narrative of William W. Brown* (1847), probably inspired by the *Narrative of the Life of Frederick Douglass* (1845). Later during his European sojourn he published *Three Years in Europe* (1852) and a novel, *Clotel: Or, The President's Daughter* (1852). Two plays, one of which, *Escape: Or, A Leap for Freedom* (1858), attracted much attention, also came from his pen. Brown had the distinction of being both the pioneer Black American novelist and playwright.

Brown also wrote a general historical sketch *The Black Man: His Antecedents, His Genius, and His Achievements* (1863). By the end of 1866, Brown had produced a significant work of contemporary history in *The Negro in the American Rebellion*. Introducing the work he tells the reader:

In collecting facts connected with the Rebellion, I have availed myself of the most reliable information that could be obtained from newspaper correspondents, as well as from those who were on the battlefield. To officers and privates of several of the colored regiments I am under many obligations for detailed accounts of engagements.

15

In the first chapter of *The Negro in the American Rebellion,* Brown reviews Black participation in the Revolution and the War of 1812, basing this on George Livermore's *An Historical Research...on Negroes as Slaves, as Citizens, and as Soldiers* (1862). Subsequent chapters deal with Denmark Vesey, Nat Turner, John Brown and the "Growth of the Slave Power." With Chapter VII, "The First Gun of the Rebellion," the Civil War story proper begins. and is treated in 330 pages divided into 39 chapters.

Of particular interest are Brown's chapters on the "contrabands," slaves who sought freedom behind the Union lines, and his account of the massacre at Fort Pillow which, while not an isolated example of Confederate practice against Black soldiers, ignited wide outrage.

Brown's literary labors continued and among other works he produced *The Rising Sun, or the Antecedents and Advancement of the Colored Race* (1874), in which he treats Egypt and Ethiopia, as well as Haiti and Liberia, and *My Southern Home, or the South and its People* (1880).

CHAPTER IX
INTELLIGENT CONTRABANDS.

I spent three weeks at Liverpool Point, the outpost of Hooker's Division, almost directly opposite Aquia Creek, waiting patiently for the advance of our left wing to follow up the army, becoming, if not a participator against the dying struggles of rebeldom, at least a chronicler of the triumphs in the march of the Union army.

During this time I was the guest of Col. Graham, of Mathias Point memory, who had brought over from that place (last November) some thirty valuable chattels. A part of the camp was assigned to them. They built log huts, and obtained from the soldiers many comforts, making their quarters equal to any in the camp.

They had friends and relatives. Negroes feel as much sympathy for their friends and kin as the whites; and, from November to the present time, many a man in Virginia has lost a very likely slave, for the camp contains now upwards of a hundred fat and healthy negroes, in addition to its original number from Mathias Point.

One of the number deserves more honor th
corded to Toussaint L'Ouverture in the brilliant
livered by Wendell Phillips. He is unquestionabl
of the Potomac, and deserves to be placed by the s.
most renowned black brethren.

The name of this negro is James Lawson , born near
Hempstead, Virginia, and he belonged to a Mr. Taylor. He
made his escape last December. On hearing his praises spoken by the captains of the gunboats on the Potomac, I was
rather indisposed to admit the possession of all the qualities
they give him credit for, and thought possible his exploits
had been exaggerated. His heroic courage, truthfulness, and
exalted Christian character seemed too romantic for their realization. However, my doubts on that score were dispelled;
and I am a witness of his last crowning act.

Jim, after making his escape from Virginia, shipped on
board of "The Freeborn," flag-gunboat, Lieut. Samuel Magaw
commanding. He furnished Capt. Magaw with much valuable intelligence concerning the rebel movements, and, from
his quiet, every-day behavior, soon won the esteem of the
commanding officer.

Capt. Magaw, shortly after Jim's arrival on board "The
Freeborn," sent him upon a scouting tour through the rebel
fortifications, more to test his reliability than anything else;
and the mission , although fraught with great danger, was
executed by Jim in the most faithful manner. Again Jim was
sent into Virginia, landing at the White House, below Mount
Vernon, and going into the interior for several miles; encountering the fire of picketguards and posted sentries; returned in safety to the shore; and was brought off in the captain's gig, under the fire of the rebel musketry.

Jim had a wife and four children at that time still in Virginia. They belonged to the same man as Jim did. He was
anxious to get them; yet it seemed impossible. One day in
January, Jim came to the captain's room, and asked for permission to be landed that evening on the Virginia side, as he
wished to bring off his family. "Why, Jim," said Capt. Magaw, "how will you be able to pass the pickets?"

"I want to try, captain: I think I can get 'em over safely,"
meekly replied Jim.

"Well, you have my permission;" and Capt. Magaw ordered one of the gunboats to land Jim that night on whatever part of the shore he designated, and return for him the following evening.

True to his appointment, Jim was at the spot with his wife and family, and was taken on board the gunboat, and brought over to Liverpool Point, where Col. Graham had given them a log-house to live in, just back of his own quarters. Jim ran the gauntlet of the sentries unharmed, never taking to the roads, but keeping in the woods, every foot-path of which, and almost every tree, he knew from his boyhood up.

Several weeks afterwards another reconnoissance was planned, and Jim sent on it. He returned in safety, and was highly complimented by Gens. Hooker, Sickles, and the entire flotilla.

On Thursday, week ago, it became necessary to obtain correct information of the enemy's movements. Since then, batteries at Shipping and Cockpit Points had been evacuated, and their troops moved to Fredericksburg. Jim was the man picked out for the occasion, by Gen. Sickles and Capt. Magaw. The general came down to Col. Graham's quarters, about nine in the evening, and sent for Jim. There were present, the general, Col. Graham, and myself. Jim came into the colonel's.

"Jim," said the general, "I want you to go over to Virginia tonight, and find out what forces they have at Aquia Creek and Fredericksburg. If you want any men to accompany you, pick them out."

"I know *two* men that would like to go," Jim answered.

"Well, get them, and be back as soon as possible."

Away went Jim over to the contraband camp, and, returning almost immediately, brought into our presence two very intelligent looking darkies.

"Are you all ready?" inquired the general.

"All ready, sir," the trio responded.

"Well, here, Jim, you take my pistol," said Gen. Sickles, unbuckling it from his belt; "and, if you are successful, I will give you $100."

Jim hoped he would be, and, bidding us good-by, started off for the gunboat "Satellite," Capt. Foster, who landed them a short distance below the Potomac Creek Batteries. They were to return early in the morning, but were unable, from the great distance they went in the interior. Long before daylight on Saturday morning, the gunboat was lying off at the appointed place. As the day dawned, Capt. Foster discovered a mounted picket guard near the beach, and almost at the same instant saw Jim to the left of them, in the woods, sighting his gun at the rebel cavalry. He ordered the "gig" to be manned, and rowed to the shore. The rebels moved along slowly, thinking to intercept the boat, when Foster gave them a shell, which scattered them. Jim, with only one of his original companions, and two fresh contrabands, came on board. Jim had *lost the other*. He had been challenged by a picket when some distance in advance of Jim, and the negro, instead of answering the summons, fired the contents of Sickles's revolver at the picket. It was an unfortunate occurrence; for at that time the entire picket-guard rushed out of a small house near the spot, and fired the contents of their muskets at Jim's companion, killing him instantly. Jim and the other three hid themselves in a hollow, near a fence, and after the pickets gave up pursuit, crept through the woods to the shore. From the close proximity of the rebel pickets, Jim could not display a light, which was the signal for Capt. Foster to send a boat.

Capt. Foster, after hearing Jim's story of the shooting of his companion, determined to avenge his death; so, steaming his vessel close in to the shore, he sighted his guns for a barn, where the rebel cavalry were hiding behind. He fired two shells: one went right through the barn, killing four of the rebels, and seven of their horses. Capt. Foster, seeing the effect of his shot, said to Jim, who stood by, "Well, Jim, I've avenged the death of poor Cornelius" (the name of Jim's lost companion).

Gen. Hooker has transmitted to the War Department an account of Jim's reconnoissance to Fredericksburg, and unites with the army and navy stationed on the left wing of the Potomac, in the hope that the Government will present Jim with a fitting recompense for his gallant services. - *War Correspondent of the New York Times.*

On Thursday, beyond Charlestown, our pickets descried a

solitary horseman, with a bucket on his arm, jogging soberly towards them. He proved to be a dark mulatto, of about thirty-five. As he approached, they ordered a halt.

"Where are you from?"

"Southern Army, cap'n," giving the military salute.

"Where are you going?"

"Coming to yous all."

"What do you want?"

"Protection, boss. You won't send me back, will you?"

"No: come in. Whose servant are you?"

"Cap'n Rhett's, of South Carliny: you's heard of Mr. Barnwell Rhett, editor of 'The Charleston Mercury'? His brother commands a battery."

"How did you get away?"

"Cap'n gove me fifteen dollars this morning, and said, 'John, go out, and forage for butter and eggs.' So you see, boss (with a broad grin), I'se out foraging! I pulled my hat over my eyes and jogged along on the cap'n's horse (see the brand S.C. on him?) with this basket on my arm, right by our guards and pickets. They never challenged me once. If they had, though, I brought the cap'n's pass." And the new comer produced this document from his pocket-book written in pencil, and carefully folded. I send you the original:-

"Pass my servant, John, on horseback, anywhere between Winchester and Martinsburg, in search of butter, &c, &c.

        "A BURNETT RHETT, *Capt. Light Artillery, Lee's Battalion.*"

"Are there many negroes in the rebel corps?"

"Heaps, boss."

"Would the most of them come to us if they could?"

"All of them, cap'n. There isn't a little pickanniny so high (waving his hand two feet from the ground) that wouldn't."

"Why did *you* expect protection?"

"Heard so in Maryland, before the Proclamation."

"Where did you hear about the Proclamation?"

"Read it, sir, in a Richmond paper."

"What is it?"

"That every slave is to be emancipated on and after the thirteenth day of January. I can't state it, boss."

"Something like it. When did you learn to read?"

"In '49, sir. I was head waiter at Mrs. Nevitt's boarding-house in Savannah, and Miss Walcott, a New-York lady, who was stopping there, taught me."

"Does your master know it?"

"Capt. Rhett doesn't know it, sir; but he isn't my master. He thinks I'm free, and hired me at twenty five dollars a month; but he never paid me any of it. I belong to Mrs. John Spring. She used to hire me out summers, and have me wait on her every winter, when she came South. After the war, she couldn't come, and they were going to sell me for Government because I belonged to a Northerner. Sold a great many negroes in that way. But I slipped away to the army. Have tried to come to you twice before in Maryland, but couldn't pass our pickets."

"Were you at Antietam?"

"Yes, boss. Mighty hard battle!"

"Who whipped?"

"Yous all, massa. They say you didn't; but I saw it, and know. If you had fought us that next day,-Thursday,-you would have captured our whole army. They say so themselves."

"Who?"

"Our officers, sir."

"Did you ever hear of old John Brown?"

"Hear of *him*? Lord bless you, yes, boss: I've read his life, and have it now in my trunk in Charleston; sent to New York by the steward of 'The James Adger,' and got it. I've read it to heaps o the colored folks. Lord, they think John Brown was almost a god. Just say you was a friend of his, and any slave will almost kiss your feet, if you let him. They say, if he was only alive now, he would be king. How it did frighten the white folks when he raised the insurrection! It was Sunday when we heard of it. They wouldn't let a negro go into the streets. I was waiter at the Mills House in Charleston. There was a lady from Massachusetts, who came down to breakfast that morning at my table. 'John,' she says, 'I want to see a negro church; where is the principal one?' 'Not any open to-day, mistress,' I told her. 'Why not?' 'Because a Mr. John Brown has raised an insurrection in Virginny.' 'Ah!' she says; 'well, they'd better look out, or they'll get the white churches shut up in that way some of these days, too!' Mr. Nicholson, one of the proprietors, was listening from the office to hear what she said. Wasn't that lady watched after that? I have a History of San Domingo, too, and a Life of Fred. Douglass, in my trunk, that I got in the same way."

"What do the slaves think about the war?"

"Well, boss, they all wish the Yankee army would come. The white folks tell them all sorts of bad stories about you all; but they don't believe them."

John was taken to Gen. McClellan, to whom he gave all the information he possessed about the position, numbers, and organization of the rebel army. His knowledge was full and valuable, and is corroborated by all the facts we have learned from other sources.

CHAPTER XI
HEROISM OF NEGROES ON THE HIGH SEAS.

In the month of June, 1861, the schooner "S.J. Waring," from New York, bound to South America, was captured on the passage by the rebel privateer "Jeff. Davis," a prize crew put on board, consisting of a captain, mate, and four seamen; and the vessel set sail for the port of Charleston, S.C. Three of the original crew were retained on board, a German as steersman, a Yankee who was put in irons, and a black man named William Tillman, the steward and cook of the schooner. The latter was put to work at his usual business, and told that he was henceforth the property of the Confederate States, and would be sold, on his arrival at Charleston, as a slave. Night comes on; darkness covers the sea; the vessel is gliding swiftly toward the South; the rebels, one after another, retire to their berths; the hour of midnight approaches; all is silent in the cabin; the captain is asleep; the mate, who has charge of the watch, takes his brandy toddy , and reclines upon the quarter-deck. The negro thinks of home and all its endearments: he sees in the dim future chains and slavery.

He resolves, and determines to put the resolution into practice upon the instant. Armed with a heavy club, he proceeds to the captain's room. He strikes the fatal blow: he feels the pulse, and all is still. He next goes to the adjoining room: another blow is struck, and the black man is master of the cabin. Cautiously he ascends to the deck, strikes the mate: the officer is wounded but not killed. He draws his revolver, and calls for help. The crew are aroused: they are hastening to aid their commander. The negro repeats his blows with the heavy club: the rebel falls dead at Tillman's feet. The African seizes the revolver, drives the crew below deck, orders the release of the Yankee, puts the enemy in irons, and proclaims himself master of the vessel.

"The Waring's" head is turned towards New York, with the stars and stripes flying, a fair wind, and she rapidly retraces her steps. A storm comes up: more men are needed to work the ship. Tillman orders the rebels to be unchained, and brought on deck. The command is obeyed; and they are put to work, but informed, that, if they show any disobedience, they will be shot down. Five days more, and "The S.J. Waring" arrives in the port of New York, under the command of William Tillman, the negro patriot.

The New-York Tribune said of this event,--

"To this colored man was the nation indebted for the first vindication of its honor on the sea." Another public journal spoke of that achievement alone as an offset to the defeat of the Federal arms at Bull Run. Unstinted praise from all parties, even those who are usually awkward in any other vernacular than derision of the colored man, has been awarded to this colored man. At Barnum's Museum he was the centre of attractive gaze to daily increasing thousands. Pictorials vied with each other in portraying his features, and in graphic delineations of the scene on board the brig; while, in one of them, Tillman has been sketched as an embodiment of black action on the sea, in contrast with some delinquent Federal officer as white inaction on land.

The Federal Government awarded to Tillman the sum of six thousand dollars as prize-money for the capture of the schooner. All loyal journals joined in praise of the heroic act; and, even when the news reached England, the negro's bravery was applauded. A few weeks later, and the same rebel privateer captured the schooner "Enchantress," bound from Boston to St. Jago, while off Nantucket Shoals. A prize-crew was put on board, and, as in the case of "The Waring," retaining the colored steward; and the vessel set sail for a Southern port. When off Cape Hatteras, she was overtaken by the Federal gunboat "Albatross," Capt. Prentice.

On speaking her, and demanding where from and whence bound, she replied, "Boston, for St. Jago." At this moment the negro rushed from the galley, where the pirates had secreted him, *and jumped into the sea*, exclaiming, "They are a privateer crew from The 'Jeff. Davis,' and bound for Charleston!" The negro was picked up, and taken on board "The Albatross." The prize was ordered to heave to, which she did. Lieut. Neville jumped aboard of her, and ordered the pirates into the boats, and to pull for "The Albatross," where they were secured in irons. "The Enchantress" was then taken in tow by "The Albatross," and arrived in Hampton Roads. On the morning of the 13th of May, 1862, the rebel gunboat "Planter" was captured by her colored crew, while lying in the port of Charleston, S.C., and brought out, and delivered over to our squadron then blockading the place. The following is the dispatch from Com. Dupont to the Secretary of War, announcing the fact:--

"U.S. STEAMSHIP AUGUSTA,
off Charleston, May 13, 1862.

"Sir,--I have the honor to inform you that the rebel armed gunboat 'Planter' was brought out to us this morning from Charleston by eight contrabands, and delivered up to the squadron. Five colored women and three children are also on board. She was the armed despatch and transportation steamer attached to the engineer department at Charleston, under Brig.-Gen. Ripley. At four in the morning, in the absence of the captain who was on shore, she left her wharf close to the government office and head-quarters, with the Palmetto and confederate flags flying, and passed the successive forts, saluting as usual, by blowing the steam-whistle. After getting beyond the range of the last gun, they hauled down the rebel flags, and hoisted a white one. "The Onward" was the inside ship of the blockading squadron in the main channel, and was preparing to fire when her commander made out the white flag.

"The armament of the steamer is a thirty-two pounder, on pivot, and a fine twenty-four-pound howitzer. She has, besides, on her deck, four other guns, one seven-inch, rifled, which were to be taken on the following morning to a new fort on the middle ground. One of the four belonged to Fort Sumter, and had been struck, in the rebel attack, on the muzzle. Robert Small, the intelligent slave, and pilot of the boat, who performed this bold feat so skilfully, is a superior man to any who have come into our lines, intel-

ligent as many of them have been. His information has been most interesting, and portions of it of the utmost importance. The steamer is quite a
valuable acquisition to the squadron by her good machinery and very light
draught. The bringing out of this steamer would have done credit to any
one. I do not know whether, in the view of the Government, the vessel will
be considered a prize; but, if so, I respectfully submit to the Department the
claims of the man Small and his associates. Very respectfully, your obedient servant,

"S.F. DUPONT,
"Flag-Officer Commanding."

The New-York "Commercial Advertiser" said of the capture, "We are forced to confess that this is a heroic act, and
that the negroes deserve great praise. Small is a middle-aged
negro, and his features betray nothing of the firmness of
character he displayed. He is said to be one of the most skillful
pilots of Charleston, and to have a thorough knowledge of
all the ports and inlets of South Carolina."

A bill was introduced in Congress to give the prize to
Robert Small and his companions; and, while it was under
consideration, the "New-York Tribune" made the following
timely remarks: "If we must still remember with humiliation that the Confederate flag yet waves where our national
colors were struck, we should be all the more prompt to recognize the merit that has put in our possession the first tro-
phy from Fort Sumter. And the country should feel doubly
humbled if there is not magnanimity enough to acknowledge a gallant action, because it was the head of a black man
that conceived, and the hand of a black man that executed it.
It would better, indeed, become us to remember that no
small share of the naval glory of the war belongs to the race
which we have forbidden to fight for us; that one negro has
captured a vessel from a Southern privateer, and another has
brought away from under the very guns of the enemy, where
no fleet of ours has yet dared to venture, a prize whose
possession a commodore thinks worthy to be announced in
a special despatch." The bill was taken up, passed both
branches of Congress, and Robert Small, together with his
associates, received justice at the hands of the American
Government.

The "New-York Herald" gave the following account of the
capture:-

"One of the most daring and heroic adventures since the war commenced was undertaken and successfully accomplished by a party of negroes in Charleston on Monday night last. Nine colored men, comprising the pilot, engineers, and crew of the rebel gunboat 'Planter,' took the vessel under their exclusive control, passed the batteries and forts in Charleston Harbor, hoisted the white flag, ran out to the blockading squadron, and thence to Port Royal, *via* St. Helena Sound and Broad River, reaching the flagship 'Wabash' shortly after ten o'clock last evening.

"'The Planter' is just such a vessel as is needed to navigate the shallow waters between Hilton Head and the adjacent islands, and will prove almost invaluable to the Government. It is proposed, I hear, by the commodore, to recommend the appropriation of $20,000 as a reward to the plucky Africans who have distinguished themselves by this gallant service, $5,000 to be given to the pilot, and the remainder to be divided among his companions.

"'The Planter' is a high-pressure, side-wheel steamer, one hundred and forty feet in length, and about fifty feet beam, and draws about five feet of water. She was built in Charleston, was formerly used as a cotton boat, and is capable of carrying about 1,400 bales. On the organization of the Confederate navy, she was transformed into a gunboat, and was the most valuable war-vessel the Confederates had at Charleston. Her armament consisted of one thirty-two-pound rifle-gun forward, and a twenty-four-pound howitzer aft. Besides, she had on board, when she came into the harbor, one seven-inch rifle-gun, one eight-inch columbiad, one eight-inch howitzer, one long thirty-two pounder, and about two hundred rounds of ammunition, which had been consigned to Fort Ripley, and which would have been delivered at that fortification on Tuesday had not the designs of the rebel authorities been frustrated. She was commanded by Capt. Relay, of the Confederate Navy, all the other employees of the vessel, excepting the first and second mates, being persons of color.

"Robert Small, with whom I had a brief interview at Gen. Benham's headquarters this morning, is an intelligent negro, born in Charleston, and employed for many years as a pilot in and about that harbor. He entered upon his duties on board 'The Planter' some six weeks since, and, as he told me, adopted the idea of running the vessel to sea from a joke which one of his companions perpetrated. He immediately cautioned the crew against alluding to the matter in any way on board the boat; but asked them, if they wanted to talk it up in sober earnestness, to meet at his house, where they would devise and determine upon a plan to place themselves under the protection of the Stars and Stripes, instead of the stars and bars. Various plans were proposed; but finally the whole arrangement of the escape was left to the discretion and sagacity of Robert, his companions promising to obey him, and be ready at a moment's notice to accompany him. For three days he kept the provisions of the party secreted in the hold, awaiting an opportunity to slip away. At length, on Monday evening, the white officers of the vessel went on shore to spend the night, intending to start on the following morning for Fort Ripley, and to be absent from the city for some days. The families of the contrabands were notified, and came stealthily on board. At about three o'clock, the fires were lit under the boilers, and the vessel steamed quietly away down the harbor. The tide was against her, and Fort Sumter was not reached till broad daylight. However, the boat passed directly under its walls, giving the usual signal-- two long pulls and a jerk at the whistle-cord--as she passed the sentinel.

"Once out of range of the rebel guns, the white flag was raised, and 'The Planter' steamed directly for the blockading steamer 'Augusta.' Capt. Parrott, of the latter vessel, as you may imagine, received them cordially, heard their report, placed Acting-Master Watson, of his ship, in charge of 'The Planter,' and sent the Confederate gunboat and crew forward to Commodore Dupont."

CHAPTER XIII
THE DISTRICT OF COLUMBIA FREE.

For many years previous to the Rebellion, efforts had been made to induce Congress to abolish slavery in the District of Columbia, without success. The "negro pens" which adorned that portion of the national domain had long made

Americans feel ashamed of the capital of their country; because it was well known that those pens were more or less connected with the American slave-trade, which, in its cruelty, was as bad as that of the African slave-trade, if not worse. It was expected, even by the democracy, that one of the first acts of the Republicans on coming into office would be the emancipation of the slaves of the district; and therefore no one was surprised at its being brought forward in the earliest part of Mr. Lincoln's administration. The bill was introduced into the Senate by Hon. Henry Wilson of Massachusetts. Its discussion caused considerable excitement among slave-holders, who used every means to prevent its passage. Nevertheless, after going through the Senate, it passed the House on the 11th of April 1862, by a large majority, and soon received the sanction of the President. The Copperhead press howled over the doings of Congress, and appeared to see the fate of the institution in this act. The "Louisville Journal" said,--

"The President, contrary to our most earnest hopes, has approved the bill for the abolition of slavery in the District of Columbia.

"We need hardly say that the President's reasons for approving the bill are not, in our opinion, such as should have governed him at this extraordinary juncture of the national history. They are not to us sufficient reasons. On the contrary, we think they weigh as nothing compared with the grave reasons in the opposite scale.

"The enemies of the country will no doubt attempt so to use the act by representing it as the first step towards the abolition of slavery in the States; but this representation, if made, will be a very gross misrepresentation. The Republicans, as a body, our readers know full well, always declared that Congress had the constitutional power to abolish slavery in the District of Columbia, and that Congress ought to exercise the power. They, however, have always declared, with the same unanimity, that Congress does not possess the constitutional power to interfere with slavery in the States. And they now declare so with especial distinctness and solemnity.

"We, of course, except from the scope of the remarks we

have now made such abolitionists as Sumner and his scattered followers in Congress. With the exception of these few *raving zealots, of whom most Republicans are heartily ashamed,* the men who voted to abolish slavery in the District of Columbia avow themselves as resolutely opposed to interfering with slavery in the States as the men who voted against the measure are known to be. Their avowals are distinct and emphatic.

"We hope that the majority in Congress are at length through with such tricks, and will henceforth leave in peace the myrtle of party eye-sores, while they split the oak of the Rebellion."

However, the predictions and hopes of the "Journal" were not to avail any thing for the slavemongers. The Rebellion had sounded the death-knell of the crime of crimes. Too many brave men had already fallen by the hands of the upholders of the barbarous system to have it stop there. The God of liberty had proclaimed that--

> "In this, the District where my Temple stands,
> I burst indignant every captive's bands;
> Here in my home my glorious work begin;
> Then blush no more each day to see this sin.
> Thus finding room to freely breathe and stand,
> I'll stretch my sceptre over all the land,
> Until, unfettered, leaps the waiting slave,
> And echoes back the blessings of the brave."

The "Press," Forney's paper, spoke thus, a few days after slavery had died in the District:--

"The emancipation of slaves in the District of Columbia was one of the most suggestive events of the age. It was an example and an illustration. The great idea of the past century, the idea which had associated and identified itself without institutions, was at last tried by a practical test. Good results came from it; none of the evils dreaded and prophesied have been manifested. It was a simple measure of legislative policy, and was established amid great opposition and feeling. Yet it was succeeded by no agitation, no outbreaks of popular prejudice. The District of Columbia is now a free Territory by the easy operation of a statute law,--by what enemies of the measure called forcible emancipation; and yet the District of

Columbia is as pleasant and as prosperous as at any period of its history. There has been no negro saturnalia, no violent outbreak of social disorder, no attempt to invade those barriers of social distinction that must forever exist between the African and Anglo-Saxon [?]. It was said that property would depreciate; that there would be excesses and violences; that the negro would become insolent and unbearable; that the city of Washington would become a desolated metropolis; that negro laber would become valueless; that hundreds of the emancipated negroes would flock to the Northern States. We have seen no such results as yet; we know that nothing of the kind is anticipated. We have yet to hear of the first emancipated negro coming to Philadelphia. Labor moves on in its accustomed way, with the usual supply and demand. We do not think a white woman has been insulted by an emancipated negro; we are confident that no emancipated negro has sought the hand of any fair damsel of marriageable age and condition.

"Society is the same in Maryland and Kentucky. In accomplishing emancipation in the District of Columbia, we have shown the timid that their fears were but of the imagination, the mere prejudices of education. Slavery has been the cancer of the Southern social system. We employ an old metaphor, perhaps, but it is a forcible and appropriate illustration. It rooted itself into the body of Southern society, attacking the glands, terminating in an ill-conditioned and deep disease, and causing the republic excruciating pain. It became schirrous and indurated. It brought disaster and grief upon them, and the sorest of evils upon us. It brought us blood and civil war, ruined commerce and desolated fields, blockaded ports, and rivers that swarm with gunboats instead of merchant vessels. It was tolerated as a necessary evil, until its extent and virulence made it incumbent upon us to terminate it as such, or to be terminated by it. The champions of this institution, not content with submitting to the toleration and protection of our great Northern free community, have made it the pretext for aggression and insult, and by their own acts are accomplishing its downfall. The emancipation of slavery in the District of Columbia was the necessary and natural result of the Southern Rebellion. It is but the beginning of the results the Rebellion must surely bring. The wedge has only entered the log, and heavy blows are falling upon it day by day."

Great was the rejoicing in Washington and throughout the Free States; for every one saw "the end from the beginning." Our own Whittier strung his harp anew, and sung,--

> "I knew that truth would crush the lie--
>   Somehow, sometime the end would be;
>   Yet scarcely dared I hope to see
> The triumph with my mortal eye.
>
> But now I see it. In the sun
>   A free flag floats from yonder dome,
>   And at the nation's hearth and home
> The justice long delayed is done."

With the abolition of slavery in the District of Columbia, commenced a new era at our contry's capital. The representatives of the Governments of Hayti and Liberia had both long knocked in vain to be admitted with the representatives of other nations. The slave power had always succeeded in keeping them out. But a change had now come over the dreams of the people, and Congress was but acting up to this new light in passing the following bill:--

"Be it enacted by the Senate and House of Representatives of the United States of America in Congress assembled, That the President of the United States be, and he hereby is, authorized,by and with the consent of the Senate, to appoint diplomatic representatives of the United States to the republics of Hayti and Liberia, respectively. Each of the said representatives so appointed shall be accredited as commissioner and consul general, and shall receive, out of any money in the treasury not otherwise appropriated, the compensation of commissioners provided for by the Act of Congress approved August 18, 1856: *Provided* that the compensation of the representative at Liberia shall not exceed $4,000."

The above bill was before the Senate some time, and elicited much discussion, and an able speech was made by Hon. Charles Sumner in favor of the recognition of the independence of Hayti and Liberia. To use his own expres-

sive words, "Slavery in the national capital is now abolished:
it remains that this other triumph shall be achieved.
Norhing but the sway of a slave-holding despotism on the
floor of Congress, hitherto, has prevented the adoption of
this righteous measure; and now that that despotism has
been exorcised, no time should be lost by Congress to see it
carried into immediate execution. All other civilized nations have ceased to make complexion a badge of superiority
or inferiority in the matter of nationality; and we should
make haste, therefore, to repair the injury we have done, as a
republic, in refusing to recognize Liberian and Haytian independence."

Even after all that had passed, the African slave-trade was
still being carried on between the Southern States and Africa.
Ships were fitted out in Northern ports for the purpose of
carrying on this infernal traffic. And, although it was
prohibited by an act of Congress, none had ever been convicted for dealing in slaves. The new order of things was to
give these traffickers a trial, and test the power by which they
had so long dealt in the bodies and souls of men whom they
had stolen from their native land. One Nathaniel Gordon
was already in prison in New York, and his trial was fast approaching: it came, and he was convicted of piracy in the
United States District Court in the city of New York; the
piracy consisting in having fitted out a slaver, and shipped
nine hundred Africans at Congo River, with a view to
selling them as slaves. The same man had been tried for the
same offence before; but the jury failed to agree, and he
accordingly escaped punishment for the time. Every effort
was made which the ingenuity of able lawyers could invent,
or the power of money could enforce, to save this miscreant
from the gallows; but all in vain: for President Lincoln
utterly refused to interfere in any way whatever, and Gordon
was executed on the 7th of February.

This blow appeared to give more offence to the commercial Copperheads than even the emancipation of the slaves
in the District of Columbia; for it struck an effectual blow at a
very lucrative branch of commerce, in which the New York-
ers were largely interested. Thus it will be seen that the nation was steadily moving on to the goal of freedom.

CHAPTER XVII
ARMING THE BLACKS.

The Northern regiments stationed at the South, or doing duty in that section, had met with so many reverses on the field of battle, and had been so inhumanly treated by the rebels, both men and women, that the new policy announced by Adjutant-Gen. Thomas, at Lake Providence and other places, was received with great favor, especially when the white soldiers heard from their immediate commanders, that the freedmen, when enlisted, would be employed in doing fatigue-duty, when not otherwise needed. The slave, regarding the use of the musket as the only means of securing his freedom permanently, sought the nearest place of enlistment with the greatest speed.

The appointment of men from the ranks of the white regiments over the blacks caused the former to feel still more interest in the new levies. The position taken by Major-Gen. Hunter, in South Carolina, and his favorable reports of the capability of the freedmen for military service, and the promptness with which that distinguished scholar and Christian gentleman, Thomas Wentworth Higginson, accepted the colonelcy of the First South Carolina, made the commanding of negro regiments respectable, and caused a wish on the part of white volunteers to seek commissions over the blacks.

The new regiments filled up rapidly; the recruits adapted themselves to their new condition with a zeal that astonished even their friends; and their proficiency in the handling of arms, with only a few days' training, set the minds of their officers at rest with regard to their future action. The following testimonial from Gen. Hunter is not without interest:--

"HEADQUARTERS DEPARTMENT OF THE SOUTH,
Hilton Head, Port Royal, S.C., May 4, 1863.
"*To His Excellency the Governor of Massachusetts, Boston, Mass.*

"I am happy to be able to announce to you my complete and eminent satisfaction with the results of the organization of negro regiments in this department. In the field, so far as tried, they have proved brave, active, enduring, and energetic, frequently outrunning, by their zeal, and familiarity with the Southern country, the restrictions deemed prudent by certain of their officers. They have never disgraced their uniform by pillage or cruelty, but have so conducted themselves, upon the whole, that even our enemies, though more anxious to find fault with these than with any other portion of our troops, have not yet been able to allege against them a single violation of any of the rules of civilized warfare.

"These regiments are hardy, generous, temperate, patient, strictly obedient, possessing great natural aptitude for arms and deeply imbued with that religious sentiment--call it fanaticism, such as like--which made the soldiers of Cromwell invincible. They believe that now is the time appointed by God for their deliverance; and, under the heroic incitement of this faith, I believe them capable of showing a courage, and persistency of purpose, which must, in the end, extort both victory and admiration.

"In this connection, I am also happy to announce to you that the prejudices of certain of our white soldiers and officers against these indispensable allies are rapidly softening, or fading out; and that we have now opening before us in this department, which was the first in the present war to inaugurate the experiment of employing colored troops, large opportunities of putting them to distinguished and profitable use.

"With a brigade of liberated slaves already in the field, a few more regiments of intelligent colored men from the North would soon place this force in a condition to make extensive incursions upon the mainland, through the most densely populated slaves regions; and, from expeditions of this character, I make no doubt the most beneficial results would arise.

   "I have the honor to be, Governor,

    "Very respectfully,

     "Your most obedient servant,

       "D. HUNTER,

       "Major-Gen. Commanding."

Reports from all parts of the South gave corroborative evidence of the deep religious zeal with which the blacks entered the army. Every thing was done for "God and liberty."

Col. T.W. Higginson, in "The Atlantic Monthly," gives the following prayer, which he heard from one of his contraband soldiers:--

"'Let me so lib dat when I die I shall *hab manners*; dat I shall know what to say when I see my heabenly Lord.

"'Let me lib wid de musket in one hand, an' de Bible in de oder--dat if I die at de muzzle of de musket, die in de water, die on de land, I may know I hab de bressed Jesus in my hand, an' hab no fear.

"'I hab lef my wife in de land o'bondage; my little ones dey say eb'ry night, "Whar is my fader?" But when I die, when de bressed mornin' rises, when I shall stan' in de glory, wid one foot on de water an' one foot on de land, den, O Lord! I shall see my wife an' my little chil'en once more.'"

"These sentences I noted down, as best I could, beside the glimmering camp-fire last night. The same person was the hero of a singular little *contre-temps* at a funeral in the afternoon. It was our first funeral. The man had died in hospital, and we had chosen a picturesque burial place above the river, near the old church, and beside a little nameless cemetery, used by generations of slaves. It was a regular military funeral, the coffin being draped with the American flag, the escort marching behind, and three volleys fired over the grave. During the services, there was singing, the chaplain deaconing out the hymn in their favorite way. This ended, he announced his text: 'This poor man cried, and the Lord heard him, and delivered him out of all his trouble.' Instantly, to my great amazement, the cracked voice of the chorister was uplifted, intoning the text, as if it were the first verse of another hymn. So calmly was it done, so imperturbable were all the black countenances that I half began to conjecture that the chaplain himself intended it for a hymn, though I could imagine no prospective rhyme for *trouble*, unless it were approximated by *debbil*; which is, indeed, a favorite reference, both with the men and with his reverence. But the chaplain, peacefully awaiting, gently repeated his text after the chant, and to my great relief the old chorister waived all further recitative, and let the funeral discourse proceed.

"Their memories are a vast bewildered chaos of Jewish history and biography; and most of the great events of the past, down to the period of the American Revolution, they instinctively attribute to Moses. There is a fine bold confidence in all their citations, however, and the record never loses piquancy in their hands, though strict accuracy may suffer. Thus one of my captains, last Sunday, heard a colored exhorter at Beaufort proclaim, 'Paul may plant, *and may polish wid water*, but it won't do,' in which the sainted Apollos would hardly have recognized himself.

A correspondent of the Burlington "Free Press" gives an account of a Freedman's meeting at Belle Plain, Va.

"Some of the negro prayers and exhortations were very simple and touching. One said in his prayer, 'O Lord! we's glad for de hour when our sins nailed us to de foot of de cross, and de bressed Lord Jesus put his soft arm around us, and tole us dat we's his chillen: we's glad we's sinners, so dat we can be saved by his grace.' Another thus earnestly prayed for the army of freedom: 'O Lord! bress de Union army; be thou their bulwarks and ditches. O Lord! as thou didst hear our prayer when we's down in de Souf country, as we held de plow and de hoe in the hot sun, so hear our prayer at dis time for de Union army. Guard 'em on de right, and on de lef', and in de rear: don't lef' 'em 'lone, though they's mighty wicked.' Another (a young man) thus energetically desired the overthrow of Satan's empire: 'O Lord! if you please, sir, won't you come forth out of de heaven, and take ride 'round about hell, and give it a mighty shake till de walls fall down.'

"A venerable exhorter got the story of the Prodigal Son slightly mixed, but not so as to damage the effect at all. He said, "He rose up and went to his fader's house. And I propose he was ragged. And I propose de road dirty. But when his fader saw him coming over de hill, ragged and dirty, he didn't say, "Dat ain't my son." He go and meet him. He throw his arms round his neck and kiss; and, while he was hugging and kissing him, he thought of dat robe in de wardroom, and he said, "Bring dat robe, and put it on him." And when dey was a putting on de robe, he though of de ring, dat splendid ring! and he said, "My son, dat was dead and is alive again, he like dat ring, cos it shine so." And he made dem bring de ring and put it on his hand; and he put shoes on his feet, and killed de fatted calf. And here, my friends, see de'fection of de prodigal for his son. But, my bredren, you are a great deal better off dan de prodigal's son. For he hadn't no gemmen of a different color to come and tell him dat his fader was glad to hab him come home again. But dese handmaid bredren has kindly come dis evening to tell us dat our heabenly Father wants us to come back now. He's ready to gib us de robe and de ring. De bressed Lord Jesus stands leaning over de bannisters of heaven, and reaching down his arms to take us up. O my friends! I ask you dis night to repent. If you lose your soul, you'll never get anoder. I tell you all, if you don't repent you're goin' straight to hell; and in de last day, when de Lord say to you, "Depart from me, ye cursed, into everlastin' fire," if you're 'onorable, you'll own up, and say it's right. O my friends! I tell you de truth: it's de best way to come to de Lord Jesus dis night."

Regiment after regiment of blacks were mustered in the United-States service, in all the rebel States, and were put on duty at once, and were sooner or later called to take part in battle.

CHAPTER XXXI
THE MASSACRE AT FORT PILLOW.

Nothing in the history of the Rebellion has equalled in inhumanity and atrocity the horrid butchery at Fort Pillow, Ky., on the 13th of April, 1864. In no other school than slavery could human beings have been trained to such readiness for cruelties like these. Accustomed to brutality and bestiality all their lives, it was easy for them to perpetrate the atrocities which will startle the civilized world, as they have awakened the indignation of our own people.

We have gleaned the facts of the fight from authentic sources, and they may be relied upon as truthful. The rebels, under Forrest, appeared, and drove in the pickets about sunrise on Tuesday morning. The garrison of the fort consisted of about two hundred of the Thirteenth Tennessee Volunteers, and four hundred negro artillery, all under command of Major Booth: the gunboat "No. 7" was also in the river. The rebels first attacked the outer forts, and, in several attempts to charge, were repulsed. They were constantly re-enforced, and extended their lines to the river on both sides of the fort. The garrison in the two outer forts was at length overpowered by superior numbers, and about noon evacuated them, and retired to the fort on the river. Here the fight was maintained with great obstinacy, and continued till about four, P.M. The approach to the fort from the rear is over a gentle declivity, cleared, and fully exposed to a raking fire from two sides of the fort. About thirty yards from the fort is a deep ravine, running all along the front, and so steep at the bottom as to be hidden from the fort, and not commanded by its guns. The rebels charged with great boldness down the declivity, and faced, without blanching, a murderous fire from the guns and smallarms of the fort, and crowded into the ravine; where they were sheltered from fire by the steep bank, which had been thus left by some unaccountable neglect or ignorance. Here the rebels organized for a final charge upon the fort, after sending a flag of truce with a demand for surrender, which was refused. The approach from the ravine was up through a deep, narrow gully, and the steep embankments of the fort. The last charge was made about four, P.M., by the whole rebel force, and was successful after a most desperate and gallant defence. The rebel army was estimated at from two thousand to four thousand, and succeeded by mere force of numbers. The gunboat had not been idle, but guided by signals from the fort, poured upon the rebels a constant stream of shot and shell. She fired two hundred and sixty shells, and, as testified to by those who could see, with marvellous precision and with fatal effect. Major Booth, who was killed near the close of the fight, conducted the defence with great coolness, skill, and gallantry. His last signal to the boat was, "We are hard pressed and shall be overpowered." He refused to surrender, however, and fought to the last. By the uniform and voluntary testimony of the rebel officers, as well as the survivors of the fight, the negro-artillery regiments fought with the bravery and coolness of veterans, and served the guns with skill and precision. They did not falter nor flinch, until, at the last charge, when it was evident they would be overpowered, they broke, and fled toward the river; and here commenced the most barbarous and cruel outrages that ever the fiendishness of rebels has perpetrated during the war.

After the rebels were in undisputed possession of the fort, and the survivors had surrendered, they commenced the indiscriminate butchery of all the Federal soldiery. The colored soldiers threw down their guns, and raised their arms, in token of surrender; but not the least attention was paid to it. They continued to shoot down all they found. A number of them, finding no quarter was given, ran over the bluff to the river, and tried to conceal themselves under the bank and in the bushes, where they were pursued by the rebel savages, whom they implored to spare their lives. Their appeals were made in vain; and they were all shot down in cold blood, and, in full sight of the gunboat, chased and shot down like dogs. In passing up the bank of the river, fifty dead might be counted, strewed along. One had crawled into a hollow log, and was killed in it; another had got over the bank into the river, and had got on a board that run out into the water. He lay on it on his face, with his face in the water. He lay there, when exposed, stark and stiff. Several had tried to hide in crevices made by the falling bank, and could not be seen without difficulty; but they were singled out, and killed. From the best information to be had, the white soldiers were, to a very considerable extent, treated in the same way. D.W. Harrison, one of the Thirteenth Tennessee on board, says, that, after the surrender, he was below the bluff, and one of the rebels presented a pistol to shoot him. He told him he had surrendered, and requested him not to fire. He spared him, and directed him to go up the bluff to the fort. Harrison asked him to go before him, or he would be shot by others; but he told him to go along. He started, and had not proceeded far before he met a rebel, who presented his pistol. Harrison begged him not to fire; but, paying no attention to his request, he fired, and shot him through the shoulder; and another shot him in the leg. He fell; and, while he lay unable to move, another came along, and was about to fire again, when Harrison told him he was badly wounded twice, and implored him not to fire. He asked Harrison if he had any money. He said he had a little money, and a watch. The rebel took from him his watch and ninety dollars in money, and left him. Harrison is, probably, fatally wounded. Several such cases have been related to me; and I think, to a great extent, the whites and negroes were indiscriminately murdered. The rebel Tennesseeans have about the same bitterness against Tennesseeans in the Federal army, as against the negroes. It was told by a rebel officer that Gen. Forrest shot one of his men, and cut another with his sabre, who were shooting down prisoners. It may be so; but he is responsible for the conduct of his men. Gen. Chalmers stated publicly, while on the Platte Valley, that, though he did not encourage or countenance his men in shooting down negro captives, yet it was right and justifiable.

The negro corporal, Jacob Wilson, who was picked up below Fort Pillow, had a narrow escape. He was down on the river-bank, and, seeing that no quarter was shown, stepped into the water so that he lay partly under it. A rebel coming along asked him what was the matter: he said he was badly wounded; and the rebel, after taking from his pocket all the money he had, left him. It happened to be near by a flat-boat tied to the bank, and about three o'clock in the morning. When all was quiet, Wilson crawled into it, and got three more wounded comrades also into it, and cut loose. The boat floated out into the channel, and was found ashore some miles below. The wounded negro soldiers aboard feigned themselves dead until Union soldiers came along.

The atrocities committed almost exceed belief; and, but for the fact that so many confirm the stories, we could not credit them. One man, already badly wounded, asked of a scoundrel who was firing at him, to spare his life. "No: damn you!" was the reply. "You fight with niggers!" and forthwith discharged two more balls into him. One negro was made to assist in digging a pit to bury the dead in, and was himself cast in among others, and buried. Five are known to have been buried alive: of these, two dug themselves out, and are now alive, and in the hospital. Daniel Tyler, of Company B, was shot three times, and struck on the head, knocking out his eye. After this, he was buried; but, not liking his quarters, dug out. He laughs over his adventurs, and says he is one of the best "dug-outs" in the world.

Dr. Fitch says he saw twenty white soldiers paraded in line on the bank of the river; and, when in line, the rebels fired upon and killed all but one, who ran to the river, and hid under a log, and in that condition was fired at a number of times, and wounded. He says that Major Bradford also ran down to the river, and, after he told them that he had surrendered, more than fifty shots were fired at him. He then jumped into the river, and swam out a little ways, and whole volleys were fired at him there without hitting him. He returned to the shore, and meeting, as the doctor supposes, some officer, was protected; but he heard frequent threats from the rebels that they would kill him.

"Yesterday afternoon," says "The Cairo News" of April 16, "we visited the United-States Hospital at Mound City, and had an interview with the wounded men from Fort Pillow.

"The Fort-Pillow wounded are doing much better than could be expected from the terrible nature of their wounds. But one, William Jones, had died, though Adjutant Learing and Lieut. John H. Porter cannot possibly long survive. Of the whole number,--fifty-two,--all except two were cut or shot after they had surrendered! They all tell the same story of the rebel barbarities; and listening to a recital of the terrible scenes at the fort makes one's blood run cold. They say they were able to keep the rebels at bay for several hours, notwithstanding the immense disparity of numbers; and, but for their treachery in creeping up under the walls of the fort while a truce was pending, would have held out until 'The Olive Branch' arrived with troops, with whose assistance they would have defeated Chalmers.

"So well were our men protected behind their works, that our loss was very trifling before the rebels scaled the walls, and obtained possession. As soon as they saw the Rebels inside the walls, the Unionists ceased firing, knowing that further resistance was useless; but the Rebels continued firing, crying out, 'Shoot them, shoot them! Show them no quarter!'

"The Unionists, with one or two exceptions, had thrown down their arms in token of surrender, and therefore could offer no resistance. In vain they held up their hands, and begged their captors to spare their lives. But they were appealing to fiends; and the butchery continued until, out of near six hundred men who composed the garrison, but two hundred and thirty remained alive: and of this number, sixty-two were wounded, and nine died in a few hours after.

"Capt. Bradford, of the First Alabama Cavalry, was an especial object of rebel hatred, and his death was fully determined upon before the assault was made. After he had surrendered, he was basely shot; but, having his revolver still at his side, he emptied it among a crowd of rebels, bringing three of the scoundrels to the ground. The massacre was acquiesced in by most of the rebel officers, Chalmers himself expressly declaring that 'home-made Yankees and negroes should receive no quarter.'"

The following is a extract from the Report of the Committee on the Conduct of the War on the Fort-Pillow Massacre:

"It will appear from the testimony that was taken, that the atrocities committed at Fort Pillow were not the results of passion elicited by the heat of conflict, but were the results of a policy deliberately decided upon, and unhesitatingly announced. Even if the uncertainty of the fate of those officers and men belonging to colored regiments, who have heretofore been taken prisoners by the rebels, has failed to convince the authorities of our Government of this fact, the testimony herewith submitted must convince even the most sceptical, that it is the intention of the rebel authorities not to recognize the officers and men of our colored regiments as entitled to the treatment accorded by all civilized nations to prisoners of war.

"The declarations of Forrest and his officers, both before and after the capture of Fort Pillow, as testified to by such of our men as have escaped after being taken by him; the threats contained in the various demands for surrender made at Paducah, Columbus, and other places; the renewal of the massacre the morning after the capture of Fort Pillow; the statements made by the rebel officers to the officers of our gunboats who received the few survivors at Fort Pillow,--all this proves most conclusively the policy they have determined to adopt.

"It was at Fort Pillow that the brutality and cruelty of the rebels were most fearfully exhibited. The garrison there, according to the last returns received at headquarters, amounted to ten officers and five hundred and thirty-eight enlisted men, of whom two hundred and sixty-two were colored troops, comprising one battalion of the Sixteenth United-States Heavy Artillery, formerly the First Alabama Artillery of colored troops, under the command of Major L.F. Booth; one section of the Second Light Artillery (colored); and a battalion of the Thirteenth Tennessee Cavalry (white), commanded by Major A.F. Bradford. Major Booth was the ranking officer, and was in command of the fort.

"Immediately after the second flag of truce retired, the rebels made a rush from the positions they had so treacherously gained, and obtained possession of the fort, raising the cry of 'No quarter.' But little opportunity was allowed for resistance. Our troops, white and black, threw down their arms, and sought to escape by running down the steep bluff near the fort, and secreting themselves behind trees and logs in the brush, and under the brush; some even jumping into the river, leaving only their heads above water. Then followed a scene of cruelty and murder without parellel in civilized warfare, which needed but the tomahawk and scalping-knife to exceed the worst atrocities ever committed by savages.

"The rebels commenced an indiscriminate slaughter, sparing neither age nor sex, white nor black, soldier nor civilian. The officers and men seemed to vie with each other in the devilish work. Men, women, and children, wherever found, were deliberately shot down, beaten, and hacked with sabres. Some of the children not more than ten years old were forced to stand up by their murderers while being shot. The sick and wounded were butchered without mercy; the rebels even entering the hospital-buildings, and dragging them out to be shot, or killing them as they lay there unable to offer the least resistance. All over the hillside the work of murder was going on. Numbers of our men were collected together in lines or groups, and deliberately shot. Some were shot while in the river; while others on the bank were shot, and their bodies kicked into the water, many of them still living, but unable to make exertions to save themselves from drowning.

"Some of the rebels stood upon the top of the hill, or a short distance from its side, and called to our soldiers to come up to them, and, as they approached, shot them down in cold blood; and, if their guns or pistols missed fire, forced them to stand there until they were again prepared to fire. All around were heard cries of 'No quarter, no quarter!' 'Kill the d--d niggers, shoot them down!' All who asked for mercy were answered by the most cruel taunts and sneers. Some wre spared for a time, only to be murdered under circumstances of greater cruelty.

"No cruelty which the most fiendish malignity could devise was omitted by these murderers. One white soldier who was wounded in the leg so as to be unable to walk was made to stand up while his tormentors shot him. Others who were wounded, and unable to stand up, were held up and again shot. One negro who had been ordered by a rebel officer to hold his horse was killed by him when he remonstrated; another, a mere child, whom an officer had taken up behind him on his horse, was seen by Gen. Chalmers, who at once ordered him to put him down and shoot him, which was done.

"The huts and tents in which many of the wounded sought shelter were set on fire, both on that night and the next morning, while the wounded were still in them; those only escaping who were able to get themselves out, or who could prevail on others less injured to help them out: and some of these thus seeking to excape the flames were met by these ruffians, and brutally shot down, or had their brains beaten out. One man was deliberately fastened down to the floor of a tent, face upwards, by means of nails driven through his clothing and into the boards under him, so that he could not possibly escape; and then the tent was set on fire. Another was nailed to the sides of a building outside of the fort, and then the building was set on fire and burned. The charred remains of five or six bodies were afterwards found, all but one so much disfigured and consumed by the flames, that they could not be identified; and the identification of that one is not absolutely certain, although there can hardly be a doubt that it was the body of Lieut. Albertson, Quartermaster of the Thirteenth Virginia Cavalry, and a native of Tennessee. Several witnesses who saw the remains, and who were personally acquainted with him while living here, testified it to be their firm belief that it was his body that was thus treated.

"These deeds of murder and cruelty closed when night came on, only to be renewed the next morning, when the demons carefully sought among the dead lying about in all directions for any other wounded yet alive; and those they found were deliberately shot. Scores of the dead and wounded were found there the day after the massacre by the men from some of our gunboats, who were permitted to go on shore, and collect the wounded, and bury the dead.

"The rebels themselves had made a pretence of burying a great many of their victims; but they had merely thrown them, without the least regard to care or decency, in the trenches and ditches about the fort, or little hollows and ravines on the hillside, covering them but partially with earth. Portions of heads and faces were found protruding through the earth in every direction; and even when your Committee visited the spot, two weeks afterwards, although parties of men had been sent on shore from time to time to bury the bodies unburied, and re-bury the others, and were even then engaged in the same work, we found the evidences of the murder and cruelty still most painfully apparent.

"We saw bodies still unburied, at some distance from the fort, of some sick men who had been met fleeing from the hospital, and beaten down and brutally murdered, and their bodies left where they had fallen. We could still see the faces and hands and feet of men, white and black, protruding out of the ground, whose graves had not been reached by those engaged in re-interring the victims of the massacre; and, although a great deal of rain had fallen withing the preceding two weeks, the ground, more especially on the side and at the foot of the bluff where most of the murders have been committed, was still discolored by the blood of our brave but unfortunate soldiers; and the logs and trees showed but too plainly the evidences of the atrocities perpetrated.

"Many other instances of equally atrocious cruelty might be mentioned; but your Committee feel compelled to refrain from giving here more of the heart-sickening details, and refer to the statements contained in the voluminous testimony herewith submitted. These statements were obtained by them from eye-witnesses and sufferers. Many of them as they were examined by your Committee were lying upon beds of pain and suffering; some so feeble that their lips could with difficulty frame the words by which they endeavored to convey some idea of the cruelties which had been inflicted on them, and which they had seen inflicted on others."

When the murderers returned, the day after the capture, to renew their fiendish work upon the wounded and dying, they found a young and beautiful mulatto woman searching among the dead for the body of her husband. She was the daughter of a wealthy and influential rebel residing at

Columbus.   With her husband, this woman was living near the fort when our forces occupied it, and joined the Union men to assist in holding the place. Going from body to body with all the earnestness with which love could inspire an affectionate heart, she at last found the object of her search. He was not dead; but both legs were broken. The wife had succeeded in getting him out from among the piles of dead, and was bathing his face, and giving him water to drink from a pool near by, which had been replenished by the rain that fell a few hours before. At this moment she was seen by the murderous band; and the cry was at once raised, "Kill the wench, kill her!" The next moment the sharp crack of a musket was heard, and the angel of mercy fell a corpse on the body of her wounded husband, who was soon after knocked in the head by the butt-end of the same weapon. Though these revolting murders were done under the immediate eye of Gen. Chalmers, the whole was planned and carried out by Gen. Forrest whose inhumanity has never been surpassed in the history of civilized or even barbarous warfare.

GEORGE WASHINGTON WILLIAMS

GEORGE WASHINGTON WILLIAMS (1849-1891)

George Washington Williams was born in Pennsylvania in 1849 and went to school there and later in Massachusetts. In 1862, at the age of 14 he ran away from home and joined the Union army. Discharged after being wounded, he reenlisted and served until the end of the war. Being discharged in Mexico, he then enlisted in the Mexican army where he rapidly became an officer. He subsequently returned to the United States, once more joined the army, leaving military service finally in 1868.

After his military career he studied theology and began his pastoral career in 1874 in Boston. He began his career as an historian with a short history of the Twelfth Street Baptist Church which he served. After a brief political appointment in the Post Office in Washington, Williams accepted a call to the Union Baptist Church in Cincinnati. He received a political appointment in the Internal Revenue Department and his attention turned to law. He was admitted to the Bar in 1881.

Williams subsequently interested himself in the exploitation of the Congo by King Leopold of Belgium and felt that there should be American involvement. His interest in the Congo was expressed in two pamphlets: "Report Upon the Congo-State and Country to the President of the U.S." (1890) and "An Open Letter...Leopold II...." (1890).

His most important books, however, are *A History of the Negro Race in America from 1669 to 1880* (1883) and *A History of the Negro Troops in the War of the Rebellion* (1888), both of which were exemplary for the time.

In *A History of the Negro Troops* he states:

Myself a soldier in the volunteer and regular army of the United States, in infantry and cavalry, an officer of artillery in the Republican forces of the Mexican army, and recently an officer of the Sixth Regiment of Massachusetts Volunteer Militia, I may claim some military experience. I par-

49

ticipated in many of the battles herein described, including some of the most severe conflicts of Negro troops with the enemy in Virginia. But I have relied very little on personal knowledge, preferring always to follow the official record.

The first two chapters of Williams's history offer a rapid survey of the military involvement of Blacks in ancient and modern times. Beginning with Chapter III he concentrates on the Civil War period, presenting a sober but critical account of Blacks in the conflict. The final chapter of the book, Chapter XVI, "The Cloud of Witnesses" is a survey of the commendation and praise received by Blacks during the war and contains Williams's proposal for a national monument with the following suggested inscription:

On the **first** side of the monument:
A GRATEFUL NATION CONSECRATES THIS MONUMENT TO THE
36,847 NEGRO SOLDIERS WHO DIED IN THE
SERVICE OF THEIR COUNTRY.
"THE COLORED TROOPS FOUGHT NOBLY."

On the **second** side of the monument:
THEY EARNED THE RIGHT TO BE FREE BY DEEDS OF DESPARATE
VALOR: AND IN THE 449 ENGAGEMENTS IN WHICH THEY PARTICI-
PATED THEY PROVED THEMSELVES WORTHY TO BE INTRUSTED
WITH A NATION'S FLAG AND HONOR.

On the **third** side of the monument:
DURING THE CIVIL WAR IN AMERICA, FROM 1861 TO 1865,
THERE WERE 178,975 NEGRO SOLDIERS ENROLLED IN THE UNITED
STATES VOLUNTEER ARMY. OF THIS NUMBER 99,337 WERE EN-
LISTED BY AUTHORITY OF THE GOVERNMENT, AND 79,638 WERE
ENLISTED BY THE SEVERAL STATES AND TERRITORIES.

On the **fourth** side of the monument:

PORT HUDSON	MILLIKEN'S BEND,
FORT WAGNER	OLUSTEE,
HONEY BILL,	FAIR OAKS,
NEW MARKET HEIGHTS,	PETERSBURG,
POISON SPRINGS,	NASHVILLE,
DEEP BOTTOM,	FORT FISHER,
FORT PILLOW,	FORT BLAKELY,
CHAFFIN'S FARM,	HATCHER'S RUN,

Williams is the subject of a biography by John Hope Franklin (1985).

CHAPTER IX
NEGRO TROOPS IN BATTLE.--
DEPARTMENT OF THE SOUTH (1862-1865)

SOUTH CAROLINA had set the other States a dangerous example in her attempts at nullification under President Jackson's administration, and was not only first in seceding, but fired the first shot of the slave-holders' rebellion against the laws and authority of the United States Government. It was eminently fitting, then, that the first shot fired at slavery by Negro soldiers should be aimed by the ex-slaves of the haughty South Carolina rebels. It was poetic justice that South Carolina Negroes should have the priority of obtaining the Union uniform, and enjoy the distinction of being the first Negro soldiers to encounter the enemy in battle. And the honor belongs to Massachusetts in furnishing a graduate of Harvard College, Thomas Wentworth Higginson, as the first colonel to lead the First South Carolina Negro Regiment of Volunteers.

Before Colonel Higginson assumed command of this regiment, in fact before it was organized as a regiment, Company A did its first fighting on Saint Helena Island. From the 3d to the 10th of November, 1862, Company A, under Captain Trowbridge, participated in the expedition along the coasts of Georgia and East Florida. The expedition was under the command of Lieutenant-colonel Oliver T. Beard, of the Forty-eighth New York Infantry. Of their fighting quality Colonel Beard in his report says:

"The colored men fought with astonishing coolness and bravery. For alacrity in effecting landings, for determination, and for bush-fighting I found them all I could desire--more than I had hoped. They behaved bravely, gloriously, and deserve all praise."

From the 13th to the 18th of November three companies of the First South Carolina Colored Volunteers participated in an expedition from Beaufort, South Carolina, to Doboy River, Georgia. In his report of the expedition General Rufus Saxton says:

"It gives me pleasure to bear witness to the good conduct of the Negro troops. They fought with the most determined bravery. Although scarcely one month since the organization of this regiment was commenced, in that short period these untrained soldiers have captured from the enemy an amount of property equal in value to the cost of the regiment for a year. They have driven back equal numbers of rebel troops, and have destroyed the salt-works along the whole line of this coast."

On the 23d of January, 1863, by order of Major-general Hunter, Colonel Higginson sailed in transports from Beaufort, South Carolina, to make a raid into Georgia and Florida. No strategic blow was to be struck, no important manoeuvre was to be executed. But there were two objects in view. Negro regiments were to be recruited in the Department, but the enemy, in retiring before the Union forces, had taken with him all effective Negroes. It was one of the objects of the expedition to secure Negro recruits in the enemy's country. The second object of the expedition was to obtain the far-famed lumber which was to be had by a bold dash into the enemy's country.   These two objects were of sufficient importance to justify the expedition, but Colonel Higginson cherished another idea that had not been canvassed at headquarters. This First South Carolina Volunteers was the only organized regiment of Negro troops in the army of the United States at this time. The tentative effort of General Hunter in raising this regiment the year before had met the inexorable disapproval of the President, and had drawn the fierce fire of the enemies of the Negro. Colonel Higginson knew that if he could get his black soldiers in battle once, the question of their employment in unlimited numbers would be finally settled. So, while he went ostensibly for recruits and lumber, his main aim was to find the enemy and engage him. His force consisted of four hundred and sixty-two officers and men. The vessels that bore the expedition were the *Ben de Ford*, Captain Hallet, carrying several six-pound guns; the *John Adams*, an army gun-boat, carrying a thirty-pound Parrott gun, two ten-pound Parrots, and an eight-inch howitzer; the *Planter*, carrying a ten-pound Parrott gun and two howitzers. The *Ben de Ford* was the largest, and carried most of the troops. It was the "flagship" of the expedition, in a manner. Major John D. Strong was in command on the *John Adams*, and Captain Charles T. Trowbridge commanded the troops on the Planter. For prudential reasons, each vessel sailed at a different hour for St. Simon's, on the coast of Georgia.

On the night of the 26th of January Colonel Higginson found himself on the right track; the enemy he was looking for was not far away. Of his purpose Colonel Higginson says: "That night I proposed to make a sort of trial trip up stream as far as Township Landing, some fifteen miles, there to pay our respects to Captain Clark's company of cavalry, whose camp was reported to lie near by. This was included in Corporal Sutton's programme, and seemed to me more inviting and far more useful to the men than any amount of mere foraging. The thing really desirable appeared to be to get them under fire as soon as possible, and to teach them, by a few small successes, the application of what they had learned in camp."

Back from the river and five miles from Township Landing the much-desired enemy was bivouacked. A troop of skirmishers was landed behind the bend below the landing, with orders to march upon the town and surround it. When the troops arrived by water the town was in possession of the force that had proceeded by land. Colonel Higginson had brought along a good supply of the Emancipation Proclamation to distribute among the Negroes, and these were rather assuring to many who had been led to believe that the "Yankees would sell them into Cuba."

After making a selection of one hundred of the best soldiers in the expedition, Colonel Higginson took up his line of march for the enemy's camp shortly after midnight. The moon shone brightly, but the command soon reached the resinous pines, and clouds of shadows hid it. The column moved on in silence until, when about two miles from its base, the advance-guard came suddenly upon the rebel cavalry and exchanged shots. Colonel Higginson gave orders to fix bayonets, and prepared to receive the enemy kneeling, and the enemy delivered his fire over the heads of the intrepid black soldiers. "My soldiers," says Colonel Higginson, "in turn fired rapidly--too rapidly, being yet beginners--and it was evident that, dim as it was, both sides had opportunity to do some execution.

"I could hardly tell whether the fight had lasted ten minutes or an hour, when, as the enemy's fire had evidently ceased or slackened, I gave the order to cease firing. But it was very difficult at first to make them desist: the taste of gunpowder was too intoxicating. One of them was heard to mutter indignantly, 'Why de cunnel order *cease* firing, when de Secesh blazin' away at de rate of ten dollar a day?'"

The enemy beat a precipitate retreat, and left Colonel Higginson's Negro troops in undisputed possession of the field. The dead and wounded were tenderly taken up by their more fortunate comrades, and the command returned to Township Landing without being again assailed by the enemy. Of the wounded, Surgeon Seth Rogers wrote: "One man killed instantly by a ball through the heart and seven wounded, one of whom will die. Braver men never lived. One man with two bullet-holes through the large muscles of the shoulders and neck brought off from the scene of action, two miles distant, two muskets, and not a murmur has escaped his lips. Another, Robert Sutton, with three wounds--one of which, being on the skull, may cost him his life--would not report himself till compelled to do so by his officers. While dressing his wounds he quietly talked of what they had done and of what they yet could do. To-day I have had the colonel *order* him to obey me. He is perfectly quiet and cool, but takes this whole affair with the religious bearing of a man who realizes that freedom is sweeter than life. Yet another soldier did not report himself at all, but remained all night on guard, and possibly I should not have known of his having had a buckshot in his shoulder if some duty requiring a sound shoulder had not been required of him to-day."

The engagement in which Colonel Higginson's Negro soldiers had courageously and unflinchingly met and returned the enemy's fire was called the *"Battle of the Hundred Pines."* It decided no important military question, but, under the circumstances, it was of great importance to Negro soldiership throughout the entire country. It was one of the first stand-up fights that ex-slaves had had with their late masters, and their splendid bravery was at once a vindication and a prophecy of valor upon other fields that were yet to be fought for freedom.

But this was not the end of the practical military experiences of this Negro regiment during the expedition up the St. Mary's River. The coveted lumber was secured, brick and railroad iron were obtained, and some "contrabands." The return trip of the expedition was signalized by a number of sharp contests with the enemy. The captain of the *John Adams* was killed in the first river engagement, but there was not the least demoralization among the troops. A Negro corporal took the wheel and guided the vessel through a hailstorm of bullets, occasionally taking a shot at the enemy from the pilot-house. The men who were detailed to man the guns fought them with the coolest courage, although they were exposed to the musket and artillery fire of the enemy.

As musketry service was valueless against the enemy upon the high bluffs, most of the troops were confined in the hot and disagreeable hold of the vessel. When the firing began it required great firmness on the part of the officers to keep the men from rushing on deck. A safety-valve to their overflowing martial zeal was permitted by the use of the port-holes under deck, through which they discharged their pieces at will. So eager were they to do service that they fought each other to secure control of the port-holes. Others begged to be put ashore, and exclaimed that it was "mighty mean" to be shut down in the hold when they might be "fightin' de Secesh in *de clar field*."

The expedition was in every way a success; and while it reflected great credit upon the commanding officer, it demonstrated the fact that Negroes well led make capable and reliable soldiers. The country was waiting for just such evidence, and Colonel Higginson's Negro soldiers furnished it. War correspondents who accompanied the expedition or received their information from the officers hurried the news to the rear, and the country was thrilled at learning that its Negro defenders had justified its hopes and disarmed all fear.

During the same week that this expedition was testing the Negro's valor another expedition from the same regiment was performing a perilous march into Georgia. On the 30th of January, 1863, Captain Charles T. Trowbridge, with the small force of thirty men, set out to destroy a rebel salt-works on the coast of Georgia. His Negro troops were familiar with the country and delighted with their military mission. The swamps were numerous and almost impassable, but they heroically dragged a boat over the country in order to cross them, and endured the fatigue, privations, and perils of the undertaking with the fortitude of veterans. They finally reached their objective point, and found thirty-two large boilers, two store-houses, and a large quantity of salt. Captain Trowbridge was a good engineer officer, and the work of destruction was complete. The commanding officer of the Department of the South was highly gratified with the results of the expedition under Colonel Higginson and that under Captain Trowbridge. Although of no great military moment, the war correspondents were easily impressed with the value of the whole affair. The *New York Times* said concerning the expedition:

"THE NEGROES IN BATTLE.

"Colonel Higginson, of the First South Carolina Volunteers, furnishes an entertaining official report of the exploits of his black regiment in Florida. He seems to think it necessary to put his case strongly and in rather exalted language, as well as in such a way as to convince the public that Negroes will fight. In this expedition his battalion was repeatedly under fire--had rebel cavalry, infantry, and, says he, 'even artillery' arrayed against them, yet in every instance came off with unblemished honor and undisputed triumph. His men made the most urgent appeals to him to be allowed to press the flying enemy. They exhibited the most fiery energy, beyond anything of which Colonel Higginson ever read, unless it may be in the case of the French Zouaves. He even says that 'it would have been madness to attempt with the bravest white troops what he successfully accomplished with black ones.' No wanton destruction was permitted, no personal outrages desired, during the expedition. The regiment, besides the victories which it achieved, and the large amount of valuable property which it secured, obtained a cannon and a flag, which the Colonel very properly askes permission for the regiment to retain. The officers and men desire to remain permanently in Florida, and obtain supplies of lumber, iron, etc., for the Government. The Colonel puts forth a very good suggestion, to the effect that a 'chain of such posts would completely alter the whole aspect of the war in the seaboard slave States, and would accomplish what no accumulation of Northern regiments can so easily effect.' This is the very use for Negro soldiers suggested in the proclamation of the President. We have no doubt that the whole State of Florida might easily be held for the Government in this way by a dozen Negro regiments."

In March, 1863, Colonel Higginson was in command of an expedition up the St. John's River, consisting of the First and Second South Carolina Volunteer Negro regiments. He re-occupied Jacksonville, and held it against the enemy until ordered to evacuate the place. In July,1863, Colonel Higginson was placed in command of another expedition, this time ordered up the South Edisto. Like the previous expeditions, this one was composed of Negro troops; and this one, while less imposing in numbers, was charged with a most arduous and perilous undertaking. The infantry force consisted of two hundred and fifty men of Colonel Higginson's First South Carolina Regiment; and besides these there was one section of the First Connecticut Battery.

While Colonel Higginson's South Carolina Negro troops were fighting their way among the rebel batteries which lined the banks of the Edisto, a regiment of Northern Negroes was learning its first lessons in the practical school of war. The Fifty-fourth Massachusetts Volunteer Infantry had already joined General A.H. Terry on James Island, and on the 16th of July, 1863, while on picket, was surprised by the enemy and hurled back upon Terry's main line. The enemy, a body of Georgians, more numerous than the Union force, was nevertheless driven off. Although the attack was a morning surprise, the black soldiers had what Napoleon styled "Two-o'clock-in-the-morning courage." Although confronted by a superior force, the Negro regiment recoiled in good order, delivering a deliberate fire. After this engagement the Fifty-fourth Regiment started the same day for Morris Island, in order to participate in a meditated assault upon Fort Wagner. The Department of the South up to this time had done little effective military service. Most of the Sea Islands had fallen into the control of the Union forces, but the way to Charleston, both by land and water, was guarded by forts, fortifications, and torpedoes. Fort Wagner was a strongly mounted and thoroughly garrisoned earthwork extending across the north end of the island; it was within twenty-six hundred yards of Fort Sumter. The reduction of this fortress left but little work to subdue Cumming's Point, and thus siege guns could be brought within one mile of Fort Sumter, and the city of Charleston--the heart of the rebellion--would be within extreme shelling distance. In this assault the Fifty-fourth Massachusetts was to participate. It had sustained a loss of fourteen killed, seventeen wounded, and thirteen missing while on James Island, and having had a taste of war, was eager for more. It was eminently proper, too, that this Northern Negro regiment from stalwart old Massachusetts should have its fighting qualities tested in Sourth Carolina before a haughty and formidable fortress, from under whose guns the most splendid valor of white troops had recoiled. Before the trying hour they had been subjected to tests not only of martial pluck, but of endurance, hunger, heat, and thirst. At the close of the engagement on the morning of the 16th these Negro soldiers were set in motion from James to Morris Island. The first shock of battle had burst upon them in the ominous silence of the early morning. All day they marched over the island under the exhausting heat of a July sun in Carolina, with the uncertain sand slipping under their weary tread. All night the march was continued through darkness and rain, amid thunder and lightning, over swollen streams, broken dikes, and feeble, shuddering, narrow causeways. Now a halt for no apparent reason, and then the column moved forward to lead in the dance of death. This dreary, weary, and exhausting march was continued till six o'clock in the morning of the 18th, when the Fifty-fourth reached Morris Island.

General Quincy A. Gillmore, an excellent engineer officer, had carefully matured his plans for the proposed assault upon Fort Wagner. It was intended to open a preliminary bombardment at daylight on the 18th, and having by heavy ordnance tranquillized Wagner, to effect its reduction by the bayonet. But a tempest came on suddenly and delayed the cruel ingenuity of war. The thunder roared, the lightning flashed, and the rain fell in torrents. The military operations were suspended in the presence of Nature's awful spectacle. About eleven o'clock aides-de-camp and mounted couriers sped in different directions, and the force on land and its naval support upon the sea began to exhibit signs of preparation for the impending conflict. The pale face and steady look of officers as they transmitted their weighty orders told the nature of their mission here and there on the island. At

12.30 P.M. a flash of fire leaped from the mouths of batteries that were ranged in semicircle for a mile across the island, and the bombardment was formally opened. The naval vessels came into action also, within a few hundred yards of the fortress, and the enemy replied promptly from Wagner, Sumter, and Cumming's Point. A storm of fire and whirring missiles was kept up all the afternoon. The enemy did not serve all his guns in Wagner, but the two operated were fought with admirable skill and daring. The infantry support clung to the bomb-proofs all the afternoon, for the commanding officer evidently knew what the Union troops would attempt at nightfall. At least one hundred great guns were engaged in an attempt to batter down this rebel fortress, and the work of destruction went on all the afternoon. Great clouds of sand were thrown into the air by the tons of metal that struck inside. A shot cut the halyards on the flag-staff, and the rebel banner went fluttering to the earth like a stricken bird.

Some of the Union officers thought the garrison was about to capitulate, but Sumter fired a shot over the fort, as much as to say, "I protest." Out from their bombs rushed a squad of men, and, with the rebel yell, hauled their colors to their place again.

As the day wore away it seemed certain, from the Union stand-point, that the garrison must yield or perish. Through a field-glass Wagner seemed little less than an unrecognizable mass of ruins, a mere heap of sand. It seemed as if the approaches to the bomb-proofs were choked with sand, and that most of the heavy guns were disabled and the fort practically dismantled. Its reduction seemed now near at hand, and the bombardment had facilitated the work of the infantry who were to consummate its reduction by a dash at the point of the bayonet. Towards evening the breaching siege guns and monitors slacked their fire. Soon the beach was filled with life. Couriers dashed in every direction, and the troops were now being disposed for an assualt. At 6 P.M. the Fifty-fourth Regiment reached General Geo. C. Strong's headquarters, about the middle of the island, wet and weary, hungry and thirsty; but there was not time for rest or refreshments. Onward the Negro regiment marched several hundred yards farther, and proudly took its place at the head of the assaulting column. General Strong and Colonel Shaw addressed it briefly, and with burning words of eloquent patriotic sentiment urged the men to valorous conduct in the approaching assault. Both officers were inspired; the siren of martial glory was sedulously luring them to the bloody and inhospitable trenches of Wagner. There was a tremor in Colonel Shaw's voice and an impressiveness in his manner. He was young and beautiful, wealthy and refined, and his heroic words soon flowered into action--bravest of the brave, leader of men! The random shot and shell that screamed through the ranks gave the troops little annoyance. The first brigade consisted of the Fifty-fourth Massachusetts, Colonel Robert Gould Shaw; the Sixth Connecticut, Colonel Chatfield; the Forty-eighth New York, Colonel Barton; the Third New Hampshire, Colonel Jackson; the Seventy-sixth Pennsylvania, Colonel Strawbridge; and the Ninth Maine, Colonel Emory. After about thirty minutes' halt, General Strong gave the order for the charge, and the column advanced quickly to its perilous work. The ramparts of Wagner flashed with small-arms, and all the large shotted guns roared with defiance. Sumter and Cumming's Point delivered a destructive cross-fire, while the howitzers in the bastions raked the ditch; but the gallant Negro regiment swept across it and gained the parapet. Here the flag of this regiment was planted; here General Strong fell mortally wounded; and here the brave, beautiful, and heroic Colonel Shaw was saluted by death and kissed by immortality. The regiment lost heavily, but held its ground under the most discouraging circumstances. The men had actually gained the inside of the fort, where they bravely contended with a desperate and determined enemy. The contest endured for contest endured for about an hour, when the regiment, shattered and torn, with nearly all of its officers dead or wounded, was withdrawn under the command of Captain Luis F. Emilio. He formed a new line of battle about seven hundred yards from the fort, and awaited orders for another charge. He despatchd a courier to the commanding officer of the second brigade that had gone to the front, stating that he was in supporting position, and was ready and willing to do what he could. Word came that the enemy was quiet and that the Firty-fourth was not needed. Captain Emilio then occupied the rifle-pits flanking the Union artillery which he found unoccupied, and being out of musket range, organized his men as best he could. The national colors of the regiment which he had brought back from the scene of the battle he sent to the rear with the wounded color-sergeant, William H. Carney, as they could not serve as a rallying point in the deep darkness. The following extracts from a letter written by a late sergeant of the Fifty-fourth to Captain Luis F. Emilio gives personal observations during this action that are not without their value:

"Regarding the assault on Fort Wagner, I recollect distinctly that when our column had charged the fort, passed the half-filled moat, and mounted to the parapet, many of the men clambered over and some entered by the lage embrasure in which one of the big guns was mounted, the firing substantially ceased there by the beach, and the rebel musketry firing steadily grew hotter on our left. An officer of our regiment called out, 'Spike that gun.' Whether this was done I do not know, for we fired our rifles and fought as hard as we could to return the fire on our right.

"But the rebel fire grew hotter on our right, and a field-piece every few seconds seemed to sweep along our rapidly thinning ranks. Men all around me would fall and roll down the scarp into the ditch. Just at the very hottest moment of the struggle a battalion or regiment charged up the the moat and halted, and did not attempt to cross it and join us, but from their position commenced to fire upon us. I was one of the men who shouted from where I stood, 'Don't fire on us! We are the Fifty-fourth!' I have heard it was a Maine regiment. This is God's living truth! Immediately after I heard an order, 'Retreat!' Some twelve or fifteen of us slid down from our position on the parapet of the fort.

"The men-of-war seemed to have turned their guns on the fort, and the fire of the Confederates on the right seemed to increase in power. The line of retreat seemed lit with infernal fire; the hissing bullets and bursting shells seemed angry demons.

"I was with Hooker's division, cooking for Colonel B. C. Tilghman, of the Twenty-sixth Pennsylvania Regiment, in the battle of Fredericksburg, when General Burnside commanded. I traversed the Hazel Dell Marr, the Stone House, when all the enemy's artillery was turned upon it; but hot as the fire was there, it did not compare to the terrific fire which blazed along the narrow approach to Wagner.

"I care not who the man is who denies the fact, our regiment did charge the fort and drove the rebels from their guns. Many of our men will join me in saying that in the early stages of the fight we had possession of the sea end of Battery Wagner. Indeed, most of the colored prisoners taken there were captured inside the battery.

"When we reached the Gatling Battery drawn up to repel the counter-attack, I remember you were the only commissioned officer present, and you placed us indiscriminately--that is, without any regard to companies--in line, and prepared to renew the charge. The commanding officer, whom I do not know, ordered us to the flanking rifle-pits, and we there awaited the expected counter-charge the enemy did not make."

Captain Emilio, who was an intelligent and experienced officer, thought that in all probability the enemy would make a counter-assault, having driven the Negro troops from the fort, and in forming a new line of battle, he was preparing for such a contingency. Fortunately for the Union forces no counter-assault was delivered, although a desultory firing was maintained nearly all night. Some time after midnight General Thomas G. Stevenson called upon Captain Emilio, where he held the front line, and personally thanked him for the dispositions he had made, and promised to relieve his gallant but weary command. Accordingly, the Tenth Connecticut relieved the Fifty-fourth Massachusetts at two o'clock the next morning, July 19th. Captain Emilio had rallied the stragglers of other regiments on the front line, and now that he was relieved he sent these men to the rear by detachments to join their regiments. With the remnant of the Fifty-fourth he went into bivouac for the night a short distance to the rear, where also some officers and men of this regiment had been swept by the tide of battle, which unfortunately had gone the wrong way that night. On the following morning Captain Emilio, still being in command of the regiment, led it to an old camp formerly occupied by the command near the south end of Morris Island.

The appalling list of casualties shows how bravely this Negro regiment had done its duty, and the unusually large number of men missing proves that the regiment had fought its way into the fort, and if properly supported, Wagner would have been captured. Colonel Shaw led about six hundred enlisted men and twenty-two officers into this action. Of the enlisted men thirty-one were killed, one hundred and thirty-five wounded, and ninety-two missing. Of the twenty-two officers participating three were killed and eleven were wounded. Nearly half of the enlisted men were killed, wounded, or missing, while more than one-half of the officers were either killed or wounded.

From a purely military stand-point the assault upon Fort Wagner was a failure, but it furnished the severest test of Negro valor and soldiership. It was a mournful satisfaction to the advocates of Negro soldiers to point the doubting, sneering, stay-at-home Negro-haters to the murderous trenches of Wagner. The Negro soldier had seen his red-letter day, and his title to patriotic courage was written in his own blood. Pleased with the splendid behavior of the regiment in particular and the special courage of several enlisted men, General Gillmore awarded a medal to the following soldiers of the Fifty-fourth: Sergeant Robert J. Simmons, Company B; Sergeant William H. Carney, Company C; Corporal Henry F. Peal, Company F; and Private George Wilson, Company A.

But it would be unjust to forget the gallant color-sergeant John Wall who fell in the outer trench. He was a brave and competent soldier, but after the United States colors had been taken up and borne to the top of the parapet, henceforth history seems to have kept her jealous eye upon Sergeant William H. Carney, the heroic self-appointed successor to Sergeant John Wall. Sergeant Carney planted his flag upon the ramparts of the rebel fort, and after having received three severe wounds, brought it to the rear stained with his own blood--

"Glares the volcanic breath,
Breaks the red sea of death,
From Wagner's yawning hold,
On the besiegers bold.
Twice vain the wild attack,
Inch by inch, sadly slow,
Fights the torn remnant back,
Face to the foe.

"Yet free the colors wave,
Borne by yon Afric brave,
In the fierce storm wind higher;
But, ah! One flashing fire:
He sinks! The banner falls
From the faint, mangled limb,
And droop to mocking walls
Those star-folds dim.

"Stay, stay the taunting laugh!
See! now he lifts the staff,
Clinched in his close-set teeth,
Crawls from dead heaps beneath,
Crowned with his starry robe,
Till he the ranks has found:
'Comrades, the dear old flag
Ne'er touched the ground.'

"O man so pure, so grand,
Sidney might clasp thy hand!
O brother! black thy skin,
But white the pearl within!
Man, who to lift thy race
Worthy, thrice worthy art,
Clasps thee, in warm embrace
A Nation's heart."

The state colors were lost in the unequal struggle at the beach end of the fort. The rebel general Ripley took them to England with him, saying that whenever Massachusetts should elect a Democrat as governor he would return the flag. Twelve years later William Gaston, the candidate of the Democratic party of the Commonwealth, was chosen governor. True to his resolve, General Ripley returned the flag to the State Government, accompanied by a polite note, and after an absence of nearly thirteen years the beautiful banner came back to Boston, that had witnessed its presentation on the Common; and on the 17th of June, 1875, on the Centennial celebration of the battle of Bunker Hill, it was borne in the imposing procession by an ex-member of the Fifty-fourth who had fought under its folds Saturday night, July 18, 1863! Its wanderings are ended forever, and now it hangs permanently in its appointed place among the regimental flags of the troops of Massachusetts. Like many of the other flags it is rent by bullets and faded by a Southern sun, but it will tell to generation after generation the matchless story of Negro patriotism and valor.

General Ripley's generous and noble letter deserves a place in history:

"8 Stanhope Terrace, Gloster Road, South Kensington,
"London, *January* 12, 1875.

"*To his Excellency the Governor of Massachusetts:*

"I have the honor to forward to your Excellency the Regimental color for the Fifty-fourth Massachusetts Volunteers, which was taken in action on the evening of the 18th of July, 1863, by the garrison of Battery Wagner, under General Taliaferro, being a part of the forces defending Charleston, South Carolina, under my command, when that work was assaulted by the Federal troops under General Gillmore.

"Since the close of the Civil War in America I have been generally absent from the country, and I have seen with regret the failure of expedients attempted to restore peace and content to the Southern States.

"It seems to me, however, that the lapse of time and the course of events have produced a less imbittered state of public feeling than that which existed just after the close of the strife. Under the existing state of things I deem it decorous, if not a positive duty, to promote the oblivion of the animosities which led to and were engendered by the war.

"Such being the case, I prefer to look upon trophies of the character of the color in question as mementos of the gallant conduct of men who like Shaw, Putnam, and other sons of Massachusetts sealed their devotion to the cause which they adopted with their lives, rather than as evidences of prowess on the one side or the other. The custodians of such a memento, I think, should be the authorities of the State served by these gallant men, and I therefore transmit the flag to your Excellency for such disposition as the authorities of Massachusetts shall determine.   Very respectfully,
Your obedient servant,
(Signed)   "R.S. RIPLEY."

At the battle of Thermoplyae three hundred Spartans held the pass against an enormous army, and yet history has made Leonidas representative of them all. Many brave soldiers fell in the forlorn assault upon Fort Wagner, but when some great painter has patriotic inspiration to give this battle an immortal representation, Colonel Shaw will be the central figure; and America will only remember one name in this conflict for all time to come--Colonel Robert Gould Shaw! This was a noble and precious life, but it was cheerfully consecrated to human freedom and the regeneration of the nation. He had good blood, splendid training, wide experience for one so young, and had inherited strong antislavery sentiments. When he had fallen, a flag of truce called for his body. A rebel officer responded, "We have buried him with his niggers." It was thought thus to cast indignity upon the hero dead, but it was a failure. The colonel and his men were united in life, and it was fitting that they should not be separated in death. In this idea his father joined, and the following letter exhibits his feelings:

"Brigadier-general Gillmore, commanding Department of the South:
"Sir,--I take the liberty to address you because I am informed that efforts are to be made to recover the body of my son, Colonel Shaw, of the Fifty-fourth Massachusetts Regiment, which was buried at Fort Wagner. My object in writing is to say that such efforts are not authorized by me or any of my family, and that they are not approved by us. We hold that a soldier's most appropriate burial-place is on the field where he has fallen. I shall therefore be much obliged, General, if, in case the matter is brought to your cognizance, you will forbid the desecration of my son's grave, and prevent the disturbance of his remains or those buried with him. With most earnest wishes for your success, I am, sir, with respect and esteem,
"Your most obedient servant,
"FRANCIS GEORGE SHAW.
"New York, *August* 24, 1863."

Instead of dishonoring the remains of Colonel Shaw by burying him with his brave black soldiers, the intended ignominy was transformed into a beautiful bow of promise that was to span forever the future of the race for which he gave his life. He was representative of all that was good in American life; he had wealth, high social position, and the broadest culture. From his exalted station he chose to fight with and for Negro troops--not only to lead them in conflict, but to die for them and the Republic; and although separated from them in civil life, nevertheless he united the rich and the poor, the learned and the unlearned, the white and black, in his military apotheosis.

"'They buried him with his niggers!'
Together they fought and died;
There was room for them all where they laid him
(The grave was deep and wide),
For his beauty and youth and valor,
Their patience and love and pain;
And at the last day together
They shall all be found again.

"'They buried him with his niggers!'
Earth holds no prouder grave;
There is not a mausoleum
In the world beyond the wave
That a nobler tale has hallowed
Or a purer glory crowned,
Than the nameless trench where they buried
The brave so faithful found.

"'They buried him with his niggers!'
A wide grave should it be.
They buried more in that shallow trench
Than human eye could see.
Ay, all the shames and sorrows
Of more than a hundred years
Lie under the weight of that Southern soil
Despite those cruel sneers.

"'They buried him with his niggers!'
But the glorious souls set free
Are leading the van of the army
That fights for liberty.
Brothers in death, in glory
The same palm-branches bear,
And the crown is a bright o'er the sable brows
As over the golden hair."

CHAPTER X
IN THE MISSISSIPPI VALLEY (1863)

BY some fateful fortuitous circumstance the first fighting of Negro troops in the Mississippi Valley was as severe and fruitless as that of their brethren and comrades in the Department of the South. Port Hudson and Fort Wagner, where the Negro soldier earned his reputation for valor, were much alike. Both were strongly fortified; one was protected by a bayou under its very guns, the other had made captive the ocean in its treacherous trenches; and in each instance the service to be performed demanded the highest qualities of courage, steadiness, endurance, and prompt obedience.

General Grant was busy with the work of reducing Vicksburg. He had proposed to General N.P. Banks, who held the lower Mississippi, to join their forces for the reduction of Port Hudson or Vicksburg first, and then to assault the other position vigorously. General Banks could not well leave New Orleans to the mercy of General Richard Taylor, who, the moment he should learn of Banks's absence up the river, would move into Louisiana from Texas with a fresh army. On the 12th of May, 1863, General Grant had crossed the Mississippi and entered upon his siege against Vicksburg. General Banks, who had been on the Atchafalaya, landed at Bayou Sara at two o'clock on the morning of the 21st of May, and immediately proceeded to embark a portion of his force on steamers, and the remainder moved up the west bank of the river. On the 23d he formed a junction with the forces under Major-general Auger and Brigadier-general Sherman, who had advanced within five miles of Port Hudson. General Gardner, commanding the rebel forces at Port Hudson, despatched Colonel Miles to defeat the proposed junction of Union troops behind his fastness. Colonel Miles attempted to strike Auger's flank while on the march, but was assaulted vigorously and driven back with severe loss. The right wing of General Banks's army, consisting of the troops under Generals Weitzel, Grover, and Dwight, struck the enemy with vigor, and compelled him to contract his outer lines and retire within his intrenchments on the 25th. The investment of Port Hudson was now complete, and on the morning of the 27th a grand assault was ordered upon the enemy's position. During the previous night the First and Third regiments of Louisiana Native Guards, the only Negro troops under General Banks, had been on the march. They had been some months in garrison, but this was their first movement towards active military service. The dust was thick, the air heavy, and the heat oppressive. The morning of the 27th dawned upon these Negro troops with a sort of sullen silence. The sky was flushed, and Nature seemed to hold her breath in horror at the terrible slaughter that was soon to take place. The enemy's works had been constructed with skill and deliberation, at a time when the slave labor of that vicinity was placed at the disposal of the military commander. The works formed a semicircle, and both ends extended towards the river. In the disposition of the troops the two Negro regiments were posted upon the right, immediately in front of two large forts. The presence of these troops in the Mississippi Valley had caused much speculation and considerable feeling. It was coldly proposed now to subject them to the severest test; and the men themselves were not less anxious to win a name than the white soldiers were desirous to see them tried in the fires of battle. The assault was intended to be simultaneous all along the line. At 5.40 A.M. General Banks's artillery opened upon the rebel works, but the attack on the right was not ordered until ten o'clock, and the left did not assault until two o'clock in the afternoon. The First Regiment of Native Guards was composed of free Negroes of means and intelligence, and all their line officers were Negroes: the regiment was under the command of Lieutenant-colonel Chauncy J. Bassett; while the Third Regiment Native Guards, mostly ex-slaves, had white line officers, and was commanded by Colonel John A. Nelson. Colonel Nelson was placed in the position of Brigadier-general, and Lieutenant-colonel Henry Finnegas assumed command of the regiment. This Negro force numbered 1,080, and was formed in four lines. The first two lines were led by Lieutenant-colonel Bassett. When the order for the assault was given, the men moved forward in quick time, and then changed it into double-quick. The line was almost perfect, and the movement was executed with spirit and dash. The enemy held his fire until the assaulting column was within four hundred yards of the point of attack. Suddenly the earth quaked, and a sheet of fire flashed along the forts; a cloud of smoke rose over the ramparts, and the air was filled with demons of destruction and death--hissing, screaming, howling, and leaping at their black victims with the rapidity of lightning. The slaughter was dreadful, but the shattered, quivering, bleeding columns only wheeled by companies to the rear, reformed at a short distance from the foe, and again gallantly dashed down through the Valley of Death and charged for the guns on the bluff. But the sixty-two pound shot, the shell, canister, and minie-ball were more than infantry could contend with in the open field; the pierced and thinned columns recoiled before such terrible odds. Lieutenant-colonel Henry Finnegas fearlessly led his columns to the assault over the same crimson path, obstructed by the dead and wounded, ploughed by shell, but lighted forever by fadeless deeds of martial valor. The mill of death was now grinding with rapacious greed. The enemy was serving his guns with rapidity and accuracy; the Union gunboats were hurling monstrous shot and shell into the river side of the enemy's work; but all eyes, of friend and foe, were turned towards the remorseless hell of conflict, bristling with bayonetts and glinting with the red flash of shotted cannon, into which Negro troops were being hurled by the inexorable orders of Brigadier-general William Dwight. It was of no avail that these troops fought like white veterans. A deep bayou ran under the guns on the bluff, and although the troops reached its edge, some fifty yards from the enemy's guns, they could not cross it. After Colonel Nelson had become convinced that his men could not carry the forts, he despatched an aide to General Dwight to report the difficulties he had to contend with. "Tell Colonel Nelson," he sternly said, "I shall consider that he has accomplished nothing unless he takes those guns."

> "Theirs not to make reply,
> Theirs not to reason why,
> Theirs but to do and die."

Not a man faltered when the torn and decimated lines were reformed and led over the same field to the same terrible fate. Shell and solid shot severed limbs from trees, tore off tops, and, in falling, these caused the men much annoyance. The colors of the First Louisiana were pierced by bullets and almost severed from the staff. The color-sergeant,

Anselmas Planciancois, was gallantly bearing the colors in front of the enemy's works when a shell cut the flag in two and carried away part of the sergeant's head. His brains and blood stained the beautiful banner, which fell over him as he embraced it in death. In a struggle for the flag the generous rivalry of two corporals was ended by a shot of a sharp-shooter which felled one of them. He dropped upon the life-less body of the color-sergeant, while his successful rival car-ried the colors proudly through the conflict. Captain Andre' Cailloux, of Company E, First Regiment Native Guards, won for himself a proud place among the military heroes of the Negro race for all time. He was of pure Negro blood, but his features showed the result of generations of freedom and culture among his ancestry. He was a man of fine presence, a leader by instinct and education. He was possessed of ample means, and yet was not alienated from his race in any inter-est. He loved to boast of genuine blackness, and his race pride made him an acceptable, successful, and formidable leader. It was the magnetic thrill of his patriotic utterances that rallied a company for the service of his country the pre-vious year. Upon all occasions he had displayed talents as a commander, and gave promise of rare courage when the trying hour should come. It had come at length: not too soon for this eager soldier, if unhappily too early for the cause he loved! During the early part of this action the enemy had trained his guns upon the colors of these Negro troops, and they especially received the closest attention of the sharp-shooters. Captain Cailloux commanded the color company. It had suffered severely from the first, but the gallant captain was seen all along the line encouraging his men by brave words and inspiring them by his noble example. His left arm was shattered, but he refused to leave the field. Now in English and then in French, with his voice faint from exhaustion, he urged his men to the fullest measure of duty. In one heroic effort he rushed to the front of his company and exclaimed, "Follow me!" When within about fifty yards of the fort a shell smote him to his death, and he fell, like the brave soldier he was, in the advance with his face to the foe. It was a soldier's death, and just what he would have chosen.

"'Still forward and charge for the guns!' said Cailloux,

And his shattered sword-arm was the guidon they knew.
But a fire rakes the flanks and a fire rakes the van;
He is down with the ranks that go down as one man."

Six desperate charges were made by these Negro troops, and after it was evident that it was by no lack of courage on their part that the guns were not taken, they were recalled from the scene of their fierce trial. The correspondent of the *New York Times* gave the following account of the conduct of these regiments:

"During this time they rallied, and *were ordered to make six distinct charges*, losing thirty-seven killed, and one hundred and fifty-five wounded, and sixteen missing, the majority, if not all, of these being in all probability now lying dead on the gory field, and without the rites of sepulture; for when by flag of truce our forces in other directions were permitted to reclaim their dead, the benefit, through some neglect, was not extended to these black regiments.

"The deeds of heroism performed by these colored men were such as the proudest white men might emulate. Their colors are torn to pieces by shot, and literally bespattered by blood and brains. The color-sergeant of the First Louisiana, on being mortally wounded, hugged the colors to his breast, when a struggle ensued between the two color-corporals on each side of him as to who should have the honor of bearing the sacred standard, and during this generous contention one was seriously wounded. One black lieutenant actually mounted the enemy's works three or four times, and in one charge the assaulting party came within fifty paces of them. Indeed, if only ordinarily supported by artillery and reserve, no one can convince us that they would not have opened a passage through the enemy's works.

"Captain Cailloux, of the First Louisiana, a man so black that he actually prided himself upon his blackness, died the death of a hero, leading on his men in the thickest of the fight. One poor wounded fellow came along with his arm shattered by a shell, and jauntily swinging it with the other, as he said to a friend of mine, 'Massa, guess I can fight no more.' I was with one of the captains, looking after the wounded going in the rear of the hospital, when we met one limping along towards the front. On being asked where he was going, he said, 'I been shot bad in the leg, captain, and dey want me to go to de hospital, but I guess I can gib 'em some more yet.' I could go on filling your columns with startling facts of this kind, but I hope I have told enough to prove that we can hereafter rely upon black arms as well as white in crushing this infernal rebellion. I long ago told you there was an army of 250,000 men ready to leap forward in defence of freedom at the first call. You know where to find them, and what they are worth.

"Although repulsed in an attempt which, situated as things were, was all but impossible, these regiments, though badly cut up, are still on hand, and burning with a passion ten times hotter from their fierce baptism of blood."

On the 30th of May, 1863, General Banks, in an elaborate report to General Halleck, spoke thus flatteringly of the conduct of his Negro troops:

"It gives me pleasure to report that they answered every expectation. Their conduct was herioc, no troops could be more determined or more daring. They made during the day three charges upon the batteries of the enemy, suffering very heavy losses, and holding their position at nightfall with the other troops on the right of our line. The highest commendation is bestowed upon them by all the officers in command on the right. Whatever doubt may have existed before as to the efficiency of organizations of this character, the history of this day proves conclusively to those who were in a position to observe the conduct of these regiments, that the Government will find in this class of troops effective supporters and defenders.

"The severe test to which they were subjected, and the determined manner in which they encountered the enemy, leave upon my mind no doubt of their ultimate success. They require only good officers, commands of limited numbers, and careful discipline to make them excellent soldiers."

Military sentiment was completely revolutionized in the Mississippi Valley respecting the Negro as a man and a soldier; and the Negro himself, with the confidence of a child just learning to walk, was now conscious of his power, and was anxious to consecrate it with lavish generosity to the Government with whose uniform and flag he had been intrusted.

CHAPTER XI
THE ARMY OF THE POTOMAC (1864).

Virginia, the mother of Presidents, was the mother of slavery, and within the limits of this ancient commonwealth the principal battles of the war were fought. Its history, traditions, institutions, topography, its water-ways and magnificent resources, furnished inspiration to the embattled armies that met upon its soil. Richmond was the capital of the Confederate Government, and Petersburg was the base of supplies and the real gate-way to the heart of the rebel Civil Government. After the Mississippi had been opened to the Gulf, the next most important military move was the reduction of Petersburg. General George B. McClellan had menaced the Confederate capital with a splendid army in 1862, but most of the veterans had returned home or had gone into other Departments. Bounty men, substitutes, and conscripts were numerous. By the spring of 1864 a numerous force of Negro troops had been added to this army, and an active and brilliant military career opened up to them.

During the winter of 1863-63 a large number of Negro troops were at persistent drill in Maryland, under Burnside, and in Virginia, under Butler. The first appearance of these troops in the field was in February, 1964, when a brigade was despatched to New Kent Courthouse to reinforce Kilpatrick, who, having made a brilliant and daring dash at Richmond in recoiling before a numerous foe, had burned bridges, destroyed railroads, and made many prisoners. The timely approach of this Negro brigade checked the impetuous and impulsive pursuit of the enemy, and gave Kilpatrick's jaded animals and weary men the relief they so much needed.

On the 7th of April, 1864, General A.E. Burnside, at the head of the Ninth Army Corps, crossed the Potomac and joined General George G. Meade's army, although actual incorporation did not occur until the Rapidan had been passed. This corps contained the majority of Negro troops who had thus far made their appearance in the Army of the Potomac, while later on the Army of the James contained, first, a full division, and subsequently an entire army corps of such troops. The reputation that Negro troops had won at Port Hudson and Fort Wagner served them well in coming in contact with the white troops in the Army of the Potomac. Most of this army was from the Middle and New England States, where Negroes were scarce, and prejudice among the working classes pronouncedly against the Negro, who was by them generally regarded as the cause of the war. But whatever doubt there was concerning the military character of the Negro, it was chiefly silent. There was, therefore, no moral or sentimental proscription to overcome; the army was eager to see the Negro soldier on trial against the flower of Lee's veteran army.

Early in the spring of 1864 Lieutenant-general Grant decided to move Meade's army across the James River, and advance upon Richmond from the south. At the same time he instructed Butler to impel his Army of the James against Petersburg. General W.F. Smith, with the majority of Butler's army, had joined Meade, and the thinned condition of Butler's lines admonished him to keep quiet within his intrenchments. But a restless and ambitious foe grudged him this quiet, and his northern outposts at Wilson's Wharf were chosen as the point of attack. This position was held by Brigadier-general E.A. Wild with a small force of Negro troops, consisting of Battery B, Second Light Artillery, and the First and Tenth Infantry regiments. Fitz-Hugh Lee, at the head of his famous cavalry force, summoned Wild to surrender on the 24th of May. Wild replied that he was there to fight, not to surrender. Lee dismounted his men and assaulted Fort Powhatan about 12.30 P.M. The Negro pickets and skirmishers retired to the intrenchments. The enemy raised a yell and rushed down upon the garrison, but the Negro troops held their fire with the coolness of veterans. When the enemy was well tangled in the abatis, General Wild delivered his fire upon the foe. Confusion and consternation followed, and the enemy recoiled and sought the cover. Lee was angered at Wild's reply, but when he saw his troops shrinking from the deadly fire of ex-slaves, he set his heart on taking the fort. The enemy was determined and desperate in the next charge, but again found the Negroes cool and deliberate in their gallant defence. Lee rightly anticipated the humiliation he would suffer if beaten off by Negro troops, and was busy among the singing bullets urging his men to desperate fighting. It was now determined to impel a massed column against the stubborn fortress, and the savagery of the onslaught told that these Virginia gentlemen were deeply chagrined. But the inferior race met the superior with a steady fire, and the Southern chivalry were driven from the field, after more than five hours' fighting, by their former slaves. Thus ended the battle of Fort Powhatan, and thus the attempt of a division of the enemy's cavalry to turn Butler's flank was a failure. The Negro had fought his first battle in this Department, and exhibited a valor which no one disputed.

General Wild sustained a loss of two killed, twenty-one wounded, and three missing: a total of twenty-six. The enemy suffered a severe loss: twenty to thirty dead were left on the field and nineteen prisoners taken, and thus his casualties footed up about two hundred in the judgement of careful officers who went over the field next day. The correspondent of the *New York Times* wrote of this battle as an eye-witness:

"In Camp, Bermuda Hundred, Virginia, *May* 26, 1864.

"The chivalry of Fitzhugh Lee and his cavalry division was badly worsted in the contest last Tuesday with Negro troops composing the garrison at Wilson's Landing. Chivalry made a gallant fight, however. The battle began at 12.30 P.M. and ended at six o'clock, when chivalry retired disgusted and defeated. Lee's men dismounted far in the rear and fought as infantry. They drove in the pickets and skirmishers to the intrenchments, and several times made valiant charges upon our works. To make an assault, it was necessary to come across an 'open' in front of our position, up to the very edge of a deep and impassable ravine. The rebels with deafening yells made furious onsets, but the Negroes did not flinch, and the mad assailants, discomfited, turned to cover with shrunken ranks. The rebel fighting was very wicked; it showed that Lee's heart was bent on taking the Negroes at any cost. Assaults on the centre having failed, the rebels tried first the left and then the right flank, with no greater success...

"There is no hesitation here in acknowledging the soldierly qualties which the colored men engaged in this fight have exhibited. Even the officers who have hitherto felt no confidence in them are compelled to express themselves mistaken. General Wild, commanding the post, says that the troops stood up to their work like veterans."

General Grant was now ready to turn his attention to the reduction of Petersburg, and General Gillmore, with three thousand five hundred men, crossed the Appomattox and moved on the city from the north over an admirable turnpike. General Kautz, with one thousand five hundred cavalry, went forward to charge the city from the southwest. In addition to these dispositions a battery and two gun-boats were to bombard Fort Clinton, defending the enemy's water aproach. These movements were to have been executed in simultaneous harmony, but for no good reason known to military critics they utterly failed. On the 10th of June Q.A. Gillmore had reached within two miles of the city, had attracted the attention and drawn the fire of the enemy, and was competent to drive the enemy's skirmishers. Instead of following up this advantage, Gillmore judged himself unequal to a vigorous assault and retired upon his own judgment. On the other side of the city, Kautz, with the fiery impetuosity of a born cavalry officer, dashed in. The menace of Gillmore had most effectually stirred the enemy, and he was massing to receive the threatened assault. But now that Gillmore had retired, the foe turned on Kautz's command, and expelled it with little effort. The failure of this movement to be concerted had appraised the enemy of the blow that Grant was about to deliver, and hence there was the necessary massing of the Confederate army to ward it off. Grant did not turn aside from his purpose, but hurried forward W.F. Smith's corps from the Chickahominy by steamers *via* the White House. Smith crossed the Appomattox at Point of Rocks and moved southward, encountering the enemy in large numbers on the 15th of June. It was a proud moment for the division of Negro troops in his command, who were now to have the post of honor and danger, and assault the enemy in his intrenched position. A brigade of Hinck's Negro division was ordered to clear a line of rifle-pits immediately in front of Smith's corps. It was about nine o'clock in the morning when the black brigade went forward with a brilliant dash that made all Union hearts thrill with pride, while the heart of the enemy quailed before the advancing columns of Negro soldiers. They carried the rifle-pits with the bayonet. General Smith, who watched the black soldiers fight for the first time, declared that they were equal to any troops, and ordered them to carry a redoubt just ahead. On the men rushed, with "Rember Fort Pillow!" as their battle-cry, and swept the enemy out of the first redoubt. The captured guns were turned upon the enemy, who was either taken or driven off. A very poetic and inspiring incident of the first charge was the advancing beyond a centre regiment of the national colors. The color-sergeant planted his flag on the enemy's works, and held it there until the regiment came came up. One gun was captured and many prisoners taken. The brigade moved on about two miles and a half, when the defences of Petersburg were confronted. From two o'clock until evening these Negro troops reconnoitred and skirmished, at all times exposed to the shells and musketry of the enemy. At about sunset the black brigade was impelled against the intrenched enemy, and it dashed at the works so quickly that the enemy could not depress his guns sufficiently to cover the space before the charging column. In a few moments the Negro soldiers were within the enemy's works, cheering lustily. An officer in one of these regiments gives the following graphic account of the fighting:

"We charged across what appeared to be an almost impassable ravine, with the right wing all the time subject to a hot fire of grape and canister, until we got so far under the guns as to be sheltered, when the enemy took to their rifle-pits as infantrymen. Our brave fellows went steadily through the swamp and up the side of a hill at an angle of almost fifty degrees, rendered nearly impassable by fallen timber. Here again our color-sergeant was conspicuous in keeping far ahead of the most advanced, hanging on to the side of the hill till he would turn about and wave the Stars and Stripes at his advancing comrades, then steadily advancing again, under the fire of the enemy, till he could almost have reached their rifle-pits with his flag-staff. How he kept from being killed I do not know, unless it can be attributed to the fact that the party advancing up the side of the hill always has the advantage of those who hold the crest. It was in this way that we got such decided advantage over the enemy at South Mountain. We took in these two redoubts four more guns, making in all five for our regiment, two redoubts, and a part of a rifle-pit as our day's work. The Fifth, Sixth, and Seventh United States Colored Troops advanced against works more to the left. The Fourth United States Colored Troops took one more redoubt, and the enemy abandoned the other. In these two we got two more guns, which made in all seven. The Sixth Regiment did not get up in time, unfortunately, to have much of the sport, as it had been previously formed in the second line. We left forty-three men wounded and eleven killed in the ravine over which our men charged the last time. Our loss in the whole day's operations was one hundred and forty-three, including six officers, one of whom was killed. Sir, there is no underrating the good conduct of these fellows during these charges; with but a few exceptions they all went in as old soldiers, but with more enthusiasm. I am delighted that our first action resulted in a decided victory.

"The commendations we have received from the Army of the Potomac, including its general officers, are truly gratifying. Hancock's corps arrived just in time to relieve us (we being out of ammunition), before the rebels were reinforced and attempted to retake these strong works and commanding positions, without which they could not hold Petersburg one hour, if it were a part of Grant's plan to advance against it on the right here.

"General Smith speaks in the highest terms of the day's work, as you have doubtless seen, and he assured me in person that our division should have the guns we took as trophies of honor. He is also making his word good in saying that he could hereafter trust colored troops in the most responsible positions. Colonel Ames. of the Sixth United States Colored Troops, and our regiment have just been relieved in the front, where we served our tour of forty-eight hours in turn with the other troops of the corps. While out we are subjected to some of the severest shelling I have ever seen, Malvern Hlll not excepted. The enemy got twenty guns in position during the night, and opened on us yesterday morning at daylight. Our men stood it, behind their works, of course, as well as any of the white troops. Our men, unfortunately, owing to the irregular features of ground, took no prisoners. Sir, we can bayonet the enemy to terms on this matter of treating colored soldiers as prisoners of war far sooner than the authorities at Washington can bring him to it by negotiation. This I am morally persuaded of. I know, further, that the enemy won't fight us if he can help it. I am sure that the same number of white troops could not have taken those works on the evening of the 15th; prisoners that we took told me so. I mean prisoners who came in after the abandonment of the fort because they could not get away. They excused themselves on the ground of pride; as one of them said to me, 'D--d if men educated as we have been will fight with niggers, and your government ought not to expect it.' The real fact is, the rebels will not stand against our colored soldiers when there is any chance of their being taken prisoners, for they are conscious of what they justly deserve. Our men went into these works after they were taken, yelling, 'Fort Pillow!' The enemy well knows what this means, and I will venture the assertion that that piece of infernal brutality enforced by them there has cost the enemy already two men for every one they so inhumanly murdered."

The result of this engagement was the capture of sixteen guns and three hundred prisoners, at the cost of six hundred killed, wounded, and missing. The action was also valuable as settling the question of the valor of Negro soldiers. It was unfortunate that a campaign opened so brilliantly should have failed so signally; not, however, on account of these troops. Instead of following up the success won by his Negro troops, General Smith bivouacked for the night. Hancock, who ought to have been within supporting distance, did not arrive until late, and then disclaimed any knowledge that an assault was meditated upon Petersburg, although he must have heard Smith's guns all day. The enemy, startled at the vehement assaults of black troops, put twenty guns in position during the night, and Lee's Confederate veterans, marching at the sound of the enemy's guns, had reached the beleagured city before sunrise next morning. With daylight came Warren and Burnside to meet the enemy. Smith's right rested on the Appomattox, while Hancock, Burnside, and Warren were disposed to the left, which was covered by Kautz's cavalry. Having returned from City Point, where he had been in consultation with General Grant, Meade ordered a general assault at 2 P.M. on the 16th of June, but it was not delivered until 6 P.M. In this assault white troops were employed mainly, but the Negro troops were despatched to Terry, who was instructed to seize Port Walthall Junction, on the Bermuda Hundred front. It was now proved that Petersburg could not be reduced by a direct assault, and the Union troops intrenched themselves and sought to subdue it by a siege.

CHAPTER XV
AS PRISONERS OF WAR.

The capture and treatment of Negro soldiers by the enemy is a subject that demands dispassionate and judicial scrutiny. No just judge of historical events would seek to tear a single chaplet from the brow of any brave soldier, it matters not what uniform he wore or what flag he fought under. Valor is valor the world over. But whatever may be said of the gallantry of Confederate soldiers or the chivalry of the South, it remains true that the treatment bestowed upon Union prisoners of war in general, and upon Negroes in particular, has no parallel in the annals of modern civilized warfare.

Slavery destroyed the Southern conscience, blunted the sensibilities and affections, and depreciated human life. The Confederate army exhibited a fierceness in battle and a cold cruelty to their prisoners that startled the civilized world. Confederate military prisons became places of torture wherein every species of cruelty was perpetrated. Among the many hells erected for the reception and retention of Union prisoners Andersonville was, perhaps, the most notorious. It was situated on the South-western Railroad, about sixty-two miles south of Macon, Georgia. On the side of a hill where the timber was thick a space was cleared for the prison, in the form of a parellelogram, 1540 feet long and 750 feet wide. The ground was of red clay, and sloped gently to the south. Logs measuring twenty-four feet in length were firmly embedded in the ground, and closely joined together all the way up, with the upper end sharpened. Beyond and outside of this was a lower stockade for greater security.

Within the main prison-wall, and thirty feet from it, a railing three feet high, upon posts ten feet apart, ran around the entire prison. This was know as the "dead-line." On the top of the main wall were thirty-five sentry boxes, while at the angles of the prison stood artillery commanding the entire space. For recapturing escaped prisoners a large pack of blood-hounds was kept constantly on hand. There was not a tree or shrub left in the entire prison, and thus the sun had full power. In the summer the thermometer registered 110° Fahrenheit, while its mean for the heated term was 88° in the shade. The only water near this prison was a little stream five feet wide and six inches deep, that had its origin in a deadly, unhealthy swamp; and this stream passed through the prison grounds, flowing from east to west.

On the 15th of February, 1864, the first detachment of Union prisoners of war, numbering eight hundred and sixty, was received. Within four months there were twelve thousand prisoners in Andersonville, and before the end of August there were 31,693--leaving about thirty-six feet for each man! The prison was in use about thirteen months, and its reports show that during that period 44,882 prisoners were received.

The prisoners were allowed as rations each day two ounces of bacon or boiled beef, one sweet potato, and one piece of bread two and one-half inches square and thick, made of corn and ground pease.

There was no shelter from rain or sun. Some men dug holes in the ground, where they remained during the day and at night wandered forth under the open sky, while others made little houses of sticks and red clay. When it rained this vast army of forlorn captives wandered about in mud a foot deep. "Into the brook there flowed the filth and excrements of more than thirty thousand men. The banks of the stream were covered with ordure, and appeared to be alive with working maggots. Through this reeking mass wandered about, elbowing and pushing one another, the shoeless, hatless, famished captives, many of them with scarcely a tatter to cover them.

The death-rate soon reached the alarming figures of 8 1/2 per hour, and of the 44,882 incarcerated 12,462 died; while a large proportion of those who lived to get out of this atrocious lazar-house died soon after in Union hospitals or at home. Those who died in the prison were piled in heaps outside of the stockade; they were hauled away by the wagon-load, cast into a common ditch without coffins and covered with quick-lime. If the dead had rings on their fingers, the axe was often used to secure these jewels.

There were three hundred men shot near the dead-line, while hundreds were torn by the half-starved blood hounds in attempting to escape. Many were put in stocks and chains for alleged breaches of the laws of the prison, and others were murdered by the hands of the keeper, Wirz, who was susequently tried by the United States authorities and hanged.

Not only physical suffering, but mental ruin, often resulted from this diabolical prison system, and men wandered about the loathsome pen raving maniacs. Some fought their battles over again, and hysterically laughed at the imaginary foes they vanquished; some wandered forth in delirium to meet kindred, and were murdered on the "dead-line;" others stood shaking their shrivelled fists at the sky pronouncing wild imprecations; while still others drifted in listless apathy from one end of the den to the other, clinching a bone or dramatically drawing their tattered garments about their emaciated forms.

But who were the victims of this organized cruelty of which the Inspector-general of the Confederate army, Colonel Chandler, said, "It is a place the horrors of which it is difficult to describe--it is a disgrace to civilization?" White officers and enlisted men from the North. Many of them had the blood of revolutionary patriots in their veins; some were from Harvard and Yale, Williams and Brown; some were justly distinguished in literature and science; many were the sons of rich men, millionaires, without food or raiment. If such men endured such hardships as prisoners of war, what was in reserve for the poor Negro?

Although the Confederate authorities had first inaugurated the policy of arming Negroes as soldiers, the moment the United States Government announced its intention to do likewise the Rebel Government proscribed the Negro as a prisoner of war. In fact, the message of Jefferson Davis on the treatment of Negroes as prisoners of war was prior to any action on this matter by either President Lincoln or Congress. The first Emancipation Proclamation of President Lincoln, issued on the 22d of September, 1862, a few days after the battle of Antietam, was rather a measure of military policy than of humanity. It was regarded by the Confederate authorities as contemplating the employment of emancipated slaves in the armed service of the United States. Before this, on the 22d of August, 1862, General B.F. Butler, then in command of the Union forces at New Orleans, had appealed to the free Negro citizens of Louisiana to rally in defence of their common country; and this fact, followed so soon by Mr. Lincoln's proclamation, imbittered and alarmed the enemy. The independent action of General Butler was regarded as indicating the policy of the Government.

On the 23d of December, 1862, Jefferson Davis, President of the Confederate States, issued the following proclamation, aimed at General Butler in particular, and all Negro soldiers and their officers in general:

"*First.* That all commissioned officers in the command of said Benjamin F. Butler be declared not entitled to be considered as soldiers engaged in honorable warfare, but as robbers and criminals, deserving death; and that they and each of them be, whenever captured, reserved for execution.

"*Second.* That the private soldiers and non-commissioned officers in the army of said Butler be considered as only the instruments used for the commission of crimes perpetrated by his orders, and not as free agents; that they, therefore, be treated, when captured, as prisoners of war, with kindness and humanity, and be sent home on the usual parole that they will in no manner aid or serve the United States in any capacity during the continuance of this war, unless duly exchanged.

"*Third.* That all Negro slaves captured in arms be at once delivered over to the executive authorities of the respective States to which they belong, to be dealt with according to the laws of said States.

"*Fourth.* That the like orders be executed in all cases with respect to all commissioned officers of the United States, when found serving in company with said slaves in insurrection against the authorities of the different States of this Confederacy.

[Signed and sealed at Richmond, December 23, 1862.]
"JEFFERSON DAVIS."

This message was laid before the Confederate Congress, and on the 12th of January, 1863, the following action was had:

"*Resolved, by the Congress of the Confederate States of America,* in response to the message of the President, transmitted to Congress at the commencement of the present session, That, in the opinion of Congress, the commissioned officers of the enemy ought *not* to be delivered to the authorities of the respective States, as suggested in the said message, but all captives taken by the Confederate forces ought to be dealt with and disposed of by the Confederate Government.

"SEC. 2. That, in the judgment of Congress, the proclamation of the President of the United States, dated respectively September 22, 1862, and January 1, 1863, and the other measures of the Government of the United States and of its authorities, commanders, and forces, designed or tending to emancipate slaves in the Confederate States, or to abduct such slaves, or to incite them to insurrection, or to employ Negroes in war against the Confederate States, or to overthrow the institution of African slavery, and bring on a servile war in these States, would, if successful, produce atrocious consequences, and they are inconsistent with the spirit of those usages which, in modern warfare, prevail among civilized nations; they may, therefore, be properly and lawfully repressed by retaliation.

"SEC. 3. That in every case wherein, during the present war, any violation of the laws of war, among civilized nations, shall be, or has been, done and perpetrated by those acting under the authority of the Government of the United States, on the persons or property of citizens of the Confederate States, or of those under the protection or in the land or naval service of the Confederate States, or of any State of the Confederacy, the President of the Confederate States is hereby authorized to cause full and ample retaliation to be made for every such violation, in such manner and to such extent as he may think proper.

"SEC. 4. That every white person, being a commissioned officer, or acting as such, who, during the present war, shall command Negroes or mulattoes in arms against the Confederate States, or who shall arm, train, organize, or prepare Negroes or mulattoes for military service against the Confederate States, or who shall voluntarily aid Negroes or mulattoes in any military enterprise, attack, or conflict in such service, shall be deemed as inciting servile insurrection, and shall, if captured, be put to death, or be otherwise punished at the discretion of the Court.

"SEC. 5. Every person, being a commissioned officer, or acting as such in the service of the enemy, who shall, during the present war, excite, attempt to excite, or cause to be excited, a servile insurrection, or shall incite, or cause to be incited, a slave or rebel, shall, if captured, be put to death, or be otherwise punished at the discretion of the Court.

"SEC. 6. Every person charged with an offence punishable under the preceding resolutions shall, during the present war, be tried before the military court attached to the army or corps by the troops of which he shall have been captured, or by such other military court as the President may direct, and in such manner and under such regulations as the President shall prescribe; and, after conviction, the President may commute the punishment in such manner and on such terms as he may deem proper.

"SEC. 7. All Negroes and mulattoes who shall be engaged in war, or be taken in arms against the Confederate States, or shall give aid or comfort to the enemies of the Confederate States, shall, when captured in the Confederate States, be delivered to the authorities of the State or States in which they shall be captured, to be dealt with acording to the present or future laws of such State or States."

This document is cited in full that the official record may be before the reader. Several points in it deserve special consideration. The Confederate Congress was unwilling, on the recommendation of Mr. Davis, to allow the prisoners which their army might take to pass into the control of the several Confederate States. While devoted to "State Rights," for once the sovereign Confederate Government raised its majestic voice and demanded possession of Union prisoners. The several States could be trusted in everything but the delicate matter of dealing with Union prisoners of war. Congress did not hesitate to take issue with President Davis. The civil and criminal law of the States in ante-bellum days had always been regarded as adequate to deal with Abolitionists, Negroes, and other criminals; but when those laws were to be applied to Union prisoners of war their efficiency was called in question, and the Confederacy now conferred upon the States authority to make new laws upon the subject. The high prerogative of murdering Union prisoners having not been delegated to the States, was reserved to the Confederate Congress.

Just where, when, and in what manner the United States ever violated "the laws or usages of war among civilized nations" is not clear. Certainly there is no record of any such violation. But of this the Confederate Government determined to be the sole judge of what constituted a violation of "the laws or usages of war;" and from its judgment there was no appeal.

Brave white officers, the laurelled leaders of gallant Negro soldiers, were marked for a felon's death. The military employment of slaves by the United States Government was justified by historical precedents ancient and modern, Christian and pagan; and last, if least, it had before it the example of the Confederate Government already alluded to. Consequently the murdering of officers who belonged to organizations composed of Negroes was "a most flagrant violation of the laws or usages of war among civilized nations." It had become manifest that either "the institution of African slavery" or the free institutions of the American Union must perish, and therefore the United States Government was justified in using the Negro as a military instrument in preserving the autonomy of the States, and in securing the freedom of the slaves.

The proclamation of Mr. Davis and the subsequent legislative action of the Confederate Congress aroused the attention and stirred the indignation of the friends of humanity everywhere. On the 14th of April, 1863, the *New York Tribune* said, editorially, "At all events, the policy of the Government to employ Black Troops in active service is definitely established, and it becomes--as indeed it has been for months--a very serious question what steps are to be taken for their protection. The Proclamation of Jefferson Davis remains unrevoked. By it he threatened death or slavery to every Negro taken in arms, and to their white officers the same fate. What is the response of our Government? Hitherto, silence. The number of Negroes in its service has already increased; in South Carolina they have already been mustered into regiments by a sweeping conscription, and now in the West apparently the same policy is adopted and rigorously enforced."

In reply to the pertinent and humane sentiments of Horace Greeley and other leaders of public sentiment at the North, the *Richmond Examiner*, speaking for the Confederate Government, said, "It is not merely the pretension of a regular Government affecting to deal with 'Rebels,' but it is a deadly stab which they are aiming at our institutions themselves, because they know that, if we were insane enough to yield this point, to treat Black men as the equals of White, and insurgent slaves as equivalent to our brave soldiers, the very foundation of Slavery would be fatally wounded."

A few bold and conscientious Southern newspapers urged that the Confederate Government had no authority to proscribe Union soldiers on account of color, and clearly pointed out the dangers that such a course as the Government had marked out would invite. The Confederate Government adhered to its views, and its army in the field carried out its policy with zeal and cruelty.

The Confederate army at Port Hudson would not permit a flag of truce to bury the brave black soldiers who fell in the memorable engagement in May, 1863. In the spring and summer of 1863 a number of Negro soldiers were made prisoners in their conflicts with the enemy, and were subjected to barbarous treatment. When an exchange of prisoners took place in front of Charleston, although the rebels held many Negro prisoners, they gave up none but white soldiers. When this fact was brought to the attention of commissioners for the exchange of prisoners on behalf of the Confederate Government, they explained that it was against the law of their Government to exchange Negro prisoners. This statement aroused the North, and President Lincoln issued the following order:

"Executive Mansion, Washington, *July* 30, 1863.

"It is the duty of every government to give protection to its citizens of whatever class, color, or condition, and especially to those who are duly organized as soldiers in the public service. The law of nations, and the usages and customs of war, as carried on by civilized powers, permit no distinction as to color in the treatment of prisoners of war as public enemies. To sell or enslave any captured person, on account of his color, and for no offence against the laws of war, is a relapse into barbarism, and a crime against the civilization of the age.

"The Government of the United States will give the same protection to all its soldiers; and if the enemy shall sell or enslave any one because of his color, the offence shall be punished by retaliation upon the enemy's prisoners in our possession.

"It is therefore ordered that, for every soldier of the United States killed in violation of the laws of war, a Rebel soldier shall be executed; and for every one enslaved by the enemy or sold into Slavery, a Rebel soldier shall be placed at hard labor on public works, and continued at such labor until the other shall be released and receive the treatment due to a prisoner of war.

ABRAHAM LINCOLN.

"By order of the Secretary of War.

"E.D. TOWNSEND,

"Assistant Adjutant-general."

On the 12th of August, 1863, the *Charleston Mercury*, an able and conservative journal, called attention to the severe treatment of Negro prisoners of war. The humane sentiments expressed appealed strongly to the general officers of the Confederate army. General Beauregard felt that the criticism applied to him. It was certainly a case of conscience, for he had sent the following despatch the year before which lowered him from the honorable position of a general and branded him forever as a murderer:

"Charleston, South Carolina, *October* 13, 1862.

"*Hon. Wm. P. Miles, Richmond, Virginia:*

"Has the bill for the execution of Abolition prisoners after January next been passed? Do it, and England will be stirred into action! It is high time to proclaim the black flag after that period. Let the execution be with the garrote.

(Signed) "G.T. BEAUREGARD."

Previous to this, on the 3d of August, 1862, General Beauregard wrote to General Wm. E. Martin from Bladen, Alabama, as follows:

"We will yet have to come to proclaiming this war ' a war to the knife,' when no quarter will be asked or granted. I believe it is the only thing which can prevent recruiting at the North. As to ourselves, I think that very few will not admit that death is preferable to dishonor and ruin."

The enemy was inflexible in his purpose to deny Negro soldiers the immunities of prisoners of war. Some whom the fortunes of civil war threw into the hands of the enemy were murdered after they had surrendered; others were placed at work on fortifications, where they were exposed to the fire of the Union army; many were crowded into common jails, and made to toil in the streets like felons, or were sold at public auction. In many instances where Negro soldiers had surrendered their arms on the battle-field they were shot down in cold blood. On the 17th of December, 1863, the *Richmond Enquirer* said: "The Yankees are not going to send their Negro troops in the field; they know as well as we do that no reliance can be placed upon them; but as depot-guards, prison-guards, etc., they will relieve their white troops. This is the use that will be made of them. Should they be sent to the field, and be put in battle, none will be taken prisoners: our troops understand what to do in such cases."

Such advice from the organ of the Confederate administration at Richmond had its influence upon the rebel army. The following correspondence between Generals Peck and Pickett needs no explanation or comment:

"Headquarters of the Army and District of North Carolina,
"Newbern, North Carolina, *February* 11, 1864.
"Major-general Pickett, Department of Virginia and North Carolina, Confederate Army, Petersburg:
"GENERAL,--I have the honor to enclose a slip cut from the *Richmond Examiner*, February 8, 1864. It is styled 'The Advance on Newbern,' and appears to have been extracted from the *Petersburg Register*, a paper published in the city where your headquarters are located.

"Your attention is particularly invited to that paragraph which states 'that Colonel Shaw was shot dead by a Negro soldier from the other side of the river, which he was spanning with a pontoon-bridge,' and that 'the Negro was watched, followed, taken, and hanged after the action at Thomasville:'

"'THE ADVANCE ON NEWBERN.--The *Petersburg Register* gives the following additional facts of the advance on Newbern: Our army, according to the report of passengers arriving from Weldon, has fallen back to a point sixteen miles west of Newbern. The reason assigned for this retrograde movement was that Newbern could not be taken by us without a loss on our part which could find no equivalent in its capture, as the place was stronger than we had anticipated. Yet, in spite of this, we are sure that the expedition will result in good to our cause. Our forces are in a situation to get large supplies from a country still abundant, to prevent raids on points westward, and keep Tories in check, and hang them when caught.

"'From a private who was one of the guard that brought the batch of prisoners through we learn that Colonel Shaw was shot dead by a Negro soldier from the other side of the river, which he was spanning with a pontoon-bridge. The Negro was watched, followed, taken, and hanged after the action at Thomasville. It is stated that when our troops entered Thomasville a number of the enemy took shelter in the houses and fired upon them. The Yankees were ordered to surrender, but refused, whereupon our men set fire to the houses, and their occupants got, bodily, a taste in this world of the flames eternal.'

"The Government of the United States has wisely seen fit to enlist many thousand colored citizens to aid in putting down the rebellion, and has placed them on the same footing in all respects as her white troops.
      *   *   *   *   *   *   *   *   *   *   *   *   *

"Believing that this atrocity has been perpetrated without your knowledge, and that you will take prompt steps to disavow this violation of the usages of war, and to bring the offenders to justice, I shall refrain from executing a rebel soldier until I learn your action in the premises.

"I am, very respectfully, your obedient servant.

"JOHN J. PECK, Major-general."

Reply of General Pickett.

"Headquarters of the Department of North Carolina,
"Petersburg, Virginia, *February* 16, 1864.

"Major-general John J. Peck, U.S.A., Commanding at Newbern:

"GENERAL,—Your communication of the 11th of February is received. I have the honor to state in reply that the paragraph from a newspaper enclosed therein is not only without foundation in fact, but so ridiculous that I should scarcely have supposed it worthy of consideration; but I would respectfully inform you that had I caught *any Negro,* who had killed either officer, soldier, or citizen of the Confederate States, I should have caused him to be immediately executed.

"To your threat expressed in the following extract from your communication, namely, 'Believing that this atrocity has been perpetrated without your knowledge, and that you will take prompt steps to disavow this violation of the usages of war, and to bring the offenders to justice, I shall refrain from executing a rebel soldier until I learn of your action in the premises,' I have merely to say that I have in my hands, and subject to my orders, captured in the recent operations in this department, some four hundred and fifty officers and men of the United States army, and for every man you hang I will hang ten of the United Staes army.

"I am, General, very respectfully, your obedient servant,
"J.E. PICKETT,
"Major-general Commanding."

On the 14th of June, 1864, a correspondent, writing from Mississippi to the *Atlanta Appeal,* speaking of Forrest's fighting in Tennessee, said:

"Very few Negroes, it seems, have been captured. Perhaps not more than forty or fifty have appeared at headquarters. Most of them fled as soon as it was known that Forrest was on the battle-field. Those that were taken escaped (?). The soldiers say that they lost them."

In plainer terms, the soldiers murdered the Negro prisoners, and Forrest knew it and approved of the butchery. As at Fort Pillow, so here and elsewhere during the Rebellion, Forrest murdered his Negro prisoners of war. His government never disapproved of his conduct, because he was simply carrying out its policy in the main.

In many instances Negro captives would be marched all day, escorted by the enemy's cavalry, and towards evening some rebel soldier would exclaim, "Halt there! These niggers are tryin' to git away!" and immediately begin an indiscriminate slaughter of their Negro prisoners. The verbal report would be that they attempted to escape and were shot by the guards. But no investigation would be instituted, and so the Confederate soldier came to understand that it was his privilege and his duty to murder Negro prisoners of war. The search has been made in vain for a single military or political protest against these enormous crimes. On the contrary, there is ample proof that the murder of Negro prisoners was authorized by the Confederate Congress, since that body regarded them as engaged in insurrection, the crime whereof was punishable with death.

The following despatch shows that the War Department knew that the Confederate Government would not treat Negro soldiers as prisoners of war, and that it was the duty of the United States Government to protect them:

"War Department, *November* 17, 1863.
"Major-general Butler, Fort Monroe:
"The whole subject of exchange of prisoners is under direction of Major-general Hitchcock, to whom, as Commissioner of Exchange, that branch of the service has been committed. He will be glad to have any aid or suggestions you may be pleased to furnish, but there should be no interference without his assent. It is known that the rebels will exchange man for man and officer for officer, except blacks, and officers in command of black troops. These they absolutely refuse to exchange. This is the point on which the whole matter hangs. Exchanging man for man and officer for officer, with the exception the rebels make, is a substantial abandonment of the Colored Troops and their officers to their fate, and would be a shameful dishonor to the Government bound to protect them. When they agree to exchange all alike there will be no difficulty.
"EDWIN M. STANTON, Secretary of War."

The men who disgraced their uniform by murdering Union prisoners of war may not be willing to remember, but will be unable to forget, their crime against the profession of arms. Every sentiment of patriotism, every instinct of humanity, every principle of justice, every element of Christian ethics, revolts at these dark deeds. The Southern conscience of to-day may seek, like Cain, to hide from the bar of public sentiment, but, like the first murder, neither the Confederate Congress nor its hired assassin, the Confederate army, can ever escape the fierce light of impartial history. A cause that could authorize and seek to justify such horrors is forever

and irrevocably "the lost cause." No descendant will be
proud of its memory, no friend of humanity will mourn at
its sepulchre. Christian civilization the world over will rejoice that such a cause has perished from among the governments of mankind; while the Negro, with unexampled
charity, if not able to forget, freely forgives the murderers of
his kinsmen under the pretext of law.

JOSEPH T. WILSON

JOSEPH T. WILSON
(1836-1895)

In *The Black Phalanx* (1890) Joseph T. Wilson undertakes to tell the history of the "Negro soldiers of the United States in the wars of 1775-1812, 1861-65." The book grew out of his presentation of episodes from Black American military history at meetings of Civil War veterans. He himself served first in the 2nd Regiment Louisiana Marine Guard (1862-63) and the 54th Massachusetts Colored Infantry (1863-64), being discharged from the latter in Boston after being wounded at the Battle of Olustee in Florida.

Born in Norfolk, Virginia, Wilson had been able to move to the Massachusetts seaport of New Bedford. From New Bedford Wilson made his way as a seaman to the South Pacific and to South America, eventually spending many years in the latter. He was in Chile in 1862 when he learned of the outbreak of the Civil War. Sensing, as nearly all Black Americans did, that this would lead to the end of slavery, Wilson set out promptly for New Orleans to seek traces of his father who had been sold in that city. It was there that he seized the occasion of enlisting in the Union Army.

Of the writing of *The Black Phalanx*, Wilson tells us in the "Preface":

> With whatever forebodings of failure I entered upon the work of collecting the literature of the war, from which to cull and arrange much of the matter contained herein, which has required years of incessant search and appeal, I can but feel that it has been thoroughly done. The public libraries of the cities of Boston, Cincinnati, New Bedford, New York, The War Department of Washington, and the private libraries of several eminent citizens, have alike been made use of by me.

The book itself is over 500 pages in length, sixty or so being devoted to the Revolution and the War of 1812, the remainder to the Civil War. Wilson, as he indicates, relied heavily on a variety of published and unpublished sources, but most fully on official dispatches in the War Department. Of particular interest to the reader are his observations on New Orleans and on Florida, where he was himself an eyewitness. For the account of the Battle of Olustee included in the book he quotes verbatim from an article he had written for *The Journal* of Toledo.

Speaking of the meaning of his researches for him, Wilson says in the "Preface":

I acknowledge it has been a labor of love to fight many of the battles of the war of rebellion over again, not because of a relish for blood and the destruction of human life, but for the memories of the past; of the bondage of a race and its struggle for freedom, awakening as they do the intense love of country and liberty, such as one who has been without either feels, when both have been secured by heroic effort.

The Black Phalanx was not an isolated piece of work. Before undertaking the monumental task of compiling that history, Wilson had written *Emancipation: Its Course From 1102 to 1875* (1881), *Voice of a New Race* (1882), and *Twenty-Two Years of Freedom* (1882).

FROM CHAPTER IV
OFFICERS

General Butler, at New Orleans, was prevented by circumstances surrounding him at the time, from choosing among the friends of the negro race, as was the case in the before mentioned regiments, men to command the first and second regiments organized by him in the above named city, in August, 1862. He was only too glad to find white men of military capꞓity to take charge of the drilling and disciplining of the troops. As an experiment he was more than lucky in the appointment of Colonels Stafford and Daniels to the command of these regiments, seconded by Lieut. Cols. Bassett and Hall, and Finnegass of the 3rd Regiment. These officers proved themselves worthy of the trust reposed in them, and made these regiments, in drill and discipline, second to none in the Department of the Gulf. Notwithstanding the captains and subordinate officers of the first and second regiments were men, who like those in a large majority of the white regiments had never made arms a profession, and, who, through American prejudice, had but very limited opportunities for acquiring even the rudiments of a common English education. Several of them, however, being mulattoes, had had some training in the schools of the parishes, and some few in the higher schools of France, and in the Islands of the Carribean Sea. Maj. Dumas, of the 2nd Regiment, whose slaves composed nearly one whole company, was a gentleman of fine tact and ability, as were others.

Considering that they were all negroes, free and slave, their dash and manly courage, no less than their military aptitude, was equal, and in many instances superior, to those found in the regiments of Maine and New York. The 3rd Regiment was officered by soldiers of undoubted character and pluck, as they proved themselves to be, during the seige of Port Hudson, especially Capt. Quinn, who won distinction and promotion, as the record shows. The regiments raised thereafter were officered, more or less, by the non-commissioned officers of the white regiments, as a reward for gallantry and meritorious service upon the field, or on account of proficiency in drill. This rule of selection held good throughout all the departments in the organizing of negro troops. In May, 1863, President Lincoln, with a view of correcting an abuse that a certain commanding general had begun to practice in assigning inferior, though brave, men to the command of negro regiments; and in keeping with his new policy of arming the negroes, for which Gen. Lorenze Thomas, Adjutant General of the Army, had gone into the Mississippi Valley region to raise twenty regiments, he appointed a Board for the examination of those applying for commands in negro regiments.

At first it was proposed to pay the officers of negro troops less than was paid the officers of white soldiers, but this plan was abandoned. Toward the close of the war nearly all the chaplains appointed to negro regiments were negroes; noncommissioned officers were selected from the ranks, where they were found as well qualified as those taken from the ranks of white regiments. In the 10th and 18th Corps it was a common thing for the orderly sergeants to call their company's roll from memory, and the records of many companies and regiments are kept at the War Department in Washington, as mementoes of their efficiency.

There were a number of negroes commissioned during
the war whose record it has not been possible to obtain.
Quite a number of mulattoes served in white regiments,
some as officers; they were so light in complexion that their
true race connection could not be told. This is true of one of
the prominent Ohioans of to-day, who served on the staff of
a Major General of volunteers. There were several among
the Pennsylvania troops, and not a few in the New York and
Massachusetts regiments. While lying on a battle-field
wounded and exhausted, an officer of the brigade to which
the writer belonged, rode up, passed me his canteen, and en-
quired if I knew him. A negative answer was given. "I am
Tom Bunting," he replied. "You know me now, don't you?
We used to play together in our boyhood days in Virginia;
keep the canteen. I will let your people know about you." So
saying he dashed away to his command; he belonged to a
Massachusetts regiment. There was quite a large number of
mulattoes who enlisted under Butler, at New Orleans, and
served in white regiments; this is also true of the confederate
army. The writer has an intimate acquaintance now living
in Richmond, Va., who served in a New York Regiment,
who, while marching along with his regiment through
Broad street, after the capture of that city, was recognized by
his mother, and by her was pulled from the ranks and embraced. A man who became United States Marshal of one of
the Southern States after the war, was Captain in the 2nd
Louisiana Native Guards Regiment. Numerous instances of
this kind could be cited.

FROM CHAPTER V
DEPARTMENT OF THE GULF

General Butler continued General Weitzel in command
but placed the negroes under another officer. However,
General Weitzel; like thousands of others, changed his mind
in regard to the colored troops. "If he was not convinced by
General Butler's reasoning," says Parton, "he must have been
convinced by what he saw of the conduct of those very colored regiments at Port Hudson, where he himself gave such
a glorious example of prudence and gallantry."

Notwithstanding these troops did good service, it did not soften or remove very much of the prejudice at the North against the negro soldiers, nor in the ranks of the army. Many incidents might be cited to show the feeling of bitterness against them. However, General Butler's example was followed very soon by every officer in command, and by the time the President's Emancipation Proclamation was issued there were not less than 10,000 negroes armed and equipped along the Mississippi river.

The not unnatural willingness of the white soldiers to allow the negro troops to stop the bullets that they would otherwise have to receive was shown in General Bank's Red River Campaign. At Pleasant Grove, Dickey's black brigade prevented a slaughter of the Union troops. The black Phalanx were represented there by a brigade attached to the first division of the 19th Corps. When the confederates routed the army under Banks at Sabine Cross Roads, below Mansfield, they drove it for several hours toward Pleasant Grove, despite the ardor of the combined forces of Banks and Franklin. It became apparent that unless the confederates could be checked at this point, all was lost. General Emory prepared for the emergency on the western edge of a wood, with an open field sloping toward Mansfield. Here General Dwight formed a brigade of the black Phalanx across the road. Hardly was the line formed when out came the gallant foe driving 10,000 men before them. Flushed with two days' victory, they came charging at double quick time, but the Phalanx held its fire until the enemy was close upon them, and then poured a deadly volley into the ranks of the exultant foe, stopping them short and mowing them down like grass. The confederates recoiled, and now began a fight such as was always fought when the Southerners became aware that black soldiers were in front of them, and for an hour and a half they fought at close quarters, ceasing only at night. Every charge of the enemy was repulsed by the steady gallantry of General Emory's brigade and the black Phalanx, who saved the army from annihilation against a foe numbering three to one. During this memorable campaign the Phalanx more than once met the enemy and accepted the face of their black flag declarations. The confederates knew full well that every man of the Phalanx would fight to the last; they had learned that long before.

As early as June, 1863, General Grant was compelled, in order to show a bold front to Gens. Pemberton and Johnston at the same time, while besieging Vicksburg, to draw nearly all the troops from Milliken's Bend to his support, leaving three infantry regiments of the black Phalanx and a small force of white cavalry to hold this, to him an all important post. Milliken's Bend was well fortified, and with a proper garrison was in condition to stand a siege. Brigadier-General Dennis was in command, and the troops consisted of the 9th and 11th Louisiana Regiments, the 1st Mississippi and a small detachment of white cavalry, in all about 1,400 men, raw recruits. General Dennis looking upon the place more as a station for organizing and drilling the Phalanx, had made no particular arrangements in anticipation of an attack. He was surprised, therefore, when a force of 3,000 men, under General Henry McCulloch, from the interior of Louisiana, attacked and drove his pickets and two companies of the 23d Iowa Cavalry,(white) up to the breastworks of the Bend. The movement was successful, however, and the confederates, holding the ground, rested for the night, with the expectation of marching into the fortifications in the morning, to begin a massacre, whether a resistance should be shown them or not. The knowledge this little garrison had of what the morrow would bring it, doubtless kept the soldiers awake, preparing to meet the enemy and their own fate. About 3 o'clock, in the early grey of the morning, the confederate line was formed just outside of the intrenchments; suddenly with fixed bayonets the men came rushing over the works, driving everything before them and shouting, "No quarter! No quarter to negroes or their officers!" In a moment the blacks formed and met them, and now the battle began in earnest, hand to hand. The gunboats "Choctaw" and "Lexington" also came up as the confederates were receiving the bayonets and the bullets of the Unionists, and lent material assistance. The attacking force had flanked the works and was pouring in a deadly, enfilading musketry fire. The defenders fell back out of the way of the gunboat's shells, but finally went forward again with what was left of their 150 white allies, and drove the enemy before them and out of the captured works. One division of the enemy's troops hesitated to leave a redoubt, when a company of brave black men dashed forward at double-quick time and engaged them. The enemy stood his ground, and soon the rattling bayonets rang out amid the thunders of the gunboats and the shouts of enraged men; but they were finally driven out, and their ranks thinned by the "Choctaw" as they went over the works. The news reached General Grant and he immediately dispatched General Mower's brigade with orders to re-enforce Dennis and drive the confederates beyond the Tensas River.

The Department of the Gulf contained a far greater proportion of the Phalanx than did any other Department, and there were very few, if any, important engagements fought in this Department in which the Phalanx did not take part.

It is unpleasant here, in view of the valuable services rendered by the Phalanx, to be obliged to record that the black soldiers were subjected to many indignities, and suffered much at the hands of their white fellow comrades in arms. Repeated assaults and ourages were committed upon black men wearing the United States' uniform, not only by volunteers but conscripts from the various States, and frequently by confederate prisoners who had been paroled by the United States; these outrages were allowed to take place, without interference by the commanding officers, who apparently did not observe what was going on.

At Ship Island, Miss., there were three companies of the 13th Maine, General Neal Dow's old regiment, and seven companies of the 2nd Regiment Phalanx, commanded by Colonel Daniels, which constituted the garrison at that point. Ship Island was the key to New Orleans. On the opposite shore was a railroad leading to Mobile by which re-enforcements were going forward to Charleston. Colonel Daniels conceived the idea of destroying the road to prevent the transportation of the confederate troops. Accordingly, with about two hundred men he landed at Pascagoula, on the morning of the 9th of April. Pickets were immediately posted on the outskirts of the town, while the main body marched up to the hotel. Before long some confederate cavalry, having been apprised of the movement, advanced, drove in the pickets, and commenced an attack on the force occupying the town. The cavalry made a bold dash upon the left of the negroes, which was the work of but a moment; the brave blacks met their charge manfully, and emptied the saddles of the front rank, which caused the rear ones first to halt and then retire. The blacks were outnumbered, however, five to one, and finally were forced to abandon the town; they went, taking with them the stars and stripes which they had hoisted upon the hotel when entering it. They fell back towards the river to give the gunboat "Jackson" a chance to shell their pursuers, but the movement resulted in an apparently revengeful act on the part of the crew of that vessel, they having previously had some of their number killed in the course of a difficulty with a black sentry at Ship Island.

The commanding officer of the land force, doubtless from prudential reasons, omitted to state in his report that the men fought their way through the town while being fired upon from house-tops and windows by boys and women. That the gunboat opened fire directly on them when they were engaged in a hand to hand coflict, which so completely cut off a number of the men from the main body of the troops that their capture appeared certain. Major Dumas, however, seeing the condition of things, put spurs to his horse and went to their succor, reaching them just as a company of the enemy's cavalry made a charge. The Major, placing himself at the head of the hard-pressed men, not only repulsed the cavalry and rescued the squad, but captured the enemy's standard-bearer. The retreating force reached their transport with the loss of only one man; they brought with them some prisoners and captured flags.

The 2nd Regiment, with the exception of the Colonel, Lieut.-Colonel and Adjutant, was officered by negroes, many of whom had worn the galling chains of slavery, while others were men of affluence and culture from New Orleans and vicinity.

The 2nd Regiment had its full share of prejudice to contend with, and perhaps suffered more from that cause than any other regiment of the Phalanx. Once while loading transports at Algiers, preparatory to embarking for Ship Island, they came in contact with a section of the famous Nim's battery, rated as one of the finest in the service. The arms of the 2nd Regiment were stacked and the men were busy in loading the vessel, save a few who were doing guard duty over the ammunition stored in a shed on the whaft. One of the battery-men attempted to enter the shed with a lighted pipe in his mouth, but was prevented by the guard. It was more than the Celt could stand to be ordered by a negro; watching for a chance when the guard about-faced, he with several others sprang upon him. The guard gave the Phalanx signal, and instantly hundreds of black men secured their arms and rushed to the relief of their comrade. The battery-men jumped to their guns, formed into line and drew their sabres. Lieut.-Colonel Hall, who was in command of the 2nd Regiment, stepped forward and demanded to know of the commander of the battery if his men wanted to take the men the guard had arrested. "Yes," was the officer's reply, "I want you to give them up." "Not until they are dealt with," said Colonel Hall. And then a shout and yell, such as the Phalanx only were able to give, rent the air, and the abortive menace was over. The gunners returned their sabres and resumed their work. Col. Hall, who always had perfect control of his men, ordered the guns stacked, put on a double guard, and the men of the 2nd Regiment resumed their labor of loading the transport. Of course this was early in the struggle, and before a general enlistment of the blacks.

The first, second and third regiments of the Phalanx were the nucleus of the one hundred and eighty that eventually did so much for the suppression of the rebellion and the abolition of slavery. The 1st and 3rd Regiments went up the Mississippi; the 2nd garrisoned Ship Island and Fort Pike, on Lake Pontchartrain, after protecting for several months the Opelousa railroad, so much coveted by the confederates.

A few weeks after the fight of the 2nd Regiment at Pascagoula, General Banks laid siege to Port Hudson, and gathered there all the available forces in his department. Among these were the 1st and 3rd Infantry Regiments of the Phalanx. On the 23rd of May the federal forces, having completely invested the enemy's works and made due preparation, were ordered to make a general assault along the whole line. The attack was intended to be simultaneous, but in this it failed. The Union batteries opened early in the morning, and after a vigorous bombardment Generals Weitzel, Grover and Paine, on the right assaulted with vigor at 10 A.M., while Gen. Augur in the center, and General W.T. Sherman on the left, did not attack till 2 P.M.

Never was fighting more heroic than that of the federal army and especially that of the Phalanx regiments . If valor could have triumphed over such odds, the assaulting forces would have carried the works, but only abject cowardice or pitiable imbecility could have lost such a position under existing circumstances. The negro regiments on the north side of the works vied with the bravest, making three desperate charges on the confederate batteries, losing heavily, but maintaining their position in the advance all the while.

The column in moving to the attack went through the woods in their immediate front, and then upon a plane, on the farther side of which, half a mile distant, were the enemy's batteries. The field was covered with recently felled trees, through the interlaced branches of which the column moved, and for two or more hours struggled through the obstacles, stepping over their comrades who fell among the entangled brushwood pierced by bullets or torn by flying missiles, and braved the hurricane of shot and shell.

What did it avail to hurl a few thousand troops against those impregnable works? The men were not iron, and were they, it would have been impossible for them to have kept erect, where trees three feet in diameter were crashed down upon them by the enemy's shot; they would have been but as so many ten-pins set up before skillful players to be knocked down.

The troops entered an enfilading fire from a masked battery which opened upon them as they neared the fort, causing the column first to halt, then to waver and stagger; but it recovered and again pressed forward, closing up the ranks as fast as the enemy's shells thinned them. On the left the confederates had planted a six-gun battery upon an eminence, which enabled them to sweep the field over which the advancing column moved. In front was the large fort, while the right of the line was raked by a redoubt of six pieces of artillery. One after another of the works had been charged, but in vain. The Michigan, New York and Massachusetts troops--braver than whom none ever fought a battle--had been hurled back from the place, leaving the field strewn with their dead and wounded. The works must be taken. General Nelson was ordered by General Dwight to take the battery on the left. The 1st and 3rd Regiments went forward at double quick time, and they were soon within the line of the enemy's fire. Louder than the thunder of Heaven was the artillery rending the air shaking the earth itself; cannons, mortars and musketry alike opened a fiery storm upon the advancing regiments; an iron shower of grape and round shot, shells and rockets, with a perfect tempest of rifle bullets fell upon them. On they went and down, scores falling on right and left. "The flag, the flag!" shouted the black soldiers, as the standard-bearer's body was scattered by a shell. Two file-closers struggled for its possession; a ball decided the struggle. They fell faster and faster; and ascended to Heaven. The ranks closed up while the column turned obliquely toward the point of fire, seeming to forget they were but men. Then the cross-fire of grape shot swept through their ranks, causing the glittering bayonets to go down rapidly. "Steady men, steady," cried bold Cailloux; his sword uplifted, his face the color of the sulphureous smoke that enveloped him and his followers, as they felt the deadly hail which came apparently from all sides. Captain Cailloux was killed with the colors in his hands; the column seemed to melt away like snow in sunshine, before the enemy's murderous fire; the pride, the flower of the Phalanx, had fallen. Then, with a daring that veterans only can exhibit, the blacks rushed forward and up to the brink and base of the fortified elevation, with a shout that rose above it. The defenders emptied their rifles, cannon and mortars upon the very heads of the brave assaulters, making of them a human hecatomb. Those who escaped found their way back to shelter as best they could.

The battery was not captured; the battle was lost to all except the black soldiers; they, with their terrible loss, had won and conquered a much greater and stronger battery than that upon the bluff. Nature seems to have selected the place and appointed the time for the negro to prove his manhood and to disarm the prejudice that at one time prompted the white troops to insult and assault the negro soldiers in New Orleans. It was all forgotten and they mingled together that day on terms of perfect equality. The whites were only too glad to take a drink from a negro soldier's canteen, for in that trying hour they found a brave and determined ally, ready to sacrifice all for liberty and country. If greater heroism could be shown than that of the regiments of the Phalanx already named, surely the 1st Regiment of Engineers displayed it during the siege at Port Hudson. This regiment, provided with picks and spades for the purpose of "mining" the enemy's works, often went forward to their labor without any armed support except the cover of heavy guns, or as other troops happened to advance, to throw up breastworks for their own protection. It takes men of more than ordinary courage to engage in such work, without even a revolver or a bayonet to defend themselves against the sallies of an enemy's troops. Nevertheless this Engineer Regiment of the black Phalanx performed the duty under such trying and perilous circumstances. Many times they went forward at a double-quick to do duty in the most dangerous place during an engagement, perhaps to build a redoubt or breastworks behind a brigade, or to blow up a bastion of the enemy's. "They but reminded the lookers on," said a correspondent of a Western newspaper, "of just so many cattle going to a slaughterhouse."

But there had been so much incredulity avowed regarding the courage of the negroes; so much wit lavished on the idea of negroes fighting to any purpose, that General Banks was justified in according a special commendation to the 1st, 2nd and 3rd Regiments, and to the 1st Engineer Regiment, of the Phalanx, saying, "No troops could be more determined or daring." The 1st lost its Cailloux, the 2nd its Paine, but the Phalanx won honor for the race it represented.

FROM CHAPTER VII
DEPARTMENT OF THE SOUTH:
"THE BATTLE OF THE OLUSTEE"

"The twentieth day of February, 1864, was one of the most

disastrous to the Federal arms, and to the administration of President Lincoln, in the annals of the war for the union. Through private advice Mr. Lincoln had received information which led him to believe that the people in the State of Florida, a large number of them, at least, were ready and anxious to identify the State with the cause of the Union, and be readily approved of the Federal forces occupying the State, then almost deserted by the rebels. Gen. Gillmore, commanding the Department of the South had a large force before Charleston, S.C., which had been engaged in the capture of Fort Wagner and the bombardment of the city of Charleston, and the reduction of Sumter.

"These objects being accomplished, the army having rested several months, Gen. Gillmore asked for leave to undertake such expeditions within his Department as he might think proper. About the middle of December, 1863, the War Department granted him his request, and immediately he began making preparations for an expedition, collecting transports, commisssary stores, drilling troops, etc., etc.

"About the 1st of January, 1864, General Gillmore wrote to the General-in-Chief, Halleck, that he was about to occupy the west bank of St. Johns river, with the view (1st) to open an outlet to cotton, lumber, etc., (2d) to destroy one of the enemy's sources of supplies, (3d) to give the negroes opportunity of enlisting in the army, (4th) to inaugurate measures for the speedy restoration of Florida to the Union.

"In accordance with instructions from President Lincoln received through the assistant Adjutant General, Major J.H. Hay, who would accompany the expedition, on the 5th of February the troops began to embark under the immediate command of General Truman Seymour, on board of twenty steamers and eight schooners, consisting of the following regiments, numbering in all six thousand troops, and under convoy of the gunboat Norwich:

"40th Massachusetts Mounted Infantry, Col. Guy V. Henry.

"7th Connecticut, Col. J.R. Hawley.

"7th New Hampshire, Col. Abbott.

"47th, 48th and 115th New York, Col. Barton's command.

"The Phalanx regiments were: 8th Pennsylvania, Col.

Fribley; 1st North Carolina, Lt.-Col. Reed; 54th Massachusetts, Col. Hollowell; 2nd South Carolina, Col. Beecher; 55th Massachusetts, Col. Hartwell, with three batteries of white troops, Hamilton's, Elder's and Langdon's. Excepting the two last named regiments, this force landed at Jacksonville on the 7th of February, and pushed on, following the 40th Massachusetts Mounted Infantry, which captured by a bold dash Camp Finnigan, about seven miles from Jacksonville, with its equipage, eight pieces of artillery, and a number of prisoners. On the 10th, the whole force had reached Baldwin, a railroad station twenty miles west of Jacksonville. There the army encamped, except Col. Henry's force, which continued its advance towards Tallahassee, driving a small force of Gen. Finnegan's command before him. This was at the time all the rebel force in east Florida. On the 18th Gen. Seymour, induced by the successful advance of Col. Henry, lead his troops from Baldwin with ten days' rations in their haversacks, and started for the Suwanee river, about a hundred and thirty miles from Baldwin station, leaving the 2d South Carolina and the 55th Massachusetts Phalanx regiments to follow. After a fatiguing march the column, numbering about six thousand, reached Barbour's Station, on the Florida Central Railroad, twenty miles from Baldwin. Here the command halted and bivouaced, the night of the 19th, in the woods bordering upon a wooded ravine running off towards the river from the railroad track.

"It is now nineteen years ago, and I write from memory of a night long to be remembered. Around many a Grand Army Camp-fire in the last fifteen years this bivouac has been made the topic of an evening's talk. It was attended with no particular hardship. The weather was such as is met with in these latitudes, not cold, not hot, and though a thick vapory cloud hid the full round moon from early eventide until the last regiment filed into the woods, yet there was a halo of light that brightened the white, sandy earth and gave to the moss-laden limbs of the huge pines which stood sentry-like on the roadside the appearance of a New England grove on a frosty night, with a shelled road leading through it.

"It was well in the night when the two Phalanx regiments

filed out of the road into the woods, bringing up the rear of the army, and took shelter under the trees from the falling dew.   Amid the appalling stillness that reigned throughout the encampment, except the tramp of feet and an occasional whickering of a battery horse, no sound broke the deep silence.   Commands were given in an undertone and whispered along the long lines of weary troops that lay among the trees and the underbrush of the pine forest.   Each soldier lay with his musket beside him, ready to spring to his feet and in line for battle, for none knew the moment the enemy, like a tiger, would pounce upon them.   It was a night of intense anxiety, shrouded in mystery as to what to-morrow would bring.   The white and black soldier in one common bed lay in battle panoply, dreaming their common dreams of home and loved ones.

"Here lay the heroic 54th picturing to themselves the memorable nights of July 17 and 18, their bivouac on the beach and their capture of Fort Wagner and the terrible fate of their comrades.   They were all veteran troops save the 8th Pennsylvania, which upon many hard-fought fields had covered themselves with gallant honor in defense of their country's cause, from Malvern Hill to Morris Island.

It was in the gray of the next morning that Gen. Seymour's order aroused the command.   The men partook of a hastily prepared cup of coffee and meat and hard-tack from their haversacks.   At sunrise the troops took up the line of march, following the railroad for Lake City.   Col. Henry, with the 40th Massachusetts Mounted Infantry and Major Stevens' independent battalion of Massachusetts cavalry, led the column.   About half-past one o'clock they reached a point where the country road crossed the railroad, about two miles east of Olustee, and six miles west of Sanderson, a station through which the troops passed about half-past eleven o'clock.   As the head of the column reached the crossing the rebel pickets fired and fell back upon a line of skirmishers, pursued by Col. Henry's command.   The enemy's main force was supposed to be some miles distant from this place, consequently General Seymour had not taken the precaution to protect his flanks, though marching through an enemy's country.   Consequently he found his troops flanked on either side.

"Col. Henry drove the skirmishers back upon their main forces, which were strongly posted between two swamps. The position was admirably chosen; their right rested upon a low, slight earthwork, protected by rifle-pits, their center was defended by an impassable swamp, and on their left was a cavalry force drawn up on a small elevation behind the shelter of a grove of pines. Their camp was intersected by the railroad, on which was placed a battery capable of operating against the center and left of the advancing column, while a rifle gun, mounted on a railroad flat, pointed down the road in front.

"Gen. Seymour, in order to attack this strongly fortified position, had necessarily to place his troops between the two swamps, one in his front, the other in the rear. The Federal cavalry, following up the skirmishers, had attacked the rebel right and were driven back, but were met by the 7th New Hampshire, 7th Connecticut, a regiment of the black Phalanx (8th Pennsylvania), and Elder's battery of four and Hamilton's of six pieces. This force was hurled against the rebel right with such impetuosity that the batteries were within one hundred yards of the rebel line of battle before they knew it. However, they took position, and supported by the Phalanx regiment, opened a vigorous fire upon the rebel earthworks. The Phalanx regiment advanced within twenty or thirty yards of the enemy's rifle-pits, and poured a volley of minie balls into the very faces of those who did not fly on their approach.

"The 7th Connecticut and the 7th New Hampshire, the latter with their seven-shooters, Spencer repeaters, Col. Hawley, commanding, had taken a stand further to the right of the battery, and were hotly engaging the rebels. The Phalanx regiment (8th), after dealing out two rounds from its advanced position, finding the enemy's force in the center preparing to charge upon them, fell back under cover of Hamilton's battery, which was firing vigorously and effectively into the rebel column. The 7th Connecticut and New Hampshire about this time ran short of ammunition, and Col. Hawley, finding the rebels outnumbered his force three to one, was about ordering Col. Abbott to fall back and out of the concentrated fire of the enemy pouring upon his men, when he observed the rebels coming in for a down upon his column.

"Here they come like tigers; the Federal column wavers a little; it staggers and breaks, falling back in considerable disorder! Col. Hawley now ordered Col. Fribley to take his Phalanx Regiment, the 8th, to the right of the battery and check the advancing rebel force. No time was to be lost, the enemy's sharpshooters had already silenced two of Hamilton's guns, dead and dying men and horses lay in a heap about them, while at the remaining four guns a few brave artillerists were loading and fixing their pieces, retarding the enemy in his onward movement.

"Deficient in artillery, they had not been able to check the Federal cavalry in its dash, but the concentrated fire from right to center demoralized, and sent them galloping over the field wildly. Col. Fribley gave the order by the right flank, double quick! and the next moment the 8th Phalanx swept away to the extreme right in support of the 7th New Hampshire and the 7th Connecticut. The low, direct aim of the enemy in the rifle-pits, his Indian sharp-shooters up in the trees, had ere now so thinned the ranks of Col. Hawley's command that his line was gone, and the 8th Phalanx met the remnant of his brigade as it was going to the rear in complete disorder. The rebels ceased firing and halted as the Phalanx took position between them and their fleeing comrades. They halted not perforce, but apparently for deliberation, when with one fell swoop in the next moment they swept the field in their front.

"The Phalanx did not, however, quit the field in a panic-stricken manner but fell hastily back to the battery, only to find two of the guns silent and their brave workers and horses nearly all of them dead upon the field. With a courage undaunted, surpassed by no veteran troops on any battle-field, the Phalanx attempted to save the silent guns. In this effort Col. Fribley was killed, in the torrent of rebel bullets which fell upon the regiment. It held the two guns, despite two desperate charges made by the enemy to capture them, but the stubbornness of the Phalanx was no match for the ponderous weight of their enemy's column, their sharp-shooters and artillery mowing down ranks of their comrades at every volley. A grander spectacle was never witnessed than that which this regiment gave of gallant courage. They left their guns only when their line officers and three hundred and fifty of their valient soldiers were dead upon the field, the work of an hour and a half. The battery lost forty of its horses and four of its brave men. The Phalanx saved the colors of the battery with its own. Col. Barton's brigade, the 47th, 48th and 115th New York, during the fight on the right had held the enemy in the front and center at bay, covering Elder's battery, and nobly did they do their duty, bravely maintaining the reputation they had won before Charleston, but like the other troops, the contest was too unequal. The rebels outnumbered them five to one, and they likewise gave way, leaving about a fouth of their number upon the field, dead and wounded.

"Col. Montgomery's brigade, comprising two Phalanx regiments, 54th Massachusetts and 1st North Carolina, which had been held in reserve about a mile down the road, now came up at double-quick. They were under heavy marching orders, with ten days' rations in their knapsacks, besides their cartridge boxes they carried ten rounds in their overcoat pockets. The road was sandy, and the men often found their feet beneath the sand, but with their wonted alacrity they speed on up the road, the 54th leading in almost a locked running step, followed closely by the 1st North Carolina. As they reached the road intersected by the railroad they halted in the rear of what remained of Hamilton's battery, loading a parting shot. The band of the 54th took position on the side of the road, and while the regiments were unstringing knapsacks as coolly as if about to bivouac, the music of the band burst out on the sulphureous air, amid the roar of artillery, the rattle of musketry and the shouts of commands, mingling its soul-stirring strains with the deafening yells of the charging columns, right, left, and from the rebel center. Thus on the very edge of the battle, nay, in the battle, the Phalanx band poured out in heroic measures 'The Star Spangled Banner.' Its thrilling notes, souring above the battles' gales, aroused to new life and renewed energy the panting, routed troops, flying in broken and disordered ranks from the field.

Many of them halted, the New York troops particularly, and gathered at the battery again, pouring a deadly volley into the enemy's works and ranks. The 54th had but a moment to prepare for the task. General Seymour rode up and appealed to the Phalanx to check the enemy and save the army from complete and total annihilation. Col. Montgomery gave Col. Hallowell the order 'Forward,' pointing to the left, and away went the 54th Phalanx regiment through the woods, down into the swamp, wading up to their knees--in places where the water reached their hips; yet on they went till they reached terra firma. Soon the regiment stood in line of battle, ready to meet the enemy's advancing cavalry, emerging from the extreme left.

"'Hold your fire!' the order ran down the line. Indeed, it was trying. The cavalry had halted but the enemy, in their rifle-pits in the center of their line, poured volley after volley into the ranks of the Phalanx, which stood like a wall of granite, holding at bay the rebel cavalry hanging on the edge of a pine grove. The 1st Phalanx regiment entered the field in front, charged the rebels in the centre of the line, driving them into their rifle-pits, and then for half an hour the carnage became frightful. They had followed the rebels into the very jaws of death, and now Col. Reid found his regiment in the enemy's enfilading fire, and they swept his line. Men fell like snowflakes. Driven by this terrific fire, they fell back. the 54th had taken ground to the right, lending whatever of assistance they could to their retiring comrades, who were about on a line with them, for although retreating, it was in the most cool and deliberate manner, and the two regiments began a firing at will against the rebels, though outnumbering them, could not face. Thus they held them till long after sunset, and firing ceased.

"The slaughter was terrible; the Phalanx lost about 800 men, the white troops about 600. It was Braddock's defeat after the lapse of a century."

CHAPTER XI
THE PHALANX IN VIRGINIA

The laurels won by the Phalanx in the Southern States,

notwithstanding the "no quarter" policy, was proof of its devotion to the cause of liberty and the old flag, which latter, until within a short period had been but a symbol of oppression to the black man; Cailloux had reddened it with his life's blood, and Carney, in a seething fire had planted it on the ramparts of Wagner. The audacious bravery of the Phalanx had wrung from Generals Banks and Gillmore congratulatory orders, while the loyal people of the nation poured out unstinted praises. Not a breach of discipline marred the negro soldier's record; not one cowardly act tarnished their fame. Grant pronounced them gallant and reliable, and Weitzel was willing to command them.

In New York City, where negroes had been hung to lamp posts, and where a colored orphan asylum had been sacked and burned, crowds gathered in Broadway and cheered Phalanx regiments on their way to the front. General Logan, author of the Illinois Black Code, greeted them as comrades, and Jefferson Davis finally accorded to them the rights due captured soldiers as prisoners of war. Congress at last took up the question of pay, and placed the black on an equal footing with the white soldiers. Their valor, excelled by no troops in the field, had finally won full recognition from every quarter, and henceforth they were to share the full glory as well as the toils of their white comrades-in-arms. Not until those just rights and attentions were attained, was the Phalanx allowed, to any great extent, to show its efficiency and prowess in the manoeuvres in Virginia and vicinity, where that magnificent "Army of Northern Virginia," the hope and the pride of the Confederacy, was operating against the Federal government. But when General Grant came to direct the movements of the Eastern armies of the United States, there was a change. He had learned from his experience at Vicksburg and other places in his western campaigns, that the negro soldiers were valuable; that they could be fully relied upon in critical times, and their patriotic zeal had made a deep impression upon him. Therefore, as before stated, there were changes, and quite a good many Phalanx regiments--numbering about 20,000 men--were taken from Southern and Western armies and transferred to the different armies in Virginia.

The 19th Army Corps sent one brigade. General Gillmore brought a brigade from the Tenth Army Corps. At least ten thousand of them were verterans, and had driven many confederates out of their breastworks.

The world never saw such a spectacle as America presented in the winter and early spring of 1864. The attempt to capture Richmond and Petersburg had failed. The Army of the Potomac lay like a weary lion under cover, watching its opponent. Bruised, but spirited and defiant, it had driven, and in turn had been driven time and again, by its equally valient foe. It had advanced marching and counter-marching, crossing and re-crossing the now historic streams of the Old Dominion. Of all this, the loyal people were tired and demanded of the Administration a change. The causes of the failures to take the confederate capitol were not so much the fault of the commanders of the brave army as that of the authorities at Washington, whose indecision and interference had entailed almost a disgrace upon McClellan, Hooker, Burnside and Meade. But finally the people saw the greatest of the difficulties, and demanded its removal, which the Administration signified its willingness to do. Then began an activity at the North, East and West, such as was never before witnessed. The loyal heart was again aroused by the President's call for troops, and all realized the necessity of a more sagacious policy, and the importance of bringing the war to a close. The lion of the South must be bearded in his lair, and forced to surrender Richmond, the Confederate Capitol, that had already cost the Government millions of dollars, and the North thousands of lives. The cockade city,-- Petersburg,--like the Gibralter of the Mississippi, should haul down the confederate banner from her breastworks; in fact, Lee must be vanquished. That was the demand of the loyal nation, and right well did they enter into preparations to consummate it; placing brave and skillful officers in command.

The whole North became a recruiting station. Sumner, Wilson, Stevens and Sherman, in Congress, and Greeley, Beecher, Philips and Curtis, with the press, had succeeded in placing the fight upon the highest plane of civilization, and linked *freedom* to the cause of the Union thus making the success of one the success of the other,--"Liberty and Union, one and inseparable." What patriotism should fail in accomplishing, bounties--National, State, county, city and township--were to induce and effect. The depleted ranks of the army were filled to its maximum, and with a hitherto victorious and gallant leader would be hurled against the fortifications of the Confederacy with new energy and determination.

Early in January, General Burnside was ordered again to take command of the Ninth Army Corps, and to recruit its strength to fifty thousand effective men, which he immediately began to do. General Butler, then in command of the Department of Virginia and North Carolina, began the organization of the Army of the James, collecting at Norfolk, Portsmouth and on the Peninsula, the forces scattered throughout his Department, and to recruit Phalanx regiments. In March, General Grant was called to Washington, and received the appointment of Lieutenant General, and placed in command of the armies of the Republic. He immediately began their reorganization, as a preliminary to attacking Lee's veteran army of northern Virginia.

As has before been stated, the negro had, up to this time, taken no very active part in the battles fought in Virginia. The seed of prejudice sown by Generals McDowell and McClellan at the beginning of hostilities, had ripened into productive fruit. The Army of the Potomac being early engaged in apprehending and returning runaway slaves to their presumed owners, had imbibed a bitter, unrelenting hatred for the poor, but ever loyal, negro. To this bitterness the Emancipation Proclamation gave a zest, through the pro-slavery press at the North, which taunted the soldiers with *"fighting to free the negroes."* This feeling had served to practically keep the negro, as a soldier, out of the Army of the Potomac.

General Burnside, upon assuming his command, asked for and obtained permission from the War Department to raise and unite a division of Negro troops to the 9th Army Corps. Annapolis, Md., was selected as the "depot and rendezvous," and very soon Camp Stanton had received its allowance of Phalanx regiments for the Corps. Early in April, the camp was broken, and the line of march taken for

Washington. It was rumored throughout the city that the 9th Corps would pass through there, and that about 6,000 Phalanx men would be among the troops. The citizens were on the *qui vive*; members of the Congress and the President were eager to witness the passage of the Corps.

At nine o'clock on the morning of the 25th of April, the head of the column entered the city, and at eleven the troops were marching down New York Avenue. Halting a short distance from the corner of 14th street, the column closed up, and prepared to pay the President a marching salute, who, with General Burnside and a few friends, was awaiting their coming. Mr. Lincoln and his party occupied a balcony over the entrance of Willard's Hotel. The scene was one of great beauty and animation. The day was superbly clear; the soft atmosphere of the early spring was made additionally pleasant by a cool breeze; rain had fallen the previous night, and there was no dust to cause discomfort to the soldiers or spectators. The troops marched and appeared well; their soiled and battered flags bearing inscriptions of battles of six States. The corps had achieved almost the first success of the war in North Carolina; it had hastened to the Potomac in time to aid in rescuing the Capitol, when Lee made his first Northern invasion; it won glory at South Mountain, and made the narrow bridge at Antietam, forever historic; it had likewise reached Kentucky in time to aid in driving the confederates from that State. Now it appeared with recruited ranks, and new regiments of as good blood as ever was poured out in the cause of right; and with a new element-- those whom they had helped set free from the thraldom of slavery--whom they were proud to claim as comrades.

Their banners were silent, effective witnesses of their valor and their sacrifices; Bull's Run, Ball's Bluff, Roanoke, Newburn, Gaines' Mills, Mechanicsville, Seven Pines, Savage Station, Glendale, Malvern, Fredericksburg, Chancellorsville, Antietam, South Mountain, Knoxville, Vicksburg, Port Hudson and Gettysburg, were emblazoned in letters of gold. The firm and soldierly bearing of the veterans, the eager and expectant countenances of the men and officers of the new regiments, the gay trappings of the cavalry, the thorough equipment and fine condition of the artillery, the clattering of hoofs, the clanking of sabres, the drum-beat, the bugle call, and the music of the bands were all subjects of interest. The President beheld the scene. Pavement, sidewalks, windows and roofs were crowded with people. A division of veterans passed, saluting the President and their commander with cheers. And then, with full ranks--platoons extending from sidewalk to sidewalk--brigades which had never been in battle, for the first time shouldered arms for their country; they who even then were disfranchised and were not American citizens, yet they were going out to fight for the flag. Their country was given them by the tall, pale, benevolent hearted man standing upon the balcony. For the first time, they beheld their benefactor. They were darker hued than their veteran comrades, but they cheered as lustily, "hurrah, hurrah, hurrah for Massa Linkun! Three cheers for the President!" They swung their caps, clapped their hands and shouted their joy. Long, loud and jubilant were the rejoicings of these redeemed sons of Africa. Regiment after regiment of stalwart men,--slaves once, but freemen now,--with steady step and even ranks, passed down the street, moving on to the Old Dominion. It was the first review of the negro troops by the President. Mr. Lincoln himself seemed greatly pleased, and acknowledged the plaudits and cheers of the Phalanx soldiers with a dignified kindness and courtesy. It was a spectacle which made many eyes grow moist, and left a life-long impression. Thus the corps that had never lost a flag or a gun, marched through the National Capitol, crossed long bridge and went into camp near Alexandria, where it remained until the 4th of May.

The Phalanx regiments composing the 4th division were the 19th, 23rd, 27th, 28th, 29th, 30th, 31st, 39th and 43rd, commanded by General E. Ferrero.

The Army of the James, under General Butler, which was to act in conjunction with the Army of the Potomac, under Meade, was composed of the 10th and 18th Corps. The 10th Corps had two brigades of the Phalanx, consisting of the 7th, 9th, 29th, 16th, 8th, 41st, 45th and 127th Regiments, commanded by Colonels James Shaw, Jr., and Ulysses Doubleday, and constituted the 3rd division of that Corps commanded by Brigadier-General Wm. Birney.

The 3rd division of the 18th Corps, commanded by Brigadier-General Charles G. Paine, was composed of the 1st, 22nd, 37th, 5th, 36th, 38th, 4th, 6th, 10th, 107th, 117th, 118th, and 2nd Cavalry, with Colonels Elias Wright, Alonzo G. Draper, John W. Ames and E. Martindale as brigade commanders of the four brigades. A cavalry force numbering about two thousand, comprising the 1st and 2nd, was under command of Colonel West, making not less than 20,000 of the Phalanx troops, including the 4th Division with the Ninth Corps, and augmenting Butler's force to 47,000 concentrated at Yorktown and Gloucester Point.

On the 28th of April, Butler received his final orders, and on the night of the 4th of May embarked his troops on transports, descended the York river, passed Fortress Monroe and ascended the James River. Convoyed by a fleet of armored war vessels and gunboats, his transports reached Bermuda Hundreds on the afternoon of the 5th. General Wilde, with a brigade of the Phalanx, occupied Fort Powhatan, on the south bank of the river, and Wilson's Wharf, about five miles below on the north side of the James, with the remainder of his division of 5,000 of the Phalanx. General Hinks landed at City Point, at the mouth of the Appomattox. The next morning the troops advanced to Trent's, with their left resting on the Appomattox, near Walthall, and the right on the James, and intrenched. In the meantime, Butler telegraphed Grant:

'OFF CITY POINT, VA., May 5th.
"LIEUT. GEN. GRANT, Commanding Armies of the United States, Washington, D.C.:

"We have seized Wilson's Wharf Landing; a brigade of Wilde's "colored" troops are there; at Fort Powhatan landing two regiments of the same brigade have landed. At City Point, Hinks' division, with the remaining troops and battery, have landed. The remainder of both the 18th and 10th Army Corps are being landed at Bermuda Hundreds, above Appomattox. No opposition experienced thus far, the movement was comparatively a complete surprise. Both army corps left Yorktown during last night. The monitors are all over the bar at Harrison's landing and above City Point. The operations of the fleet have been conducted to-day with energy and success. Gens. Smith and Gillmore are pushing the landing of the men. Gen. Graham with the army gunboats, lead the advance during the night, capturing the signal station of the rebels. Colonel West, with 1800 cavalry, made several demonstrations from Williamsburg yesterday morning. Gen. Rantz left Suffolk this morning with his cavalry, for the service indicated during the conference with the Lieut.-General. The New York flag-of-truce boat was found lying at the wharf with four hundred prisoners, whom she had not time to deliver. She went up yesterday morning. We are landing troops during the night, a hazardous service in the face of the enemy.

> "BENJ. F. BUTLER,
> "A.F. PUFFER, Capt. and A.D.C.   *Maj. Gen. Commanding.*

About two miles in front of their line ran the Richmond & Petersburg Railroad, near which the enemy was encountered. Butler's movements being in concert with that of the Army of the Potomac and the 9th Corps,--the latter as yet an independent organization.

General Meade, with the Army of th Potomac, numbering 120,000 effective men, crossed the Rapidan *en route* for the Wilderness, each soldier carrying fifty rounds of ammunition and three days rations. The supply trains were loaded with ten days forage and subsistence. The advance was in two columns, General Warren being on the right and General Hancock on the left. Sedgwick followed closely upon Warren and crossed the Rapidan at Germania Ford. The Ninth Corps received its orders on the 4th, whereupon General Burnside immediately put the Corps in motion toward the front. Bivouacking at midnight, the line of march was again taken up at daylight, and at night the Rapidan was crossed at Germania Ford. The corps marched on a road parallel to that of its old antagonist, General Longstreet's army, which was hastening to assist Lee, who had met the Army of the Potomac in the entanglements of the wilderness, where a stubborn and sanguinary fight raged for two days. General Ferrero's division, composed of the Phalanx regiments, reached Germania Ford on the morning of the 6th, with the cavalry, and reported to General Sedgwick, of the 6th Corps, who had the care of the trains. The enemy was projecting an attack upon the rear of the advancing columns. Gen. Ferrero was ordered to guard with his Phalanx division, the bridges, roads and trains near and at the Rapidan river. That night the confederates attacked Sedgwick in force; wisely the immense supply trains had been committed to the care of the

Phalanx, and the enemy was driven back before daylight, while the trains were securely moved up closer to the advance. General Grant, finding that the confederates were not disposed to continue the battle, began the movement toward Spottsylvania Court House on the night of the 7th. The 9th Corps brought up the rear, with the Phalanx division and cavalry covering the trains.

Butler and his Phalanx troops, as we have seen, was within six miles of Petersburg, and on the 7th, Generals Smith and Gillmore reached the railroad near Port Walthall Junction, and commenced destroying it; the confederates attacked them, but were repulsed. Col. West, on the north side of the James River, forded the Chickahominy with the Phalanx cavalry, and arrived opposite City Point, having destroyed the railroad for some distance on that side.

Leaving General Hinks with his Phalanx division to hold City Point, on the 9th Butler again moved forward to break up the railroad which the forces under Smith and Gillmore succeeded in doing, thus separating Beaureguard's force from Lee's. He announced the result of his operation's in the following message to Washington:

"May 9th, 1864.

"Our operations may be summed up in a few words. With one thousand and seven hundred cavalry we have advanced up the Peninsula, forced the Chickahominy and have safely brought them to our present position. These were *colored cavalry*, and are now holding our advanced pickets toward Richmond. General Kautz, with three thousand cavalry from Suffolk, on the same day with our movement up James river, forced the Blackwater, burned the railroad bridge at Stony Creek, below Petersburg, cutting in two Beauregard's force at that point. We have landed here, intrenched ourselves, destroyed many miles of railroad, and got possession, which, with proper supplies, we can hold out against the whole of Lee's army. I have ordered up the supplies. Beauregard, with a large portion of his force, was left south, by the cutting of the railroad by Kautz. That portion which reached Petersburg under Hill, I have whipped to-day, killing and wounding many, and taking many prisoners, after a well contested fight. General Grant will not be troubled with any further re-inforcements to Lee from Beaureguard's force.   'BENJ. F. BUTLER,
Major-General."

But for having been misinformed as to Lee's retreating on Richmond,--which led him to draw his forces back into his intrenchments,--Butler would have undoubtedly marched triumphantly into Petersburg. The mistake gave the enemy holding the approaches to that city time to be re-enforced, and Petersburg soon became well fortified and garrisoned. Beaureguard succeeded in a few days time in concentrating in front of Butler 25,000 troops, thus checking the latter's advance toward Richmond and Petersburg, on the south side of the James, though skirmishing went on at various points.

General Grant intended to have Butler advance and capture Petersburg, while General Meade, with the Army of the Potomac, advanced upon Richmond from the north bank of the James river. Gen. Butler failed to accomplish more than his dispatches related, though his forces entered the city of Petersburg, captured Chester Station, and destroyed the railroad connection between Petersburg and Richmond. Failure to support his troops and to intrench lost him all he had gained, and he returned to his intrenchments at Bermuda Hundreds.

The Phalanx (Hinks division) held City Point and other stations on the river, occasionally skirmishing with the enemy, who, ever mindful of the fact that City Point was the base of supplies for the Army of the James, sought every opportunity to raid it, but they always found the Phalanx ready and on the alert.

After the battle of Drewry's Bluff, May 16th, Butler thought to remain quiet in his intrenchments, but Grant, on the 22nd, ordered him to send all his troops, save enough to hold City Point, to join the Army of the Potomac; whereupon General W.F. Smith, with 16,000 men, embarked for the White House, on the Pamunky river, Butler retaining the Phalanx division and the Cavalry. Thus ended the operations of the Army of the James, until Grant crossed the river with the army of the Potomac.

On the 13th of May, Grant determined upon a flank movement toward Bowling Green, with a view of making Port Royal, instead of Fredericksburg, his depot for supplies. Sending his reserve artillery to Belle Plain, he prepared to advance. It was in this manoeuvre that Lee, for the last time, attacked the Federal forces, outside of cover, in any important movement. The attempt to change the base of supply was indeed a hazardous move for Grant; it necessitated the moving of his immense train, numbering four thousand wagons, used in carrying rations, ammunition and supplies for his army, and transportation of the badly wounded to the rear, where they could be cared for.

Up to this time, the Wilderness campaign had been a continuous fight and march. The anxiety which Grant felt for his train, is perhaps best told by himself:

"My movements are terribly embarrassed by our immense wagon train. It could not be avoided, however."

It was the only means by which the army could obtain needful supplies, and was consequently indispensable. It was the near approach to the train that made the confederates often fight so desperately, for they knew if they could succeed in capturing a wagon they would probably get something to eat. Soon after the advance began, it was reported to Grant, that the confederate cavalry was in the rear, in search of the trains. On the 14th he ordered General Ferrero to "keep a sharp lookout for this cavalry, and if you can attack it with your (Phalanx) infantry and (white) cavalry, do so." On the 19th Ferrero, with his Phalanx division, (4th division, 9th Corps) was on the road to Fredericksburg, in rear of and to the right of General Tyler's forces, in the confederates' front. The road formed Grant's direct communication with his base, and here the confederates, under Ewell attacked the Federal troops. Grant sent this dispatch to Ferrero:

"The enemy have crossed the Ny on the right of our lines, in considerable force, and may possibly detach a force to move on Fredericksburg. Keep your cavalry pickets well out on the plank road, and all other roads leading west and south of you. If you find the enemy moving infantry and artillery to you, report it promptly. In that case take up strong positions and detain him all you can, turning all your trains back to Fredericksburg, and whatever falling back you may be forced to do, do it in that direction."

The confederates made a dash for the train and captured twenty-seven wagons, but before they had time to feast off of their booty the Phalanx was upon them. The enemy fought with uncommon spirit; it was the first time "F.F.V's," the chivalry of the South,--composing the Army of Northern

Virginia,--had met the negro soldiers, and true to their instinctive hatred of their black brothers, they gave them the best they had; lead poured like rain for a while, and then came a lull. Ferrero knew what it meant, and prepared for their coming. A moment more and the accustomed yell rang out above the roar of the artillery. The confederates charged down upon the Phalanx, but to no purpose, save to make the black line more stable. They retaliated, and the confederates were driven as the gale drives chaff, the Phalanx recapturing the wagons and saving Grant's line of communication. General Badeau, speaking of their action, in his military history of Grant, says:

"It was the first time at the East when colored troops had been engaged in any important battle, and the display of soldierly qualities won a frank acknowledgment from both troops and commanders, not all of whom had before been willing to look upon negroes as comrades. But after that time, white soldiers in the army of the Potomac were not displeased to receive the support of black ones; they had found the support worth having."

SUSIE KING
TAYLOR

SUSIE KING TAYLOR
(1848-1912)

One of the most informative books about the participation of Blacks as soldiers in the Civil War is *Army Life in A Black Regiment* by Thomas Wentworth Higginson. Higginson had himself begun to recruit a regiment in the spring of 1862, the Forty-first Massachusetts. It is an interesting coincidence that at the same time he entered into a life-long correspondence with the poet Emily Dickinson, whose "Dear Preceptor" he was to become. However, when the Fifty-first was on the verge of leaving for duty, Higginson was invited to take command of the First South Carolina Volunteers in South Carolina of Union-held Port Royal. The First South Carolina was a regiment of freed slaves, and it is Higginson's experience with this group, later known as the Thirty-third U.S. Colored Troops, which provides the substance of his classic work.

A slight volume, by Susie King Taylor, a remarkable Black woman born in slavery, *Reminiscences of My Life in Camp* (1902), provides an interesting pendant to the ampler volume by Higginson, who wrote in his introduction to Taylor's book:

> Actual military life is rarely described by a woman, and this is especially true of a woman whose place was in the ranks, as the wife of a soldier and herself a regimental laundress. No such description has ever been given, I am sure by one thus connected with a colored regiment; so that the nearly 200,000 Black soldiers (178,975) of our Civil War have never before been delineated from the woman's point of view.

In her account, Susie Taylor mentions a great-great-grandmother who died at 120 years and who had five sons who served in the Revolutionary War. Her great-grandmother lived to be 100 years old. Taylor was herself born near Savannah in August, 1848 and was reared by her grandmother in Savannah, where she and her brother were taught to read and write by a widowed free Black woman, a

Mrs. Woodhouse:

> We went every day about nine o'clock, with our books wrapped in paper
> to prevent the police or white persons from seeing them. We went in, one at
> a time, through the gate, into the yard to the L kitchen, which was the
> schoolroom. She had twenty-five or thirty children whom she taught, as-
> sisted by her daughter, Mary Jane. The neighbors would see us going in
> sometimes, but they supposed we were there learning trades...

In April of 1862, after a long period of speculation and
hope among Savannah's Blacks concerning the possibility of
seeking freedom with the Union Troops, the 14 year old Taylor was taken by an uncle, along with his own seven children, behind the Union lines. She describes her arrival at St.
Simon's Island and subsequent events in her narrative written years later. What Taylor gives us in her account is a
sense of day-to-day life in the encampment and of the haz-
ards both ordinary and extraordinary which are the fortunes
of war.

After the war Taylor returned with her husband to
Savannah where she opened a school to teach ex-slave children and adults, an undertaking similar no doubt to hundreds and even thousands of such enterprises in the South in
the years following the war. Her husband died shortly after,
and after a series of reverses she was forced to turn to domestic service to support her young child. In 1874, having
previously travelled to the North with an employer, she
moved to Boston and in 1879 married Russell L. Taylor. She
devoted much of her time in subsequent years to veteran's
activities, organizing and holding various offices in a
women's auxiliary to the G.A.R.

From the vantage point of 1902, looking back at the war
years, Taylor wrote:

> There are many people who do not know what some of the colored
> women did during the war. There were hundreds of them who assisted the
> Union soldiers by hiding them and helping them to escape. Many were
> punished for taking food to the prison stockades for the prisoners.... These
> things should be kept in history before the people. There has never been a
> greater war in the United States than the one of 1861, where so many lives
> were lost—not men alone but noble women as well.

Comparing 1861 with 1902, Taylor concluded:

What a wonderful revolution! In 1861 the Southern papers were full of advertisements for 'slaves,' but now, despite all the hindrances and 'race problems,' my people are striving to attain the full standard of all other races born free in the sight of God, and in a number of instances have succeeded. Justice we ask--to be citizens of these United States, where so many of our people have shed their blood with their white comrades, that the stars and stripes should never be polluted.

CHAPTER III
ON ST. SIMON'S ISLAND
1862

NEXT morning we arrived at St. Simon's, and the captain told Commodore Goldsborough about this affair, and his reply was, "Captain Whitmore, you should not have allowed them to return; you should have kept them." After I had been on St. Simon's about three days, Commodore Goldsborough heard of me, and came to Gaston Bluff to see me. I found him very cordial. He said Captain Whitmore had spoken to him of me, and that he was pleased to hear of my being so capable, etc., and wished me to take charge of a school for the children on the island. I told him I would gladly do so, if I could have some books. He said I should have them, and in a week or two I received two large boxes of books and testaments from the North. I had about forty children to teach, beside a number of adults who came to me nights, all of them so eager to learn to read, to read above anything else. Chaplain French, of Boston, would come to the school, sometimes, and lecture to the pupils on Boston and the North.

About the first of June we were told that there was going to be a settlement of the war. Those who were on the Union side would remain free, and those in bondage were to work three days for their masters and three for themselves. It was a gloomy time for us all, and we were to be sent to Liberia. Chaplain French asked me would I rather go back to Savannah or go to Liberia. I told him the latter place by all means. We did not know when this would be, but we were prepared in case this settlement should be reached. However, the Confederates would not agree to the arrangement, or else it was one of the many rumors flying about at the time, as we heard nothing further of the matter. There were a number of settlements on this island of St. Simon's, just like little villages, and we would go from one to the other on business, to call, or only for a walk.

One Sunday, two men, Adam Miller and Daniel Spaulding, were chased by some rebels as they were coming from Hope Place (which was between the Beach and Gaston Bluff), but the latter were unable to catch them. When they reached the Beach and told this, all the men on the place, about ninety, armed themselves, and next day (Monday), with Charles O'Neal as their leader, skirmished the island for the "rebs." In a short while they discovered them in the woods, hidden behind a large log, among the thick underbrush. Charles O'Neal was the first to see them, and he was killed; also John Brown, and their bodies were never found. Charles O'Neal was an uncle of Edward King, who later was my husband and a sergeant in Co. E., U.S.I. Another man was shot, but not found for three days. On Tuesday, the second day, Captain Trowbridge and some soldiers landed, and assisted the skirmishers. Word having been sent by the mail-boat Uncas to Hilton Head, later in the day Commodore Goldsborough, who was in command of the naval station, landed about three hundred marines, and joined the others to oust the rebels. On Wednesday, John Baker, the man shot on Monday, was found in a terrible condition by Henry Batchlott, who carried him to the Beach, where he was attended by the surgeon. He told us how, after being shot, he lay quiet for a day. On the second day he managed to reach some wild grapes growing near him. These he ate, to satisfy his hunger and intense thirst, then he crawled slowly, every movement causing agony, until he got to the side of the road. He lived only three months after they found him.

On the second day of the skirmish the troops captured a boat which they knew the Confederates had used to land in, and having this in their possession, the "rebs" could not return; so pickets were stationed all around the island. There was an old man, Henry Capers, who had been left on one of the places by his old master, Mr. Hazzard, as he was too old to carry away. These rebels went to his house in the night, and he hid them up in the loft. On Tuesday all hands went to this man's house with a determination to burn it down, but Henry Batchlott pleaded with the men to spare it. The rebels were in hiding, still, waiting a chance to get off the island. They searched his house, but neglected to go up into the loft, and in so doing missed the rebels concealed there. Late in the night Henry Capers gave them his boat to escape in, and they got off all right. This old man was allowed by the men in charge of the island to cut grass for his horse, and to have a boat to carry this grass to his home, and so they were not detected, our men thinking it was Capers using the boat. After Commodore Goldsborough left the island, Commodore Judon sent the old man over to the mainland and would not allow him to remain on the island.

There were about six hundred men, women, and children on St. Simon's, the women and children being in the majority, and we were afraid to go very far from our own quarters in the daytime, and at night even to go out of the house for a long time, although the men were on the watch all the time; for there were not any soldiers on the island, only the marines who were on the gunboats along the coast. The rebels, knowing this, could steal by them under cover of the night, and getting on the island would capture any persons venturing out alone and carry them to the mainland. Several of the men disappeared, and as they were never heard from we came to the conclusion they had been carried off in this way.

The latter part of August, 1862, Captain C.T. Trowbridge, with his brother John and Lieutenant Walker, came to St. Simon's Island from Hilton Head, by order of General Hunter, to get all the men possible to finish filling his regiment which he had organized in March, 1862. He had heard of the skirmish on this island, and was very much pleased at the bravery shown by these men. He found me at Gaston Bluff teaching my little school, and was much interested in it. When I knew him better I found him to be a thorough gentleman and a staunch friend to my race.

Captain Trowbridge remained with us until October, when the order was received to evacuate, and so we boarded the Ben-De-Ford, a transport, for Beaufort, S.C. When we arrived in Beaufort, Captain Trowbridge and the men he had enlisted went to camp at Old Fort, which they named "Camp Saxton." I was enrolled as laundress.

The first suits worn by the boys were red coats and pants, which they disliked very much, for, they said, "The rebels see us, miles away."

The first colored troops did not receive any pay for eighteen months, and the men had to depend wholly on what they received from the commissary, established by General Saxton. A great many of these men had large families, and as they had no money to give them, their wives were obliged to support themselves and children by washing for the officers of the gunboats and the soldiers, and making cakes and pies which they sold to the boys in camp. Finally, in 1863, the government decided to give them half pay, but the men would not accept this. They wanted "full pay" or nothing. They preferred rather to give their services to the state, which they did until 1864, when the government granted them full pay, with all the back pay due.

I remember hearing Captain Heasley telling his company, one day, "Boys, stand up for your full pay! I am with you, and so are all the officers." This captain was from Pennsylvania, and was a very good man; all the men liked him. N.G. Parker, our first lieutenant, was from Massachusetts. H.A. Beach was from New York. He was very delicate, and had to resign in 1864 on account of ill health.

I had a number of relatives in this regiment,--several uncles, some cousins, and a husband in Company E, and a number of cousins in other companies. Major Strong, of this regiment, started home on a furlough, but the vessel he was aboard was lost, and he never reached his home. He was one of the best officers we had. After his death, Captain C.T. Trowbridge was promoted major, August, 1863, and filled Major Strong's place until December, 1864, when he was promoted lieutenant-colonel, which he remained until he was mustered out, February, 6, 1866.

In February, 1863, several cases of varioloid broke out among the boys, which caused some anxiety in camp. Edward Davis, of Company E (the company I was with), had it very badly. He was put into a tent apart from the rest of the men, and only the doctor and camp steward, James Cummings, were allowed to see or attend him; but I went to see this man every day and nursed him. The last thing at night, I always went in to see that he was comfortable, but in spite of the good care and attention he received, he succumbed to the disease.

I was not in the least afraid of the small-pox. I had been vaccinated, and I drank sassafras tea constantly, which kept my blood purged and prevented me from contracting this dread scourge, and no one need fear getting it if they will only keep their blood in good condition with this sassafras tea, and take it before going where the patient is.

CHAPTER IV
CAMP SAXTON--
PROCLAMATION AND BARBECUE
1863

ON the first of January, 1863, we held services for the purpose of listening to the reading of President Lincoln's proclamation by Dr. W. H. Brisbane, and the presentation of two beautiful stands of colors, one from a lady in Connecticut, and the other from Rev. Mr. Cheever. The presentation speech was made by Chaplain French. It was a glorious day for us all, and we enjoyed every minute of it, and as a fitting close and the crowning event of this occasion we had a grand barbecue. A number of oxen were roasted whole, and we had a fine feast. Although not served as tastily or correctly as it would have been at home, yet it was enjoyed with keen appetites and relish. The soldiers had a good time. They sang or shouted "Hurrah!" all through the camp, and seemed overflowing with fun and frolic until taps were sounded, when many, no doubt, dreamt of this memorable day.

I had rather an amusing experience; that is, it seems amusing now, as I look back, but at the time it occurred it was a most serious one to me. When our regiment left Beaufort for Seabrooke, I left some of my things with a neighbor who lived outside of the camp. After I had been at Seabrooke about a week, I decided to return to Camp Saxton to get them. So one morning, with Mary Shaw, a friend who was in the company at that time, I started off. There was no way for us to get to Beaufort other than to walk, except we rode on the commissary wagon. This we did, and reached Beaufort about one o'clock. We then had more than two miles to walk before reaching our old camp, and expected to be able to accomplish this and return in time to meet the wagon again by three o'clock that afternoon, and so be taken back. We failed to do this, however, for when we got to Beaufort the wagon was gone. We did not know what to do. I did not wish to remain overnight, neither did my friend, although we might easily have stayed, as both had relatives in the town.

It was in the springtime, and the days were long, and as the sun looked so bright, we concluded to walk back, thinking we should reach camp before dark. So off we started on our ten mile tramp. We had not gone many miles, however, before we were all tired out and began to regret our undertaking. The sun was getting low, and we grew more frightened, fearful of meeting some animal or of treading on a snake on our way. We did not meet a person, and we were frightened almost to death. Our feet were so sore we could hardly walk. Finally we took off our shoes and tried walking in our stocking feet, but this made them worse. We had gone about six miles when night overtook us. There we were, nothing around us but dense woods, and as there was no house or any place to stop at, there was nothing for us to do but continue on. We were afraid to speak to each other.

Meantime at the camp, seeing no signs of us by dusk, they concluded we had decided to remain over until next day, and so had no idea of our plight. Imagine their surprise when we reached camp about eleven P.M. The guard challenged us, "Who comes there?" My answer was, "A friend without a countersign." He approached and saw who it was, reported, and we were admitted into the lines. They had the joke on us that night, and for a long time after would tease us; and sometimes some of the men who were on guard that night would call us deserters. They used to laugh at us, but we joined with them too, especially when we would tell them our experience on our way to camp. I did not undertake that trip again, as there was no way of getting in or out except one took the provision wagon, and there was not much dependence to be put in that returning to camp. Perhaps the driver would say one hour and he might be there earlier or later. Of course it was not his fault, as it depended when the order was filled at the Commissary Department; therefore I did not go any more until the regiment was ordered to our new camp, which was named after our hero, Colonel Shaw, who at the time was at Beaufort with his regiment, the 54th Massachusetts.

I taught a great many of the comrades in Company E to read and write, when they were off duty. Nearly all were anxious to learn. My husband taught some also when it was convenient for him. I was very happy to know my efforts were successful in camp, and also felt grateful for the appreciation of my services. I gave my services willingly for four years and three months without receiving a dollar. I was glad, however, to be allowed to go with the regiment, to care for the sick and afflicted comrades.

CHAPTER V
MILITARY EXPEDITIONS

IN the latter part of 1862 the regiment made an expedition into Darien, Georgia, and up the Ridge, and on January 23, 1863, another up St. Mary's River, capturing a number of stores for the government; then on to Fernandina, Florida. They were gone ten or twelve days, at the end of which time they returned to camp.

March 10, 1863, we were ordered to Jacksonville, Florida. Leaving Camp Saxton between four and five o'clock, we arrived at Jacksonville about eight o'clock next morning, accompanied by three or four gunboats. When the rebels saw these boats, they ran out of the city, leaving the women behind, and we found out afterwards that they thought we had a much larger fleet than we really had. Our regiment was kept out of sight until we made fast at the wharf where it landed, and while the gunboats were shelling up the river and as far inland as possible, the regiment landed and marched up the street, where they spied the rebels who had fled from the city. They were hiding behind a house about a mile or so away, their faces blackened to disguise themselves as negroes, and our boys, as they advanced toward them, halted a second, saying, "They are black men! Let them come to us, or we will make them know who we are." With this, the firing was opened and several of our men were wounded and killed. The rebels had a number wounded and killed. It was through this way the discovery was made that they were white men. Our men drove them some distance in retreat and then threw out their pickets.

While the fighting was on, a friend, Lizzie Lancaster, and I stopped at several of the rebel homes, and after talking with some of the women and children we asked them if they had any food. They claimed to have only some hard-tack, and evidently did not care to give us anything to eat, but this was not surprising. They were bitterly against our people and had no mercy or sympathy for us.

The second day, our boys were reinforced by a regiment of white soldiers, a Maine regiment, and by cavalry, and had quite a fight. On the third day, Edward Herron, who was a fine gunner on the steamer John Adams, came on shore, bringing a small cannon, which the men pulled along for more than five miles. This cannon was the only piece for shelling. On coming upon the enemy, all secured their places, and they had a lively fight, which lasted several hours, and our boys were nearly captured by the Confederates; but the Union boys carried out all their plans that day, and succeeded in driving the enemy back. After this skirmish, every afternoon between four and five o'clock the Confederate General Finnegan would send a flag of truce to Colonel Higginson, warning him to send all women and children out of the city, and threatening to bombard it if this was not done. Our colonel allowed all to go who wished, at first, but as General Finegan grew more hostile and kept sending these communications for nearly a week, Colonel Higginson thought it not best or necessary to send any more out of the city, and so informed General Finegan. This angered the general, for that night the rebels shelled directly toward Colonel Higginson's headquarters. The shelling was so heavy that the colonel told my captain to have me taken up into the town to a hotel, which was used as a hospital. As my quarters were just in the rear of the colonel's, he was compelled to leave his also before the night was over. I expected every moment to be killed by a shell, but on arriving at the hospital I knew I was safe, for the shells could not reach us there. It was plainly to be seen now, the ruse of the flag of truce coming so often to us. The bearer was evidently a spy getting the location of the headquarters, etc., for the shells were sent too accurately to be at random.

Next morning Colonel Higginson took the cavalry and a regiment on another tramp after the rebels. They were gone several days and had the hardest fight they had had, for they wanted to go as far as a station which was some distance from the city. The gunboats were of little assistance to them, yet notwithstanding this drawback our boys returned with only a few killed and wounded, and after this we were not troubled with General Finegan.

We remained here a few weeks longer, when, about April first, the regiment was ordered back to Camp Saxton, where it stayed a week, when the order came to go to Port Royal Ferry on picket duty. It was a gay day for the boys. By seven o'clock all tents were down, and each company, with a commissary wagon, marched up the shell road, which is a beautiful avenue ten or twelve miles out of Beaufort. We arrived at Seabrooke at about four o'clock, where our tents were pitched and the men put on duty. We were here a few weeks, when Company E was ordered to Barnwell plantation for picket duty.

Some mornings I would go along the picket line, and I could see the rebels on the opposite side of the river. Sometimes as they were changing pickets they would call over to our men and ask for something to eat, or for tobacco, and our men would tell them to come over. Sometimes one or two would desert to us, saying, they "had no negroes to fight for." Others would shoot across at our picket, but as the river was so wide there was never any damage done, and the Confederates never attempted to shell us while we were there.

I learned to handle a musket very well while in the regiment, and could shoot straight and often hit the target. I assisted in cleaning the guns and used to fire them off, to see if the cartridges were dry, before cleaning and reloading, each day. I thought this great fun. I was also able to take a gun all apart, and put it together again.

Between Barnwell and the mainland was Hall Island. I went over there several times with Sergeant King and other comrades. One night there was a stir in camp when it was found that the rebels were trying to cross, and next morning Lieutenant Parker told me he thought they were on Hall Island; so after that I did not go over again.

While planning for the expedition up the Edisto River, Colonel Higginson was a whole night in the water, trying to locate the rebels and where their picket lines were situated. About July the boys went up the Edisto to destroy a bridge on the Charleston and Savannah road. This expedition was twenty or more miles into the mainland. Colonel Higginson was wounded in this fight and the regiment nearly captured. The steamboat John Adams always assisted us, carrying soldiers, provisions, etc. She carried several guns and a good gunner, Edward Herron. Henry Batchlott, a relative of mine, was a steward on this boat. There were two smaller boats, Governor Milton and the Enoch Dean, in the fleet, as these could go up the river better than the larger ones could. I often went aboard the John Adams. It went with us into Jacksonville, to Cole and Folly Island, and Gunner Herron was always ready to send a shell at the enemy.

One night, Companies K and E, on their way to Pocotaligo to destroy a battery that was situated down the river, captured several prisoners. The rebels nearly captured Sergeant King, who, as he sprang and caught a "reb," fell over an embankment. In falling he did not release his hold on his prisoner. Although his hip was severely injured, he held fast until some of his comrades came to his aid and pulled them up. These expeditions were very dangerous. Sometimes the men had to go five or ten miles during the night over on the rebel side and capture or destroy whatever they could find.

While at Camp Shaw, there was a deserter who came into Beaufort. He was allowed his freedom about the city and was not molested. He remained about the place a little while and returned to the rebels again. On his return to Beaufort a second time, he was held a spy, tried, and sentenced to death, for he was a traitor. The day he was shot, he was placed on a hearse with his coffin inside, a guard was placed either side of the hearse, and he was driven through the town. All the soldiers and people in town were out, as this was to be a warning to the soldiers. Our regiment was in line on dress parade. They drove with him to the rear of our camp, where he was shot. I shall never forget this scene.

While at Camp Shaw, Chaplain Fowler, Robert Defoe, and several of our boys were captured while tapping some telegraph wires. Robert Defoe was confined in the jail at Walterborough, S.C., for about twenty months. When Sherman's army reached Pocotaligo he made his escape and joined his company (Company G). He had not been paid, as he had refused the reduced pay offered by the government. Before we got to camp, where the pay-rolls could be made out, he sickened and died of small-pox, and was buried at Savannah, never having been paid one cent for nearly three years of service. He left no heirs and his account was never settled.

In winter, when it was very cold, I would take a mess-pan, put a little earth in the bottom, and go to the cook-shed and fill it nearly full of coals, carry it back to my tent and put another pan over it; so when the provost guard went through camp after taps, they would not see the light, as it was against the rules to have a light after taps. In this way I was heated and kept very warm.

A mess-pan is made of sheet iron, something like our roasting pans, only they are nearly as large round as a peck measure, but not so deep. We had fresh beef once in a while, and we would have soup, and the vegetables they put in this soup were dried and pressed. They looked like hops. Salt beef was our stand-by. Sometimes the men would have what we called slap-jacks. This was flour, made into bread and spread thin on the bottom of the mess-pan to cook. Each man had one of them, with a pint of tea, for his supper, or a pint of tea and five or six hard-tack. I often got my own meals, and would fix some dishes for the non-commissioned officers also.

Mrs. Chamberlain, our quartermaster's wife, was with us here. She was a beautiful woman; I can see her pleasant face before me now, as she, with Captain Trowbridge, would sit

and converse with me in my tent two or three hours at a
time. She was also with me on Cole Island, and I think we
were the only women with the regiment while there. I remember well how, when she first came into camp, Captain
Trowbridge brought her to my tent and introduced her to
me. I found her then, as she remained ever after, a lovely
person, and I always admired her cordial and friendly ways.

Our boys would say to me sometimes, "Mrs. King, why is
it you are so kind to us? you treat us just as you do the boys
in your own company." I replied, "Well, you know, all the
boys in other companies are the same to me as those in my
Company E; you are all doing the same duty, and I will do
just the same for you." "Yes," they would say, "we know
that, because you were the first woman we saw when we
came into camp, and you took an interest in us boys ever
since we have been here, and we are very grateful for all you
do for us."

When at Camp Shaw, I visited the hospital in Beaufort,
where I met Clara Barton. There were a number of sick and
wounded soldiers there, and I went often to see the comrades. Miss Barton was always very cordial toward me, and I
honored her for her devotion and care of those men.

There was a man, John Johnson, who with his family was
taken by our regiment at Edisto. This man afterwards
worked in the hospital and was well known to Miss Barton. I
have been told since that when she went South, in 1883, she
tried to look this man up, but learned he was dead. His son
is living in Edisto, Rev. J.J. Johnson, and is the president of
an industrial school on that island and a very intelligent
man. He was a small child when his father and family were
captured by our regiment at Edisto.

CHAPTER VI
ON MORRIS AND OTHER ISLANDS

FORT WAGNER being only a mile from our camp, I went
there two or three times a week, and would go up on the
ramparts to watch the gunners send their shells into
Charleston (which they did every fifteen minutes), and had a
full view of the city from that point. Outside of the fort were

many skulls lying about; I have often moved them one side out of the path. The comrades and I would have quite a debate as to which side the men fought on. Some thought they were the skulls of our boys; others thought they were the enemy's; but as there was no definite way to know, it was never decided which could lay claim to them. They were a gruesome sight, those fleshless heads and grinning jaws, but by this time I had become accustomed to worse things and did not feel as I might have earlier in my camp life.

It seems strange how our aversion to seeing suffering is overcome in war,--how we are able to see the most sickening sights, such as men with their limbs blown off and mangled by the deadly shells, without a shudder; and instead of turning away, how we hurry to assist in alleviating their pain, bind up their wounds, and press the cool water to their parched lips, with feelings only of sympathy and pity.

About the first of June, 1864, the regiment was ordered to Folly Island, staying there until the latter part of the month, when it was ordered to Morris Island. We landed on Morris Island between June and July, 1864. This island was a narrow strip of sandy soil, nothing growing on it but a few bushes and shrubs. The camp was one mile from the boat landing, called Pawnell Landing, and the landing one mile from Fort Wagner.

Colonel Higginson had left us in May of this year, on account of wounds received at Edisto. All the men were sorry to lose him. They did not want him to go, they loved him so. He was kind and devoted to his men, thoughtful for their comfort, and we missed his genial presence from the camp.

The regiment under Colonel Trowbridge did garrison duty, but they had troublesome times from Fort Gregg, on James Island, for the rebels would throw a shell over on our island every now and then. Finally orders were received for the boys to prepare to take Fort Gregg, each man to take 150 rounds of cartridges, canteens of water, hard-tack, and salt beef. This order was sent three days prior to starting, to allow them to be in readiness. I helped as many as I could to pack haversacks and cartridge boxes.

The fourth day, about five o'clock in the afternoon, the call was sounded, and I heard the first sergeant say, "Fall in, boys, fall in," and they were not long obeying the command. Each company marched out of its street, in front of their colonel's headquarters, where they rested for half an hour, as it was not dark enough, and they did not want the enemy to have a chance to spy their movements. At the end of this time the line was formed with the 103d New York (white) in the rear, and off they started, eager to get to work. It was quite dark by the time they reached Pawnell Landing. I have never forgotten the goodbys of that day, as they left camp. Colonel Trowbridge said to me as he left, "Good-by, Mrs. King, take care of yourself if you don't see us again." I went with them as far as the landing, and watched them until they got out of sight, and then I returned to camp. There was no one at camp but those left on picket and a few disabled soldiers, and one woman, a friend of mine, Mary Shaw, and it was lonesome and sad, now that the boys were gone, some never to return.

Mary Shaw shared my tent that night, and we went to bed, but not to sleep, for the fleas nearly ate us alive. We caught a few, but it did seem, now that the men were gone, that every flea in camp had located my tent, and caused us to vacate. Sleep being out of the question, we sat up the remainder of the night.

About four o'clock, July 2, the charge was made. The firing could be plainly heard in camp. I hastened down to the landing and remained there until eight o'clock that morning. When the wounded arrived, or rather began to arrive, the first one brought in was Samuel Anderson of our company. He was badly wounded. Then others of our boys, some with their legs off, arm gone, foot off, and wounds of all kinds imaginable. They had to wade through creeks and marshes, as they were discovered by the enemy and shelled very badly. A number of the men were lost, some got fastened in the mud and had to cut off the legs of their pants, to free themselves. The 103d New York suffered the most, as their men were very badly wounded.

My work now began. I gave my assistance to try to alleviate their sufferings. I asked the doctor at the hospital what I could get for them to eat. They wanted soup, but that I could not get; but I had a few cans of condensed milk and some turtle eggs, so I thought I would try to make some custard. I had doubts as to my success, for cooking with turtle eggs was something new to me, but the adage has it, "Nothing ventured, nothing done," so I made a venture and the result was a very delicious custard. This I carried to the men, who enjoyed it very much. My services were given at all times for the comfort of these men. I was on hand to assist whenever needed. I was enrolled as company laundress, but I did very little of it, because I was always busy doing other things through camp, and was employed all the time doing something for the officers and comrades.

After this fight, the regiment did not return to the camp for one month. They were ordered to Cole Island in September, where they remained until October. About November 1, 1864, six companies were detailed to go to Gregg Landing, Port Royal Ferry, and the rebels in some way found out some of our forces had been removed and gave our boys in camp a hard time of it, for several nights. In fact, one night it was thought the boys would have to retreat. The colonel told me to go down to the landing, and if they were obliged to retreat, I could go aboard on of our gunboats. One of the gunboats got in the rear, and began to shell General Beauregard's force, which helped our boys retain their possession.

About November 15, I received a letter from Sergeant King, saying the boys were still lying three miles from Gregg Landing and had not had a fight yet; that the rebels were waiting on them and they on the rebels, and each were holding their own; also that General Sherman had taken Fort McAllister, eight miles from Savannah. After receiving this letter I wanted to get to Beaufort, so I could be near to them and so be able to get news from my husband. November 23 I got a pass for Beaufort. I arrived at Hilton Head about three o'clock next day, but there had been a battle, and a steamer arrived with a number of wounded men; so I could not get a transfer to Beaufort. The doctor wished me to remain over until Monday. I did not want to stay. I was anxious to get off, as I knew no one at Hilton Head.

I must mention a pet pig we had on Cole Island. Colonel Trowbridge brought into camp, one day, a poor, thin little pig, which a German soldier brought back with him on his return from a furlough. His regiment, the 74th Pennsylvania, was just embarking for the North, where it was ordered to join the 10th corps, and he could not take the pig back with him, so he gave it to our colonel. That pig grew to be the pet of the camp, and was the special care of the drummer boys, who taught him many tricks; and so well did they train him that every day at practice and dress parade, his pigship would march out with them, keeping perfect time with their music. The drummers would often disturb the devotions by riding this pig into the midst of evening praise meeting, and many were the complaints made to the colonel, but he was always very lenient towards the boys, for he knew they only did this for mischief. I shall never forget the fun we had in camp with "Piggie."

CHAPTER VII
CAST AWAY

THERE was a yacht that carried passengers from Hilton Head to Beaufort. There were also five small boats which carried people over. The only people here, beside the soldiers, were Mrs. Lizzie Brown, who came over on a permit to see her husband, who was at this place, and was very ill (he died while she was there), Corporal Walker's wife, with her two years old child, and Mrs. Seabrooke. As soon as we could get the yacht, these persons I have mentioned, together with a comrade just discharged, an officer's boy, and myself, took passage on it for Beaufort. It was nearly dark before we had gone any distance, and about eight o'clock we were cast away and were only saved through the mercy of God. I remember going down twice. As I rose the second time, I caught hold of the sail and managed to hold fast. Mrs. Walker held on to her child with one hand, while with the other she managed to hold fast to some part of the boat, and we drifted and shouted as loud as we could, trying to attract the attention of some of the government boats which were going up and down the river. But it was in vain, we could not make ourselves heard, and just when we gave up all hope, and in the last moment (as we thought) gave one more despairing cry, we were heard at Ladies' Island. Two boats were put off and a search was made, to locate our distressed boat. They found us at last, nearly dead from exposure. In fact, the poor little baby was dead, although her mother still held her by her clothing, with her teeth. The soldier was drowned, having been caught under the sail and pinned down. The rest of us were saved. I had to be carried bodily, as I was thoroughly exhausted. We were given the best attention that we could get at this place where we were picked up. The men who saved us were surprised when they found me among the passengers, as one of them, William Geary, of Darien, Georgia, was a friend of my husband. His mother lived about two miles from where we were picked up, and she told me she had heard cries for a long time that night, and was very uneasy about it. Finally, she said to her son, "I think some poor souls are cast away." "I don't think so, mother," he replied; "I saw some people going down the river to-day. You know this is Christmas, and they are having a good time." But she still persisted that these were cries of distress, and not of joy, and begged him to go out and see. So to satisfy her, he went outside and listened, and then he heard them also, and hastened to get the boats off to find us. We were capsized about 8.15 P.M. and it was near midnight when they found us. Next day, they kept a sharp lookout on the beach for anything that might be washed in from the yacht, and got a trunk and several other things. Had the tide been going out, we should have been carried to sea and lost.

I was very ill and under the doctor's care for some time, in Beaufort. The doctor said I ought to have been rolled, as I had swallowed so much water. In January, 1865, I went back to Cole Island, where I could be attended by my doctor, Dr. Miner, who did all in his power to alleviate my suffering, for I was swollen very much. This he reduced and I recovered, but had a severe cough for a long time afterward.

CHARLOTTE L. FORTEN

CHARLOTTE L. FORTEN
(1838-1914)

Born into a serious and high-thinking Black abolitionist milieu Charlotte Forten, as her journal shows, was in many ways a typical nineteenth blue stocking, but for her the liberation and uplift of her race were persistent and primary concerns. Her Philadelphia ancestry included several generations of freedmen going back to the early eighteenth century and she was the granddaughter of James Forten who had served as a youth in the Revolutionary War and who had been taken prisoner. After the war he was apprenticed to a sailmaker. He became prosperous and during the War of 1812 he enlisted 2500 Philadelphia Blacks to aid in constructing defense works for the city. His subsequent career in the cause of abolition is well attested. He disposed of most of a large fortune in the cause before his death in 1842. The funeral procession of her grandfather, joined by hundreds of whites and thousands of blacks must have greatly impressed the young Charlotte. Her own father, Robert Bridges Forten, served in the Forty-Third United States Colored Regiment. Dying in 1864, he was buried with full military honors.

In 1854 her father decided to send her to Salem, Massachusetts to continue her education which had been largely conducted at home to avoid segregated schools. She was received there into the family of the Black abolitionist Charles Lenox Remond, at one time better known than Frederick Douglass as an orator. Both he and his sister Sarah P. Remond became well-known in England as anti-slavery speakers. Graduating from the Salem Normal School, she was appointed a teacher in the Epes Grammar School of Salem in 1856. In 1858, because of delicate health, she returned to Philadelphia, though she was in Salem both in 1860 and in 1861.

Beginning in the fall of 1861, the Union Blockade of the Confederacy was strengthened by the capture of coastal installations and the islands off the coast of South Carolina, Hilton Head, Port Royal, and Beaufort, passed into Union hands and were incorporated into the Military Department of the South. Not only were thousands of slaves resident in the territory thus acquired, but into this and other captured areas, more thousands of slaves sought freedom behind the Union lines. The decision to set up an educational and work program for these ex-slaves was rapidly put into place and the Port Royal Experiment, as it came to be called, was placed into motion. A call for volunteers went out in 1862. Charlotte Forten was one of those who responded and her journal provides an interesting inside report on events of this exciting story. We also learn of her reaction to military events taking place a short distance away, such as the fearful carnage experienced by the Fifty-Fourth Massachusetts Colored Infantry and the loss of its colonel, Robert Gould Shaw, at the second assault on Fort (Battery) Wagner on Morris Island on July 18, 1863.

After her return to Philadelphia in 1864, Charlotte Forten contributed an account of her experiences to the *Atlantic Monthly*, but her journal remained unpublished until 1953.

Her activities for the next fourteen years were principally literary, including articles for journals and at least one translation of a French historical novel, *Madame Therese*, by the writing team known as Erckmann-Chartrian. In 1878 she married Francis J. Grimke, then on the verge of graduating from Princeton Theological Seminary.

The Reverend Francis Grimke's story was as fascinating as her own. He had been born near Charleston in 1850, the son of a planter whose sisters had quit the South because of their abolitionist sentiments and had become distinguished in the cause. The planter died in 1852, leaving his slaves to his son with the proviso that his slave sons be freed. The half-brother did not honor the request, and at the age of 10 the young Francis ran away. Eventually he was imprisoned and sold by his half-brother, but soon after the war ended and both Francis and his brother Archibald attracted the attention of federal officials and were first sent to Massachusetts and later to Lincoln University, from which they were graduated with high honor in 1870. The Grimke aunts learned of their existence at this time and acknowledged them.

Charlotte Forten came to Washington, D.C. with her husband who had a long career as the pastor of the Fifteenth Street Presbyterian Church. Francis J. Grimke, who died in 1937, named as their joint literary executor Anna J. Cooper, a friend of his wife. It was in her custody that the *Journal* was kept, passing to Howard University at Dr. Cooper's death, at the age of 105 in 1964.

JOURNAL
1862

At Sea. Oct. 27. Monday. Let me see. Where am I? What do I want to write? I am in a state of utter bewilderment. It was on Wednesday I rec'd the note. On Thursday I said "good bye" to the friends that are so dear, and the city that is so hateful, and went to New York...The next morn did not hurry myself, having heard that the steamer "United States" w'ld not sail till twelve...I went to "Lovejoy's" to meet the Hunns and found there a card from Mr. Hunn bidding me hasten to the steamer, as it was advertised to sail at nine. It was then between ten and eleven. After hurrying down and wearying ourselves, found when I got on board that it was not to sail till twelve. But I did not go ashore again. It was too bad, for I had no time to get several things that I wanted much, among them "Les Miserables," which my dear brother Henry had kindly given me the money for. He had not had time to get it in Philadelphia.

Enjoyed the sail down the harbor perfectly. The shipping is a noble sight. Had no symptoms of sea-sickness until eve when, being seated at the table an inexpressibly singular sensation caused me to make a hasty retreat to the aft deck, where, by keeping perfectly still sitting on a coil of ropes spent a very comfortable eve. and had a pleasant conversation with one of the passengers. Did not get out of sight of land until after dark. I regretted that.

Went below for the night into the close ladies' cabin with many misgivings which proved not unfounded. Was terribly sea-sick that night and all the next morning. Did not reappear on deck till noon of the next day--Saturday. What an experience! Of all doleful, dismal, desperate experiences sea-sickness is certainly the dolefulest, dismalest, and desperate-est!

T'was rather a miserable afternoon. Was half sick all the time and scarcely dared to move. There was highly pleasant talk going on around me, to which I c'ld listen in silence-- that was all. My companion Lizzie Hunn was sick all the time. Poor girl, she c'ld take no pleasure in anything.

When night came, we both determined that we w'ldn't go below and have a repetition of the agonies of the night before. We heroically resolved to pass the night on deck. A nice little nook was found for us "amidships," and there enveloped in shawls and seated in arm chairs we were made as comfortable as possible, and passed the night without being sick. Two of the passengers--young men from Hilton Head, who were very gentlemanly and attentive, entertained us for some time with some fine singing; then they retired, and we passed the rest of the night in the society of Old Ocean alone. How wild and strange it seemed there on the deck in the dark night, only the dim outlines of sea and sky to be seen, only the roaring of the waves to be heard. I enjoyed it much. The thought that we were far, far, away from land was a pleasant one to me.

The next day--Sunday--was emphatically a *dismal* day. It rained nearly all the time so that we c'ld not be on deck much of the time. As soon as we established ourselves nicely outside down came the rain and we were driven into the close cabin, which was almost unendurable to me. Tried to read a little in the French Bible which Henry gave me, but in vain. The day was mostly spent in the interesting occupation of preventing sea-sickness by keeping perfectly quiet and watching the rain drops.

Before night a storm came on. And a terrible storm it was. The steward arranged mattresses and blankets for us in the covered passage way "amidships," and we lay down, but not to rest. It was a veritable grand storm at sea. The vessel rocked and plunged, the planks creaked and groaned, the sea broke upon the bows with thunderous roars, and within one w'ld have thought that all the crockery in the establishment was going to pieces. Such a noise I never heard in my life. Such roaring and plunging, and creaking. Afterward we were told that one of the chains of the vessel broke, and indeed for a time she seemed to be at the mercy of the waves. Some one near us--one of the waiters, I think, was dreadfully frightened, and commenced praying and moaning most piteously, crying "Oh Jesus, dear Jesus," in most lamentable tones, till I began to think we must really be in danger. Then the water came into the ladies cabin, below. One lady who had a baby with her woke up in the night and c'ld not find the child. It had been rolled away from her by the tossing of the ship, the lamps were out, and after some time, and much terror on the part of the poor woman the baby was found by one of the waiters under the berth. She was very quiet, and did not seem at all alarmed at her involuntary journey. Despite all the alarm and distress and anxiety we c'ld not help being amused at this little episode. During all the storm, however, I felt no fear; and now that the danger has passed, I feel really glad that I have at last experienced a "veritable storm at sea." The most astonishing thing was that I had two or three most refreshing sleeps in the very height of the storm.

This morning the sea was still very rough, but I struggled up, and dressed with great difficulty, and with the aid of one of the waiters made my way on deck. The sky was still very much overcast, the great, white capped waves were rising to a great height and breaking against the sides of the vessel. It was a grand sight, and I enjoyed it greatly. It has quite cleared off now, and the day is most lovely. I am feeling well and *luxuriating* in the glorious beauty of sea and sky. But my poor companion is still quite sick, and while I write, sits before me on a coil of ropes, enveloped in shawls, and looking the picture of dolefulness and despair.

How grand, how glorious the sea is, to-day! It far more than realizes my highest expectations of it. The sky too is beautiful--a deep, delicious blue, with soft, white, fleecy clouds floating over it. We have seen several sails today, in the distance, but still no land, whereat I am rejoiced.

There's not much to be said about the passengers on board. There are about a dozen beside ourselves, none of whom seem to me especially interesting, except perhaps our friend from Hilton Head, Mr.B. He is very intelligent, and I sh'ld think even a talented young man. He has read and admires all my favorite authors, and I enjoy talking with him about them. I have rarely found a *man* with so keen and delicate an appreciation of the beautiful, both in Nature and Art. There are no soldiers on board but one officer who stalks about the boat looking well pleased with himself and evidently trying to look quite grand, but *sans* success, for he was rather insignificant despite his good figure, fierce moustaches, and epaulettes.

Of the three ladies on board two go South to join their husbands, and the third accompanies hers. The first two are quite talkative, the latter very quiet. I believe that is all that can be said of them. There is a sea captain here whom I like very much. He is a Cape Cod man; has been to sea ever since he was nine years old. Has visited many lands, and I enjoy hearing him talk about them. The other gentlemen do not interest me, so I shall let them pass.

Have only been able to go to the table twice. Then there was no difficulty as I feared there might be. People were as kind and polite as possible. Indeed I have had not the least trouble since I have been on board. The waiters are as obliging and attentive as they can be, and bring us our meals out on deck every day.--

Afternoon.--I have just beheld the most glorious sight I ever saw in my life...I staggered to the bow of the ship (which still rolls and pitches terribly) and there saw the sea in all its glory and grandeur. Oh, how beautiful those great waves were as they broke upon the sides of the vessel, into foam and spray, pure and white as new fallen snow. People talk of the monotony of the sea. I have not found it monotonous for a moment, since I have been well. To me there is "infinite variety," constant enjoyment in it.

I have tried to read, but in vain; there is so much to take off one's attention, besides reading makes my head dizzy. One of the most beautiful sights I have yet seen is the phosphorescence in the water at night--the long line of light in the wake of the steamer, and the stars, and sometimes balls of fire that rise so magically out of the water. It is most strange and beautiful. Had it not been for the storm we should have reached Port Royal to-day. But we shall not get there till to-morrow.

Tuesday, A.M. Oct. 28. How very, very lovely it was last night. Saw at last what I have so longed to see--the ocean in the moonlight. There was a beautiful young moon. Our ship rode gently along over a smooth sea leaving a path of silver behind it. There was something inexpressibly sweet and soothing and solemn in that soft moonlight. We sat on deck a long time, and the friends from Hilton Head, both of whom have very fine voices, sang beautifully. They were kind enough to change state rooms with us, and we slept up stairs very quietly.

Early this morn Mr. Hunn came to our door to tell us that we were in sight of the blockading fleet in Charleston harbor. Of course we sprang to the window eagerly, and saw the masts of the ships looking like a grove of trees in the distance. We were not near enough to see the city. It was hard to realize that we were even so near that barbarous place.--

Later--We were again in sight of land. Have passed Edisto and several other islands, and can now see Hilton Head. Shall reach it about one. Tis nearly eleven now. The South Carolina shore is flat and low;--a long line of trees. It does not look very inviting. We are told that the oranges will be ripe when we get to Beaufort, and that in every way this is just the loveliest season to be there, which is very encouraging.

We approach Hilton Head. Our ship has been boarded by Health Officer and Provost Marshal. We shall soon reach the landing. All is hurry and confusion on board. I must lay thee aside, friend journal, and use my eyes for seeing all there is to be seen. When we reach our place of destination. I will give to thee, oh faithful friend, the result of my observations. So *au revoir.*--

Tuesday Night. T'was a strange sight as our boat approached the landing at Hilton Head. On the wharf was a motley assemblage,--soldiers, officers, and "contrabands" of every hue and size. They were mostly black, however, and certainly the most dismal specimens I ever saw. Hilton Head looks like a very desolate place; just a long low, sandy point running out into the sea with no visible dwellings upon it but the soldiers' white roofed tents.

Thence, after an hour's delay, during which we signed a

paper, which was virtually taking the oath of allegiance, we left the "United States," most rocking of rockety propellers,-- and took a steamboat for Beaufort. On board the boat was General Saxton to whom we were introduced. I like his face exceedingly. And his manners were very courteous and affable. He looks like a thoroughly *good* man.--From Hilton Head to Beaufort the same low long line of sandy shore bordered by trees. Almost the only object of interest to me were the remains of an old Huguenot Fort, built many, many years ago.

Arrived at Beaufort we found that we had yet not reached our home. Went to Mr. French's, and saw there Reuben Tomlinson, whom I was very glad to meet, and Mrs. Gage, who seemed to be in a rather dismal state of mind. Beaufort looks like a pleasant place. The houses are large and quite handsome, built in the usual Southern style with verandahs around them, and beautiful trees. One magnolia tree in Mr. French's yard is splendid,--quite as large as some of our large shade trees, and, with the most beautiful foliage, a dark rich glossy green.

Went into the Commissary's Office to wait for the boat which was to take us to St. Helena's Island which is about six miles from Beaufort. T'is here that Miss Towne has her school, in which I am to teach, and that Mr. Hunn will have his store. While waiting in the Office we saw several military gentlemen, *not* very creditable specimens, I sh'ld say. The little Commissary himself...is a perfect little popinjay, and he and a Colonel somebody who didn't look any too sensible, talked in a very smart manner, evidently for our special benefit. The word "nigger" was plentifully used, whereupon I set them down at once as *not* gentlemen. Then they talked a great deal about rebel attacks and yellow fever, and other alarming things, with significant nods and looks at each other. We saw through them at once, and were not at all alarmed by any of their representations. But if they are a fair example of army officers, I sh'ld pray to see as little of them as possible.

To my great joy found that we were to be rowed by a crew of negro boatmen. Young Mr. French whom I like--accompanied us, while Mr. Hunn went with a flat to get our bag-

gage. The row was delightful. It was just at sunset--a grand
Southern sunset; and the gorgeous clouds of crimson and
gold were reflected in the waters below, which were smooth
and calm as a mirror. Then, as we glided along, the rich
sonorous tones of the boatmen broke upon the evening stillness. Their singing impressed me much. It was so sweet and
strange and solemn, "Roll, Jordan, Roll" was grand and another

> *"Jesus make de blind to see*
> *Jesus make de deaf to hear*
> *"   "   " cripple walk*
> *Walk in, dear Jesus,"*

and the refrain

> *"No man can hender me."*

It was very, very impressive. I want to hear these men sing
Whittier's "Song of the Negro Boatmen." I am going to see if
it can't be brought about in some way.

It was nearly dark when we reached St. Helena's, where
we found Miss Towne's carriage awaiting us, and then we
three and our driver, had a long drive along the lonely roads
in the dark night. How easy it w'ld have been for a band of
guerillas--had any chanced that way--to seize and hang us.
But we feared nothing of the kind. We were in a jubilant
state of mind and sang "John Brown" with a will as we drove
through the pines and palmettos. Arrived at the Superintendent's house we were kindly greeted by him and the
ladies and shown into a lofty *ceilinged* parlor where a cheerful wood fire glowed in the grate, and we soon began to feel
quite at home in the very heart of Rebeldom; only that I do
not at all realize yet that we are in South Carolina. It is all a
strange wild dream, from which I am constantly expecting to
awake. But I can write no more now. I am tired, and still
feel the motion of the ship in my poor head. Good night,

Wednesday, Oct. 29. A lovely day, but rather cool, I sh'ld
think, for the "sunny South." The ship still sings in my
head, and everything is most unreal, yet I went to drive. We
drove to Oaklands, our future home. It is very pleasantly situated, but the house is in rather a dilapidated condition, as
are most of the houses here, and the yard and garden have a
neglected look, when it is cleaned up, and the house made

habitable I think it will be quite a pleasant place. There are some lovely roses growing there and quantities of ivy creeping along the ground, even under the house, in wild luxuriance.--The negroes on the place are very kind and polite. I think I shall get on amicably with them.

After walking about and talking with them, and plucking some roses and ivy to send home, we left Oaklands and drove to the school. It is kept by Miss Murray and Miss Towne in the little Baptist Church, which is beautifully situated in a grove of live oaks. Never saw anything more beautiful than these trees. It is strange that we do not hear of them at the North. They are the first objects that attract one's attention here. They are large, noble trees with small glossy green leaves. Their great beauty consists in the long bearded moss with which every branch is heavily draped. This moss is singularly beautiful, and gives a solemn almost funereal aspect to the trees.

We went into the school, and heard the children read and spell. The teachers tell us that they have made great improvement in a very short time, and I noticed with pleasure how bright, how eager to learn many of them seem. The singing delighted me most. They sang beautifully in their rich, sweet clear tones, and with that peculiar swaying motion which I had noticed before in the older people, and which seems to make their singing all the more effective. Besides several other tunes they sang "Marching Along" with much spirit, and then one of their own hymns "Down in the Lonesome Valley," which is sweetly solemn and most beautiful. Dear children! born in slavery, but free at last! May God preserve to you all the blessings of freedom, and may you be in every possible way fitted to enjoy them. My heart goes out to you. I shall be glad to do all that I can to help you.--

As we drove homeward I noticed that the trees are just beginning to turn; some beautiful scarlet berries were growing along the roadside; and everywhere the beautiful live oak with its moss drapery. The palmettos disappoint me much. Most of them have a very jagged appearance, and are yet stiff and ungraceful. The country is very level--as flat as that in eastern Pennsylvania. There are plenty of woods, but I think they have not the grandeur of our Northern woods. The cotton fields disappoint me too. They have a very straggling look, and the pods are small, not at all the great snowballs that I had imagined. Altogether the country w'ld be rather desolate looking were it not for my beautiful and evergreen live oaks.

Friday, Oct. 31. Miss Towne went to Beaufort to-day, and I taught for her. I enjoyed it much. The children are well-behaved and eager to learn. It will be a happiness to teach them.

I like Miss Murray so much. She is of English parentage, born in the Provinces. She is one of the most whole-souled warm-hearted women I ever met. I felt drawn to her from the first (before I knew she was English) and of course I like her none the less for that.

Miss Towne also is a delightful person. "A charming lady" Gen. Saxton calls her and my heart echoes the words. She is housekeeper, physician, everything, here. The most indispensable person on the place, and the people are devoted to her....And indeed she is quite a remarkable young lady. She is one of the earliest comers, and has done much good in teaching and superintending the negroes. She is quite young; not more than twenty-two or three I sh'ld think, and is superintendent of two plantations. I like her energy and decision of character. Her appearance too is very interesting.

Mr. Soule the Superintendent is a very kind, agreeable person. I like him.

Sunday, Nov. 2. Drove to church to-day,--to the same little Baptist Church that the school is held in. The people came in slowly. They have no way of telling the time. About eleven they had all assembled; the church was full. Old and young were there assembled in their Sunday dresses. Clean gowns on, clean head handkerchiefs, bright colored, of course, I noticed that some had even reached the dignity of straw hats, with bright feathers.

The services were very interesting. The minister, Mr. Phillips is an earnest New England man. The singing was very beautiful. I sat there in a kind of trance and listened to it, and while I listened looked through the open windows into the beautiful grove of oaks with their moss drapery. "Ah wld that my tongue c'ld utter The thoughts that arise in me."

But it cannot. The sermon was quite good. But I enjoyed nothing so much as the singing--the wonderful, beautiful singing. There can be no doubt that these people have a great deal of musical talent. It was a beautiful sight,--their enthusiasm. After the service two couples were married. Then the meeting was out. The various groups under the trees forming a very pretty picture.

We drove to the Episcopal Church afterwards where the aristocracy of Rebeldom used to worship. The building is much smaller than the others, but there is a fine organ there on which Miss W played while some of the young Superintendents sang very finely, and then we came home.

It is all like a dream still, and will be for a long time, I suppose; a strange wild dream. When we get settled in our own house and I have fairly entered into teaching, perhaps I shall begin to realize it all. What we are to do for furniture I know not. Our sole possessions now consist of two bureaus and a bedstead. Mr. Hunn had not time to get the mattresses in New York. So I suppose we must use blanket substitutes till we can do better. I am determined not to be discouraged at anything. I have never felt more hopeful, more cheerful than I do now--

Oaklands, Tuesday, Nov. 4. Came to our new home to-day. Felt sorry to leave the friends who have been so kind to us, but as they are only three miles distant; hope to see them occasionally. But nobody here has much time for visiting.

Wednesday, Nov. 19. A steamer is in! Miss Towne had letters from Philadelphia to-day. The mail is not yet all distributed. If I don't get any I shall be *perfectly* desperate. But I surely will get some to-morrow. To-night had another pupil--Robert--brighter than Harry --not so bright as Harry. He will do well I think.-   *Thursday, Nov. 20.* ...Wrote to-night to... Whittier asking him to write a little Christmas hymn for our children to sing. I hope he will do it....

Saturday, Nov. 22. Had the loveliest walk this afternoon to Mr. Ruggle's our nearest neighbor's. The path lay partly through beautiful woods principally pines and live oaks.

The air was delicious, the sunlight bright, the brown pine leaves odorous as usual, and I noticed some maple leaves that had turned a rich dark, almost copper color. Plucked some for my dear Miss Murray whom I heard express a wish for some a day or two ago.

Found that Miss Ruggles was not at home. They have a pleasant little place, rather more civilized looking than ours. Returning, just at sunset saw a beautiful sight. In some parts of the wood the branches of the live oak formed a perfect ceiling overhead and from them depended long sprays of that exquisite moss lighted up by the sun's last rays. I c'ld think only of some fairy palace, at first, then the sight suggested the Mammoth cave as I had seen it once in an excellent Panorama. Those sprays of moss, glowing in the sunlight, were perfect stalactites, as I saw them illuminated. If they lacked the sparkling crystals they quite made up for the loss in airy grace and lightness. I wanted you my dearest A.,-- and several dear friends of mine who like you have a most keen and delicate perception of the beautiful--to look upon that scene with me. And since that c'ld not be, I longed to be an artist that I might make a sketch and send it to you.

Sunday, Nov. 23. Attended church to-day. T'was even a pleasanter experience than before. Saw several new arrivals there--old ones returned, rather--among them Mr. Samuel Phillips, a nephew of *the* Phillips. He has not the glorious beauty of the illustrious relative, but still has somewhat the Phillips style of face. He is not at all handsome; has bright red hair, but a pleasant face, and an air *distingue.*

After the sermon an old negro prayed a touching and most effective prayer. Then the minister read. Gen. Saxton's Proclamation for Thanksgiving--which is grand--the very best and noblest that c'ld have been penned. I like and admire the Gen. more than ever now.

Six couples were married to-day. Some of the dresses were unique. Am sure one must have worn a cast-off dress of her mistress's. It looked like white silk covered with lace. The lace sleeves, and other trimmings were in rather a decayed state and the white cotton gloves were well ventilated. But the bride looked none the less happy for that. Only one had the slightest claim to good looks. And she was a demure lttle thing with a neat, plain silk dress on. T'was amusing to see some of the headdresses. One, of tattered flowers and ribbons, was very ridiculous. But no matter for that. I am *truly* glad that the poor creatures are trying to live right and virtuous lives. As usual we had some fine singing. It was very pleasant to be at church again. For two Sundays past I had not been, not feeling well.

This eve. our boys and girls with others from across the creek came in and sang a long time for us. Of course we had the old favorites "Down in the Lonesome Valley," and "Roll, Jordan, Roll," and "No man can hender me," and beside those several shouting tunes that we had not heard before; they are very wild and strange. It was impossible for me to understand many of the words although I asked them to repeat them for me. I only know that one had something about "De Nell Am Ringing." I think that was the refrain; and of another, some of the words were "Christ build the church widout no hammer nor nail." "Jehovah Halleluhia," which is a grand thing, and "Hold the light," an especial favorite of mine--they sang with great spirit. The leader of the singing was Prince, a large black boy, from Mr. Ruggle's place. He was full of the shouting spirit, and c'ld not possibly keep still. It was amusing to see his gymnastic performances. They were quite in the Ethiopian Methodists' style. He has really a very fine bass voice. I enjoyed their singing so much, and sh'ld have enjoyed it so much more if some dear ones who are far away c'ld have listened to it with me. How delighted they would have been.

The effect of the singing has been to make me feel a little sad and lonely to-night. A yearning for congenial companionship *will* sometimes come over me in the few leisure moments I have in the house. T'is well they are so few. Kindness, most invariable,--for which I am most grateful--I meet with constantly but congeniality I find not at all in this house. But silence, foolish murmurer. He who knows all things knows that it was for no selfish motive that I came here, far from the few who are so dear to me. Therefore let me not be selfish now. Let the work to which I have solemnly pledged myself fill up my whole existence to the exclusion of all vain longings.

Tuesday, Nov. 25. ...Miss Murray is teaching the children in school "Sound the Loud Timbrel." They like the words so much that I think they will soon learn them.

Saw the Standard to-night. Twas welcome as the face of an old friend. Read also a few numbers of "Salem Chapel," which is as intensely interesting and exciting as ever. This eve. gave Harry and Robert their lesson.

Yesterday had some visitors in school--Miss T and her brother, and a Miss Merrick from Syracuse. I liked the latter's face. She looks like an earnest worker.

Wednesday, Nov. 26. Miss Towne was not at school, and Miss Murray and I had sole charge. After school told the children a little about the sun, stars etc., and then Miss Murray taught them some verses of "Sound the Loud Timbrel" which she wants them to learn for the New Year. Had a lovely walk in the woods gathering leaves and berries wherewith to decorate the church to-morrow.

Thursday, Nov. 27. Thanksgiving Day. This, according to Gen. Saxton's noble Proclamation, was observed as a day of Thanksgiving and praise. It has been a lovely day--cool, delicious air, golden, gladdening sunlight, deep blue sky, with soft white clouds floating over it. Had we no other causes the glory and beauty of the day alone make it a day for which to give thanks. But we have other causes, great and glorious, which unite to make this peculiarly a day of thanksgiving and praise. It has been a general holiday. According to Gen. Saxton's orders an animal was killed on each plantation that the people might to-day eat fresh meat, which is a great luxury to them, and indeed to all of us here.

This morning a large number--Superintendents, teachers and freed people, assembled in the little Baptist church. It was a sight that I shall not soon foget--that crowd of eager, happy black faces from which the shadow of slavery had forever passed. "Forever free!" Forever free!" Those magical words were all the time singing themselves in my soul, and never before have I felt so truly grateful to God. The singing was, as usual, very beautiful. I thought I had never heard my favorite "Down in the Lonesome Valley" so well sung.

After an appropriate prayer and sermon by Rev. Mr. Phillips, Gen. Saxton made a short but spirited speech to the people--urging the young men to enlist in the regiment now forming under Col. T.W. Higginson. That was the first intimation I had had of Mr. Higginson's being down here. I am greatly rejoiced thereat. He seems to me of all fighting men the one best fitted to command a regiment of colored soldiers. The mention of his name recalled the happy days passed last summer in Massachusetts, when day after day, in the streets of Worcester we used to see the indefatigable *Capt.* Higginson drilling his white company. I never saw him so full of life and energy--entering with his whole soul into his work--without thinking what a splendid general he w'ld make. And that too may come about. Gen. Saxton said to-day that he hoped to see him commander of an army of black men. The Gen. told the people how nobly Mr. Higginson had stood by Anthony Burns, in the old dark days, even suffering imprisonment for his sake; and assured them that they might feel sure of meeting no injustice under the leadership of such a man; that he w'ld see to it that they were not wronged in any way.

Then he told them the story of Robert Smalls, and added. "To-day Robert came to see me. I asked him how he was getting on in the store which he is keeping for the freed people. He said he was doing very well--making fifty dollars a week, sometimes, "But" said he "Gen. I'm going to stop keeping store. I'm going to enlist." "What," said I. "Are you going to enlist when you can make fifty dollars a week keeping store?" "Yes Sir," he replied "I'm going to enlist as a private in the black regiment. How can I expect to keep my freedom if I'm not willing to fight for it? Suppose the Secesh sh'ld get back here again? what good w'ld my fifty dollars do me then? Yes, Sir I sh'ld enlist if I were making a thousand dollars a week."

Mrs. Frances D. Gage then made a few beautiful and earnest remarks. She told the people about the slaves in Santa Cruz, how they rose and conquered their masters, and declared themselves free, and no one dared to oppose them. And how, soon after, the governor rode into the market-place and proclaimed emancipation to all people of the Danish West Indies. She then made a beautiful appeal to the mothers, urging them not to keep back their sons from the war fearing they might be killed but to send them forth willingly and gladly as she had done hers, to fight for liberty. It must have been something very novel and strange to them to hear a woman speak in public, but they listened with great attention and seemed much moved by what she said.

Then Gen. Saxton made a few more remarks. I think what he said will have much effect on the young men here. There has been a good deal of distrust about joining the regiment. The soldiers were formerly so unjustly treated by the Government. But they trust Gen. Saxton. He told them what a victory the black troops had lately won on the Georgian coast, and what a great good they had done for their race in winning; they had proved to their enemies that the black man can and will fight for his freedom. After the Gen. had done speaking the people sang "Marching Along," with great spirit.

After church there was a wedding. This is a very common occurrence here. Of course the bridal costumes are generally very unique and comical, but the principal actors are fortunately quite unconscious of it, and look so proud and happy while enjoying this--one of the many privileges that freedom has bestowed upon them--that it is quite pleasant to see them.

Beside the Gen. and Mrs. Gage there were several other strangers present;--ladies from the North who come down here to teach.

In Miss Towne's box came my parcel--so long looked for--containing letters from my dear Mary Shepard, and Aunt Margaretta...and a Liberator, the first that I have seen since leaving home. How great a pleasure it is to see it. It is familiar and delightful to look upon as the face of an old friend. It is of an old date--Oct 31st but it is not the less welcome for that. And what a significant fact it is that one may now sit here in safety--here in the rebellious little Palmetto State and read the Liberator, and display it to one's friends, rejoicing over it in the fulness of one's heart as a very great treasure. It is fitting that we sh'ld give to this--the Pioneer Paper in the cause of human rights--a hearty welcome to the land where, until so recently, those rights have been most barbarously trampled upon. We do not forget that it is in fact directly

traceable to the exertions of the editor of this paper and those
who have labored so faithfully with him, that the Northern
people now occupy in safety the South Carolina Shore; that
freedom now blesses it, that it is, for the first time, a place
worth living in.

This eve. commenced a long letter to Mr. William Lloyd
Garrison, composed partly of to-day's journalism, and partly
of other things that I thought w'ld interest him. He can publish it in the Liberator, if he thinks it worth printing, which I
do not.

Truly this has been a delightful day to me. I recall with
pleasure the pleasant Thanksgiving Days passed in New
England in Massachusetts which I believe I am in the habit of
considering as *all* New England. But this has been the happiest, the most jubilant Thanksgiving Day of my life. We hear
of cold weather and heavy snowstorms up in the North land.
But here roses and oleanders are blooming in the open air.
Figs and oranges are ripening, the sunlight is warm and
bright, and over all shines gloriously the blessed light of
Freedom--Freedom forevermore!--

Friday, Nov. 28. Kept store nearly all day, and found constant sources of interest and amusement in it. I had nearly
forgotten to tell you, dear A., to tell you about a very old
man--Dr. Crofts, they call him--(his name is Scipio rightly)
who came into the store yesterday. He was rejoicing over the
new state of things here, and said to Mr. Hunn. "Don't hab
me feelins hurt now. Used to hab me feelins hurt all de
time. But don't hab em hurt now, no more." Poor old soul!
We rejoiced with him that he and many like him no longer
have their "feelins hurt," as in the old time.

This eve. finished my letter to Mr. Garrison...Mr. Hunn
brought me a paper from the office--a Boston Transcript, sent
by Sarah Putnam. It is pleasant to see a Boston paper.

Saturday, Nov. 29. Have decorated our little sitting room
with ivy and autumn leaves and berries till it looks quite
bright. Have hung a wreath of ivy around my lovely Evangeline which makes her, if possible, lovelier than ever. We
have a clock, which is quite a treasure here. It is like the face
of an old friend...This eve. devoured "Aurora Leigh" for the
very manyth time. Every time I read it I discover new beauty

in it.

Christmas Day 1862. A bright and lovely Christmas day. We were waked early by the people knocking at our window and shouting "Merry Christmas." After breakfast we went out and distributed the presents;--to each of the babies a bright red dress, and to little Jessie a white apron trimmed with crochet braid, and to each of the other children an apron and an orange. To each of the workers a pie--an apple pie, which pleased them much.

Then we went to school. How pretty the evergreens looked in the bright light, after we had thrown open the windows. T'was a long time before the other teachers got there, and I had to keep all the children from getting restless. I kept them out of doors, and had them sing old songs and new. They sang with great spirit. After the others came, we opened school, and at once commenced distributing the presents. First Miss Murray's class, then mine, then Miss Towne's. Most of the children were much delighted with their gifts, and well they might be, for they were very useful ones,--principally dresses for the girls, and material for shirts and pantaloons for the boys. For the larger ones, also there were little bags, nicely fitted out with sewing utensils which Miss Murray and Miss Towne arranged. The larger children behaved well, and by great exertions I managed to keep the "babies" quiet.

After the gifts were distributed, they were addressed by Lieut. Col. Billings of the 1st regiment South Carolina Volunteers. He is a New England man of very gentlemanly and pleasing manners.--A good man, and much interested in the people, I sh'ld think. I liked him. Then Mr. Fairfield spoke to them about the birth of Christ. Afterward they sang; Among other things, "John Brown," Whittier's "Hymn," "Sing, oh Graveyard," and "Roll, Jordan Roll." There was no one present beside the teachers, our household, Lt. Col. Billings, Mr. Thorpe, Mr. Fairfield and Miss Rosa Towne and Miss Ware.

I enjoyed the day very much. Was too excited and interested to feel weariness then, but am quite exhausted to-night. The children have been in, singing for us. My pet *petite* Amaretta has a sweet voice and quite strong for such a little one. She was full of music to-night. "All I want to do is sing and shout" she said to me with her pretty, dimply smile. There is something very bewitching about that child. All the children had the shouting spirit to-night. They had several grand shouts in the entry. "Look upon the Lord," which they sang to-night, seems to me the most beautiful of all their shouting tunes. There is something in it that goes to the depths of one's soul.--I am weary and must stop.

Dear friends, up North! my heart is with you to-night. What w'ld I not give for one look at your dear faces, one grasp of your kindly hands! Dear ones! I pray with my whole heart that this may have been to you a very, very happy Christmas.

Friday, Dec. 26. Kept store nearly all day. I like it occasionally. It amuses and interests me. There was one very sensible man in to-day, whose story interested me much. He had been a carpenter, and had been taken up by his master on the mainland, on "the main," as they call it, to help build houses to which the families of the rebels might retreat when the Yankees sh'ld come. His master sent him back again to this island to bring back a boat and some of the people. He was provided with a pass. On reaching the island, he found that the Union troops had come, so he determined (indeed he had determined before) to remain here with his fmily, as he knew his master w'ld not dare to come back after them. Some of his fellow servants whom he had left on the "main," hearing that the Union troops had come resolved to try to make their escape. They found a boat of the master's, out of which a piece about six feet square had been cut. In the night, secretly, they went to the boat which had been sunk near the edge of the creek, measured the hole, and went to the woods and, after several nights' work, made a piece large enough to fit in. With this they mended the boat, by another night's work, and then sunk it in the same position in which they had found it. The next night five of them embarked, and after passing through many perils in the shape of the enemy's boats, near which they were obliged to pass, and so making very slow progress, for they c'ld travel only at night, and in the day time, ran their boat close up to the shore, out of sight--they at last passed the enemy's lines and reached one of our gunboats in safety.   They were taken on board, and their wants attended to, for their provisions had given out and they were much exhausted.   After being there some time they were sent to this island, where their families, who had feared they w'ld never see them again welcomed them rejoicingly.   I was much interested in the story of their escape, and give it for yr especial benefit, Dear A.

Spent the eve. in making wreaths for our windows and my love Evangeline....

A letter from Sarah Putnam delights me much, for it tells me that my dear friend Dr. Rogers, sailed last week for Port Royal so of course he has come in this steamer. I c'ld clap my hands and shout for joy. I am so very, very glad. This is the very place for him, and he is of all men, the man for the place. He is to be surgeon in Col. Higginson's regiment South Carolina Volunteers. I am most impatient to see him.

Sat. Dec. 27. A rather dreary day. So the less said about it the better. Worked quite hard. The Miss Townes and Miss Murray paid us a brief visit. Capt. Hooper whom everybody likes, has come, and brought me a letter, which I rec'd wonderingly from Miss Murray's hands. The handwriting was strange to me. It was postmarked "Boston." On opening it I found it to be from a stranger--a lady in West Gloucester, who says she has read with interest my letter in the paper, and expresses her great interest in the work here. A very kind and pretty letter. Enclosed in it was a "Proclamation Song," written by a friend of hers, to be sung to the air "Glory Hallelujah," on 1st Jan. Not exquisite poetry, but a very good and appropriate song. It touched me receiving such a letter from a stranger. I think I must write and thank her for it. Had a lovely walk in the woods this morn. Twas almost like June.

Sunday, Dec. 28. At church had the pleasure of seeing Gen. Saxton and his father, who has come down to visit him. The General presented him to me. He is a pleasant old gentleman, and spoke warmly in praise of Dr. Rogers who came on the same steamer with him. Saw also the much loved Capt. Hooper, whose looks and manners I like much. He made a very good speech to the people, as also did Gen. Saxton urging them to enlist, and inviting them all to come to the camp near Beaufort on New Year's Day, and join in the grand Celebration, which is to take place there. I long to go, and hope I shall.

Capt. Hooper handed me a letter from my dear Mary Shepard. It was unexpected, and so all the more delightful. I sh'ld have been very, very glad to have had letters from home and from Henry for Christmas gifts. But so it was not. I must try to be content.

Tuesday, Dec. 30. This eve. Mr. and Miss Ruggles spent with us quite pleasantly. It is very rarely we have company, and so I note it down.

Wednesday, Dec. 31. Mr. Thorpe and Mr. Hooper dined with us to-day. I think they are--Mr. Thorpe especially, the most anti-slavery of the Superintendents. And they are very gentlemenly, and I like them. This afternoon Mr. and Mrs. Wells called. He is very agreeable, she *not* so agreeable, to me. I count the hours till to-morrow, the glorious, glorious day of freedom.

1863

Thursday, New Year's Day. The most glorious day this nation has yet seen, *I* think. I rose early--an event here--and early we started, with an old borrowed carriage and a remarkably slow horse. Whither were we going? thou wilt ask, dearest A. To the ferry; thence to Camp Saxton, to the Celebration. From the Ferry to the camp the "Flora" took us.

How pleasant it was on board! A crowd of people, whites and blacks, and a band of music--to the great delight of the negroes. Met on board Dr. and Mrs. Peck and their daughter, who greeted me most kindly. Also Gen. Saxton's father whom I like much, and several other acquaintances whom I was glad to see. We stopped at Beaufort, and then proceeded to Camp Saxton, the camp of the 1st Regiment South Carolina Volunteers. The "Flora" could not get up to the landing, so we were rowed ashore in a row boat.

Just as my foot touched the plank, on landing, a hand grasped mine and well known voice spoke my name. It was my dear and noble friend, Dr. Rogers. I cannot tell you, dear A., how delighted I was to see him; how *good* it was to see the face of a friend from the North, and *such* a friend. I think myself particularly blessed to have him for a friend. Walking on a little distance I found myself being presented to Col. Higginson, whereat I was so much overwhelmed, that I had no reply to make to the very kind and courteous little speech with which he met me. I believe I mumbled something, and grinned like a simpleton, that was all. Provoking, isn't it? that when one is most in need of sensible words, one finds them not.

I *cannot* give a regular chronicle of the day. It is impossible. I was in such a state of excitement. It all seemed, and seems still, like a brilliant dream. Dr. Rogers and I talked all the time, I know, while he showed me the camp and all the arrangements. They have a beautiful situation, on the grounds once occupied by a very old fort, "De La Ribanchine," built in 1629 or 30. Some of the walls are still standing. Dr. Rogers has made quite a good hospital out of an old gin house. I went over it. There are only a few invalids in it, at present. I saw everything; the kitchens, cooking arrangements, and all. Then we took seats on the platform.

The meeting was held in a beautiful grove, a live-oak grove, adjoining the camp. It is the largest one I have yet seen; but I don't think the moss pendants are quite as beautiful as they are on St. Helena. As I sat on the stand and looked around on the various groups, I thought I had never seen a sight so beautiful. There were the black soldiers, in their blue coats and scarlet pants, the officers of this and other regiments in their handsome uniforms, and crowds of lookers-on, men, women and children, grouped in various attitudes, under the trees. The faces of all wore a happy, eager, expectant look.

The exercises commenced by a prayer from Rev. Mr. Fowler, Chaplain of the regiment. An ode written for the occasion by Prof. Zachos, originally a Greek, now Superintendent of Paris island--was read by himself, and then sung by the whites. Col. Higginson introduced Dr. Brisbane in a few elegant and graceful words. He read the President's Proclamation, which was warmly cheered. Then the beautiful flags presented by Dr. Cheever's Church were presented to Col. Higginson for the Regiment in an excellent and enthusiastic speech, by Rev. Mr. Manfield French. Immediately at the conclusion, some of the colored people--of their own accord sang "My Country Tis of Thee." It was a touching and beautiful incident, and Col. Higginson, in accepting the flags made it the occasion of some happy remarks. He said *that* tribute was far more effective than any speech he c'ld make. He spoke for some time, and all that he said was grand, glorious. He seemed inspired. Nothing c'ld have been better, more perfect. And Dr. Rogers told me afterward that the Col. was much affected. That tears were in his eyes. He is as Whittier says, truly a "sure man." The men all admire and love him. There is a great deal of personal magnetism about him, and his kindness is proverbial. After he had done speaking he delivered the flags to the color-bearers with a few very impressive remarks to them. They each then, Sgt. Prince Rivers and Cpl. Robert Sutton, made very good speeches indeed, and were loudly cheered. Gen. Saxton and Mrs. Gage spoke very well. The good Gen. was received with great enthusiasm, and throughout the morning--every little while it seemed to me three cheers were given for him. A Hymn written I believe, by Mr. Judd, was sung, and then all the people united with the Regiment in singing "John Brown." It was grand. During the exercises, it was announced that Fremont was appointed Commander-in-chief of the Army, and this was received with enthusiastic and prolonged cheering. But as it is picket news, I greatly fear that it is not true.

We dined with good Dr. Rogers at the Col. T.W. Higginson's table, though, greatly to my regret he, (the Col.) was not there. He partook of some of the oxen, (of which ten had been roasted) with his men. I like his doing that. We had quite a sumptuous dinner. Our party consisted of Dr. Rogers, Adjuntant Dewhurst, Capt. Rogers, Mr. and Miss Ware (Mrs. Winsor's brother and sister), Mr. Hall, their cousin, whom I like much, and Mr. and Miss Hunn and me. We had a merry, delightful dinner. The only part that I did not enjoy was being obliged to read Whittier's Hymn aloud at the table. I wanted Dr. Rogers to do it. But he w'ld insist on my doing it. So of course it was murdered. I believe the older I grow the more averse I get to doing anything in public. I have no courage to do such things.

Col. Higginson invited us into his tent--a very nice, almost *homelike* one. I noticed a nice secretary, with writing utensils and "Les Miserables" on it. A *wreath* of beautiful oranges hung against the wall, fronting the door. I wanted to have a good look at this tent; but we were hardly seated when the Dr. and Col. were called away for a moment, and Lieut. Col. Billings coming in w'ld insist upon our going into his tent. I did not want to go at all, but he was so *persistent* we had to. I fear he is a somewhat vain person. His tent was very comfortable too, and I noticed quite a large piece of "Secesh" furniture, something between a secretary and a bureau, and quite a collection of photographs and daguerres. But I did not examine them, for my attention was occupied by Col. Higginson to whom I showed Whittier's poem, letter and photo. "He looks old," he said to me sadly, as he handed back the picture.

Dr. Rogers introduced me to Dr. Hawks and his wife-- pleasant people, and *good* anti-slavery. They mentioned having Liberators with my letters in them. I am sorry they have come down here.

Col. Higginson asked me to go out and hear the band play, which I very gladly did. But it stopped just as we stepped outside of the tent. 'Just then one of the soldiers came up to the Col. and said "Do Cunnel, do ask 'em to play Dixie, just for me, for my lone self." The Col. made the request, but the leader of the band said he feared they w'ld not be able to play the whole tune as they had not the necessary pieces. "Nebber mind," said the man "jus' half a tune will do." It was found impossible to play even that but the leader promised that the next time they came they would be fully prepared to play Dixie for him.

The Dress Parade--the first I had ever seen--delighted me. It was a brilliant sight--the long line of men in their brilliant uniform, with bayonets gleaming in the sunlight. The Col. looked splendid. The Dr. said the men went through with the drill remarkably well. It seemed to me nothing c'ld be more perfect. To me it was a grand triumph--that black regiment doing itself honor in the sight of the white officers, many of whom, doubtless "came to scoff." It was typical of what the race so long downtrodden and degraded will yet achieve on this Continent.

After the Parade, we went to the Landing, intending to take a boat for Beaufort. But the boat was too crowded, and we decided to wait for another. It was the softest, loveliest moonlight. We sat down among the ruins of the old fort. Just as the boat had reached a favorable distance from the shore the band in it commenced playing Home, sweet Home. It was exquisitely beautiful. The lovely moonlight on the water, the perfect stillness around seemed to give new beauty to that ever beautiful old song. And then as my dear friend, Dr. Rogers said, "It came *very near* to us all."

Finding the night air damp we went to the tent of Mr. Fowler, the chaplain, whom I like much better in private conversation than as a orator. He is a thoroughly good, earnest man. Thither came Col. Higginson and Dr. Hawks. We sat around the nice fire--the tent has *chimney* and fire place, made by Mr. Fowler's own skilful hands. Col. Higginson is a perfectly delightful person in private.--So genial, so witty, so kind. But I noticed when he was silent, a careworn almost sad expression on his earnest, noble face. My heart was full when I looked at him. I longed to say "I thank you, I thank you, for that noble glorious speech." And yet I *c'ld not.* It is always so. I do not know how to talk. Words always fail me when I want them most. The more I feel the more impossible it is for me to speak. It is very provoking. Among other things, Col. Higginson said how amusing it was to him--their plan of housekeeping down here. "This morning I was asked "Well, Colonel, how many oxen shall we roast today." And I said, just as calmly as I w'ld have ordered a pound or two of beef, at home.--well I think *ten* will do. And then to be consulted as to how many gallons of molasses, and of vinegar, and how many pounds of ginger w'ld be wanted seemed very odd." I wish I c'ld reproduce for you the dry humorous tones in which this was said. We had a pleasant chat, sitting there in the firelight, and I was most unwilling to go, for besides the happiness of being in the society of the Col. and the Dr. we wanted dreadfully to see the "shout" and grand jubilee which the soldiers were going to have that night. But it was already late, and hearing that the "Flora" was coming we had to hasten to the Landing. I was sorry to say good-bye to Dr. Rogers. What an *unspeakable* happiness it was to see him. But I fear for his health. I fear the exposure of a camp life. Am glad to see that he has warm robes and blankets, to keep him comfortable. I wish I c'ld do something for him. He has done so much for me.

Ah, what a grand, glorious day this has been. The dawn of freedom which it heralds may not break upon us at once; but it will surely come, and sooner, I believe, than we have ever dared hope before. My soul is glad with an exceeding great gladness. But before I close, dear A., I must bring our little party safe home to Oaklands. We had a good time on the Flora. Lizzie Hunn and I promenaded the deck, and sang John Brown, and Whittier's Hymn and "My Country Tis of Thee." And the moon shone bright above us, and the waves beneath, smooth and clear, glistened in the soft moonlight. At Beaufort we took the row boat, and the boatmen sang as they rowed us across. Mr. Hall was with us, and seemed really to appreciate and enjoy everything. I like him. Arrived at St. Helena's we separated, he to go to "Coffin's Point" (a dreadful name, as Dr. Rogers says) and we to come hither. Can't say that I enjoyed the homeward drive very much. T'was so intensely cold, yes *intensely*, for these regions. I fear some of the hot enthusiasm with which my soul was filled got chilled a little but it was only for a short time.

Old friend, my good and dear A. a very, very happy New Year to you! Dear friends in both my Northern homes a happy, happy New Year to you, too! And to us all a year of such freedom as we have never yet known in this boasted but hitherto wicked land. The hymn, or rather one of the hymns that those boatmen sung is singing itself to me now. The refrain "Religion so...sweet" was so sweet and touching in its solemnity.

Saturday, Jan. 24. Had to-day the pleasantest visit I've had since I've been here. Lizzie and I drove to Mr. Thorpe's plantation...The gentlemen took us around to see the people of whom there are 150 on the place. 100 have come from Edisto. There were no houses to accommodate so many, and they had to find shelter in barns, outhouses and any other place they could get. They have constructed rude houses for themselves--many of them--which do not, however afford them much protection in bad weather. I am told that they are all excellent, industrious people.

One old woman interested me deeply. Her name is Daphne, and she is probably at least a hundred years old. She has had fifty grandchildren, sixty-five greatgrandchildren, and three great, greatgrandchildren. She is entirely blind, but seems quite cheerful and happy. She told us that she was brought from Africa to this country just after the Revolution. I asked her if she was glad that all her numerous family were now and forever free. Her bright old face grew brighter as she answered. "Oh yes, yes missus." She retains her faculties remarkably well for one so old. It interested me greatly to see her. As Mr. H said "It was worth coming to South Carolina to see that old relic of a past time."

15 of the people on this place escaped from the main land, last spring. Among them was a man named Michael. After they had gone some distance--their masters in pursuit--Michael's master overtook him in the swamp. A fierce grapple ensued--the master on horseback, the man on foot:--the former drew a pistol and shot the slave through the arm, shattering it dreadfully. Still the brave man fought desperately and at last succeeded in unhorsing the master, and beat him until he was senseless. He then with the rest of the company escaped. With them was a woman named Rina, now a cook at Mr. Thorpe's. She was overtaken by her master's cousin, and nearly run over by his horse. But he, having a liking for her, wheeled his horse around, when he saw who it was, without saying a word, and allowed her to escape.--A story which I record because it is a rare thing to hear anything good of a rebel. I had the pleasure of shaking hands with Rina, and congratulating her on her escape. She is a very neat, sensible looking black woman.

Mr. Thorpe's place--which used to be the property of one of the numerous family of Fripps--Thomas by name--is most beautifully situated in the midst of noble pine trees, and on the banks of a large creek which deserves--almost--to be dignified by the name of the river. Tis the pleasantest place I've seen yet. And Mr. Thorpe says it is quite healthy.

Of course we lost our way coming back, and I, in trying to turn the horse, ran up against a tree and there our *"shay"* staid. In vain did Lizzie and I try to move the horse, and then the wheels. Both were equally immovable, till fortunately we saw a man at a little distance and called him to our aid. With his assistance we soon got righted again. All this I tell you, dear A. as a great secret. Wouldn't have anybody else know of my unskilfulness. Despite this little *contretemps* we had a delightful sunset drive home.

Sunday, Jan. 25. Saw a wonderful sight to-day. 150 people were baptized in the creek near the church. They looked very picturesque--many of them in white aprons, and bright dresses and handkerchiefs. And as they, in procession, marched down to the water, they sang beautifully. The most perfect order and quiet prevailed throughout.

Monday, Jan. 26. Rec'd another kind note from Dr. Rogers written prior to the other. In it he gives me some account of what he is doing; and I am so glad to know. It is so good to hear from him, I fear he has not got my note. Not that t'was of much importance, but I w'ld like him to know how constantly I think of him.

Tuesday, Jan. 27. J brought me from Beaufort to-day a package from home containing a letter from Aunt Margaretta, some delicious candy from our good Emma, and a pair of quite nice pants, from Mrs. Chew, sent especially to Cupid. How delighted he was to get them. He couldn't say much, but I wish Mrs. Chew c'ld have seen the marvelous bows and *scrapings* which he made.

Wednesday, Jan. 28. A memorable day because we had a snowstorm--in miniature. When I got up this morning some of the roofs had a white layer on them, but it did not stay on the ground. The "storm" lasted but a little while. Towards eve. there was another slight attempt at snow, which was unsuccessful. A cold, dreary day. Miss Ruggles sent me "Say and Seal," and a bunch of lovely white flowers, which it does my soul good to see. She is very kind....

Friday, Jan. 30. Finished "Say and Seal," some of which I like very much. But it is rather religious to suit me. I don't know but it seems to me the author's works have a little *cant* about them. Now Mrs. Stowe always has something about religion in her books, but it is so differently *administered*, that it is only pleasant and beautiful....

Saturday, Jan. 31. Lizzie and I went to Beaufort--after bread. We had a lovely row across,--at noon--in the brightest sunlight. But neither going or coming did the boatmen sing, which disappointed me much. The Sergeant said these were not singers--*That* is most surprising. I thought *everybody* sang down here. Certainly every boat crew *ought*. As we drove to the ferry, we noticed how fresh and green everything looked;--so unlike winter. The trees are nearly all evergreen. Bare branches are rarely to be seen. What a lovely morning it was!--like a May morn. up North. Birds singing on every side. Deep green in the pines and "deep delicious blue" in the sky. Why is it that green and blue together are so lovely in Nature, and so *un*lovely elsewhere?

In Beaufort we spent nearly all our time at Harriet Tubman's--otherwise "Moses." She is a wonderful woman--a real heroine. Has helped off a large number of slaves, after taking her own freedom. She told us that she used to hide them in the woods during the day and go around to get provisions for them. Once she had with her a man named Joe, for whom a reward of $1500 was offered. Frequently, in different places she found handbills exactly describing him, but at last they reached in safety the Suspension Bridge over the Falls and found themselves in Canada. Until then, she said, Joe had been very silent. In vain had she called his attention to the glory of the Falls. He sat perfectly still-moody, it seemed, and w'ld not even glance at them. But when she said, "Now we are in Canada" he sprang to his feet with a great shout, and sang and clapped his hand in a perfect delirium of joy. So when they got out, and he first touched *free* soil, he shouted and hurrahed "as if he were crazy"-- she

How exciting it was to hear her tell the story. And to hear her sing the very scraps of jubilant hymns that he sang. She said the ladies crowded around them, and some laughed and some cried. My own eyes were full as I listened to her--the heroic woman! A reward of $1000 was offered for her by the Southerners, and her friends deemed it best that she sh'ld, for a time find refuge in Canada. And she did so, but only for a short time. She came back and was soon at the good brave work again. She is living in Beaufort now; keeping an eating house. But she wants to go North, and will probably do so ere long. I am glad I saw her--*very* glad!

At her house we met one of the Superintendents from Port Royal Island, a Boston man--Mr. S--who is intelligent and very agreeable. He kindly went with us to Mrs. Hawkes's--the wife of the Surgeon 1st Regiment South Carolina Volunteers but she was at the camp with her husband who did not go with the Expedition. Was sorry not to see her.

Went, afterward, to Mr. Judd's for letters, and found there one from Annie. Am delighted to have it, and to know she is not ill. Mr. Judd's house is beautifully situated. In the same street with Gen. Saxton's. On the Bay--as they call it. Saw the building which was once the Public Library. It is now a shelter for "contrabands" from Fernandino. How disgusted the rebels w'ld be. I suppose they w'ld upturn their aristocratic noses and say "To what base uses etc." It does *me* good to see how the tables are turned. The market place also we saw. Mr. S said doubtless human beings had been sold there. But there is not a certainty of it, as that business was generally transacted in Charleston. The Arsenal is a fine large stone structure--fine--I should say--for this region. The entrance is guarded by two handsome brass cannon, and a fierce looking sentinel. Nearly all the houses in Beaufort have a dismantled, desolate look. Few persons are to be seen in the streets some soldiers and "contrabands." I believe we saw only three ladies. But already Northern improvements have reached this southern town. One of them is a fine new wharf which is a convenience that one wonders how the "Secesh" c'ld have done without. They were an uncivilized people. I noticed more mulattoes there than we have on St. Helena. Some were very good-looking. Little colored children--of every hue playing about the streets looking as merry and happy as children ought to look--now that the dark shadow of slavery hangs over them no more.

We did our few errands and were quite ready for the four o'clock boat, which was not, however, ready for us until sometime afterward. I missed the singing, in our row back.

Sunday, Feb. 1. Quite a number of strangers at church to-day,--among them our good Gen. Saxton; whom it is always a pleasure to see. Reuben Tomlinson was there. I was glad to see him. It recalled the old Philadelphia days--the pleasantest of them.

This afternoon went into the woods, and gathered some casino berries and beautiful magnolia leaves and exquisite ferns. How beautifully they contrast, on my table, with the daffodils and narcissus which are in full bloom now. Think of these flowers blooming out of doors in January and February. Isn't it wonderful? I cant tell you how much pleasure they give me. What sunbeams they are to warm and cheer my heart.

Monday, Feb. 2. Have just heard to-night of the return of the 1st Regiment. They came back with laurels and Secesh prisoners. Have heard no particulars, but am *glad*, emphatically glad to know that they come back completely successful. That is grand, glorious! In the joy of my heart sat down and wrote a congratulatory note, to my dear friend, Dr. Rogers. I know how rejoiced he must be. Thank God that he and the noble Col. have come back safe.

Saturday, Feb. 7. One day this week Tina, an excellent woman from Palawana, came in, and told us a very interesting story about two girls, one about ten the other fifteen, who, having been taken by their master up into the country about the time of "Gun Shoot," determined to try to get back to their parents who had been left on this island. They stole away at night, and travelled through woods and swamps, for two days without eating. Sometimes their strength w'ld fail and they w'ld sink down in the swamps, and think they c'ld go no further, but they had brave little hearts, and struggled on, till at last they reached Port Royal Ferry. There they were seen by a boat-load of people who had also made their escape. The boat was too full to take them but the people, as soon as they reached these islands, told the father of the children, who immediately hastened to the Ferry for them. The poor little creatures were almost wild with joy, despite their exhausted state, when they saw their father coming to them. When they were brought to their mother she fell down "jus' as if she was dead" as Tina expressed it. She was so overpowered with joy. Both children are living on Dalta now. They are said to be very clever. I want to see the heroic little creatures.

Another day, one of the black soldiers came in and gave us *his* account of the Expedition. No words of mine, dear A can give you any account of the state of exultation and enthusiasm that he was in. He was eager for another chance at "de Secesh." I asked him what he would do if his master and others sh'ld come back and try to reenslave him. "I'd fight um Miss, I'd fight um till I turned to dust!" He was especially delighted at the ire which the sight of the black troops excited in the minds of certain Secesh women whom they saw. These vented their spleen by calling the men "baboons dressed in soldiers clothes," and telling them that they ought to be at work in their masters' rice swamps, and that they ought to be lashed to death. "And what did you say to them?" I asked. "Oh muss, we only tell um 'Hole your tongue, and dry up.' You see *we* wusn't feared of *dem, dey couldn't hurt us now.* Whew! didn't we laugh...to see dem so mad!" The spirit of resistance to the Secesh is strong in these men.

Sunday, Feb. 8. ...Towards night, after the others had gone, Dr. Rogers came. Wasn't I glad to see him. He looks none the worse for his later experience. He brought his notes of the Expedition taken on the spot, and very kindly read them to us, to-night. They are very, very interesting, more so to me even than Col. Higginson's excellent Report, (which the Dr. also brought) because entering more into particulars. He will not have them printed for which I am sorry. They ought to be. They, and the report also, show plainly how noble and bravely the black soldiers can fight. I am delighted. I think the contemputuous white soldiers will cease to sneer soon. Dr. Rogers described beautifully the scenes through which they passed, particularly the night journey up St. Mary's River, with the grand old funereal oaks on either side. How strange and solemn it must have been.

At one place, Alberti's Mills, they went up to the plantation, and found the mistress, living in solitary splendor. She and her husband (now dead) came from the North, but have lived a long time down South, and had a large plantation and great wealth. Dr. Rogers describes Madam Alberti as a very superior woman. She spent a long time in trying to convince Dr. Rogers that she and her husband had devoted themselves to the good of their slaves, and lamented their ingratitude in all deserting her--as they have all done except one or two petted house servants. Robert Sutton, now Corporal in the Regiment was formerly her slave, and said the people were cruelly treated, and the jail on the place, where chains and handcuffs were found, bears witness to that.

The soldiers brought off cattle, horses and lumber, all of great value to the Government. They behaved gallantly under fire from the rebels, and entered into their work with zeal. Three of them saved the life of their brave Col. Higginson. He, as usual, was at one time in advance, when a rebel pistol was fired at him by an officer, who immediately drew another and was about to take more fatal aim (the Col. not perceiving it) when three of the soldiers seeing his danger, fired at once, killing the rebel officer. Dr. Rogers says that several who were badly wounded did not report to him, fearing that they w'ld be obliged to leave their posts. The noble Robert Sutton whom Col. Higginson calls "the Leader of the Expedition" was wounded in three places, and still kept at his post. Dr. Rogers speaks of him as does Col. Higginson--in the highest terms. He says he thinks he must be the descendant of some Nubian king. He is a grand man. My heart is filled with an exceeding great joy to-night.

I can never thank Dr. Rogers sufficiently for bringing me those notes. It was very kind. And it makes me so happy to see him safe back again. The kind, loving words he spoke to me to-night sank deep into my heart. "As a brother," he told me to consider him. And I will gladly do so. He read me Emerson's noble Hymn, written for the grand Jubilee Concert, on Emancipation Day in Boston. Dr. Rogers read it to the Regiment he told me, during service, this morning. I am glad. He was in full uniform to-day. Makes a splendid looking officer. I looked at him and his horse with childish admiration.

Monday, Feb. 9. Dr. Rogers walked part of the way to school with me, and we had a nice, long talk. He said he wished he lived nearer that he might come in and read to me sometimes. Ah! wouldn't *I* enjoy that, unspeakably! It is too bad that I can see so seldom the only old friend I have here,-- and such a friend! Dear Miss Towne was not well enough to be at school to-day. I am very sorry. With what eager interest and delight Miss Murray speaks of the success of the Regiment. I believe she is as rejoiced as I am, and that's saying a great deal. It does me good to see it.

Frogmore, Wednesday, Feb. 11. Quite unwell yesterday and to-day. This morn. the Townes--my good physician and her sister--came in and declaring that I needed change of air, forcibly bore me off to Frogmore. Well, I was glad to go, and here I am. The place is delightfully situated, on an arm of the sea, which, at high tide, comes up to within a few feet of the house. There are lovely trees around, and an almost sea air, which is most invigorating after the somewhat oppresive atmosphere farther inland. This is a very large plantation. There are nearly 200 people living on it. Ah! how pleasant this salt smell is. It recalls the dear old Marblehead days.

Thursday, Feb. 12. Have done little else but sleep. It is very quiet here. Have had most delicious rest, both for soul and body. Miss Rosa Towne is as kind as possible. Hers is a beautiful kindness, that does one good thoroughly. I love her...

Found the first snowdrop to-day;--a lovely, pure, little darling, growing at the foot of the piazza steps. Welcome, welcome a thousand times!

Friday, Feb. 13. Miss Laura Towne came to-day. To-night some of the little boys came in and danced for us. It was *deliciously* comical. Miss Laura rewarded them by giving them belts with bright buckles, which pleased them mightily. To-night there was a bit of a shout in the "Praise House," but there were not enough to make it very enjoyable. They sang beautifully however. One song I have not heard before. Must try to get the words. "Jacob" and "would not let me go," are in it.

Saturday, Feb. 14. Valentine's day *at home.* Who will send me one? A dark, gloomy, stormy day without, but cheery within. Miss W and Miss Murray came to-day, and we have quite a large party--five ladies and two gentlemen. Stormed so much this afternoon they c'ld not go, and will be obliged to spend the night with us. This is *jolly.* I know Mr. F thinks so. *Wasn't* he rejoiced to see Miss Murray. Ah! this love. Tis a queer thing, but very amusing--to lookers-on.

Helped Miss Rosa fill bags with sewing utensils for the people--a pleasant task. We both enjoyed it.

To-night--a wild stormy night--went out on the piazza and listened to the roaring of the sea. How wild it sounded. Occasionally we c'ld hear a great wave break upon the shore. That sound of the sea is music to my ears. I c'ld not bear to come away from it. It brought New England near to me. But the air is dangerously damp, and I had to tear myself away. Miss Laura Towne told us some delightfully horrible stories and then Mr. F told us some stories from Vergil, in which he seems well read. We had a very pleasant, social evening.-- Good bye, old Journal friend.

Saturday, April 11. Had a perfect ride to-day with Col Higginson and Dr. Rogers. Went to Rose's plantation, and Capers. There the Col. left us to go on board one of the gun boats. Dr. Rogers and I rode on to Barnwell's Plantation, which is the most beautiul place I have yet seen. It is filled with magnificent live oaks, magnolias, and other trees. Saw there a grand old oak said to be the largest on the islands, some of its branches have been cut off, but the circumference of those remaining is more than a hundred feet. It is a wonderful tree. The grounds slope down to the water--Broad River, and here again we went to a point whence the rebels are sometimes to be seen and though we, and one of the black soldiers, strained our eyes we c'ld discover none.

How shall I tell you, dear A. about our ride home first through an avenue of beautiful trees--mostly live oaks draped with moss--and then for miles and miles through the Pine Barrens. The air was soft, Italian, only a low faint murmur c'ld be heard among the pines,--hardly "the slow song of the sea." The ground was thickly carpeted with ferns of a most delicious green, and to crown all we found Azaleas of a deep pink color and perfect fragrance. Found also sand violets, very large purple ones, and some kind of grass which bears an exquisite fine white flower, some of the petals just tinged with a delicate lilac. The flower is a little spicea. We rode slowly through the Barrens. I think I never enjoyed anything so perfectly, I *luxuriated* in it. It was almost "too much, too much." Dr. Rogers and I had a long and interesting talk. How kind, how good he is! It is very pleasant to know he cared so much for me, even although I *know* he thinks far better of me than I deserve. The brightest and most delightful experiences must come to an end, and at last but too soon we emerged from the Pine Barrens and came out into the shell road. It was like leaving Paradise. Yet this is a very pleasant road, too. Noticed the finest live oak, almost the finest, I ever saw. Not quite so large as the Barnwell, but far more beautiful. Found also the most exquisite white violets I ever saw--such delicate, wonderful penciling. They were fragrant too. Had a good canter on the nice hard road.

On reaching home we were met by the news that the rebels were supposed to be bringing up pontoon bridges, were expected to make an attempt to cross near the Ferry, at a place about two miles distant from here. The news created quite a little excitement. The Col. had not yet returned. A messenger was dispatched for him, and another to Gen. Saxton at Beaufort that gunboats and artillery may be sent up. Capt. James S. Rogers seems to enjoy the prospect of a fight, promises me I shall see a shell this afternoon.--The Col. has now returned. Couriers are coming in every few minutes. One of the Superintendent's whose place is near the Ferry has been watching thro' his glass the movements opposite, and reports that the rebels are gathering in large force. Meanwhile I sit composedly down taking notes; and shall now occupy myself with darning a pair of stockings for the doctor until something further occurs which is *writable*. Have no fear.

Night. Finished the stockings, then took a pleasant walk with Dr. Minor in the garden; where we discovered a lovely magnolia just opened, some perfect rosebuds, and a *strawberry* nearly ripe. At supper everybody in good spirits, gay and cheerful. We heard that the gunboats had arrived, and all this eve at intervals, we hear the guns. Did not know at first which side they were on, but am incapable of fear. Can hear plainly the explosion of shells. Are sure now that the firing is from our gunboats. Being so very near us, of course it sounds heavy. The Col. has just been reading me (a magnificent reader he is) some of the ballads of the old Cavaliers. How grand, how stirring they are. And how Robert *Brown-*

ing is too. Afterward the Dr. read me a little of the "Faerie Queene" and then some letters which have just come. The battery has arrived from Beaufort. And I am told young Mr. Merriam of Boston is here. He is always ready for a fight. Mrs. Dewhurst and I will now composedly retire. We don't fear an attack; but if it comes--why let it. Our men will fight bravely we know. As for myself, I do not fear. W'ld far rather be killed than that our noble Col. Higginson or the equally noble and good Dr. Rogers should be.

This has been an exciting day, I have enjoyed it, yes truly enjoyed it. The Arago sailed this morn. So I shall not see my good friend Mr. Pierce again, for which I am sorry. Regret very much that he will not be here to-morrow to speak to the soldiers. I like so much his kind genial way of speaking to these people, and Dr. Rogers says he does too. It gives them entire confidence in him. He has promised to call and see grandmother in Philadelphia. I am very glad.

Sunday, Apr. 12. Slept more soundly last night than I have before. Was only wakened once or twice by couriers coming "in hot haste." That was all. Woke quite late, to find a lovely morning.

Dr. Minor and I had a grand ride. Same programme as yesterday--Rose's Capers' and then Barnwells'; thence another perfect ride thro' the Pine Barrens. Found exquisite white azaleas this time, and the largest violets I've yet seen. T'was a lovely, dreamy kind of morning--half sunlight, half shade. How exquisite the shades of green are now. The bright, fresh green of the young oaks and plums, and gum trees contrasting most beautifully with the dark, sombre pines. I think the air to-day must be like that of Italy. Had a pleasant talk with Dr. Minor. He is very young, full of enthusiasm and courage. I like him much. Dr. Rogers has a very high opinion of him. There's something so earnest, singlehearted about him. He has talent, too. Lives in Connecticut now. Was born in Ceylon he tells me. I enjoyed hearing him talk about that far away island. Rode his horse, a noble, spirited fellow, but gentle as can be. He canters splendidly; but a little more roughly that the roan I've ridden hitherto. The Col. has a splendid horse, Rinoldo. So has the Dr. They came from Florida. Had nearly four hours ride.

Got home just so as to miss seeing Gens. Hunter and Saxton, who have been paying us a visit. Wanted to see Gen. Hunter. Found that Mr. Judd had come...to take me to Beaufort. And so unwillingly had to take my leave. How very, very much I have enjoyed this visit. Have promised the Col. that when another person can be found to take my place in school here, I will come and teach the soldiers. I shall be glad to do it. Found it hard to leave my kind friend Dr. Rogers. He has been very good to me.

Had a pleasant drive to Beaufort with Mr. Judd and Miss Ruggles. Passed the fortifications which are quite complete now. Thee was a Negro funeral at the burying grounds. We c'ld see the crowd of people and hear them singing hymns;-- not their own beautiful hymns, I am sorry to say. I do so fear these will be superseded by ours, which are poor in comparison, and which they do not sing well at all. From Beaufort saw Gen. Hunter in the street, but had not a good look at him.

The Oaks. Monday, morn. Apr. 13. Came hither last eve., and spent the night. In the night was sure I heard some one try my door. Asked "Who's there?" No answer. The noise was repeated--the question asked again. Still no answer. Woke Miss Ware who had the adjoining room. She lit the candle and we took our revolvers,--all ready for rebels. Waited awhile. Then as all continued quiet, put our pistols under our heads and composed ourselves to sleep. The wind or rats, I supposed afterward. At first I was sure it was some person but thought it more likely to be a robber than a rebel.

Oaklands--Night. Have had a wearisome day at school. So many little ones. And nearly all in a state of rebellion, owing to their teacher's long absence. Had some newspapers, but no letters, which disappoints me greatly. Spent the eve. in writing.

Tuesday, Apr. 14. Windy, disagreeable day. Very small school. How deliciously fragrant the air is now with orange blossoms. They've been open a week. Roses too in full bloom. We have some superb buds in our garden. The largest I ever saw; and of an exquisite color--something between a pink and a buff.

To-night it is rumored that there are rebels--cavalry--on

the island. I do not believe it. It is said they can blow brandy into their horses' noses and that will enable them to swim a long distance. And so it is tho't they may have been able to cross from Edisto over some of the little creeks. There's no probability of it. Mrs. Hunn is somewhat alarmed. Reports are most numerous here, always. So it is better not to believe them at all.

Some rebels were nicely caught a few days ago. They were at a picket station on or near Edisto. Capt. Dutch of the Kingfisher, hearing that they were there from a Negro, one of their servants, went with some of his men to the house and took them all prisoners. There were nine or ten of them.-- The aristocracy of the islands. Am delighted to think they were taken.

Seaside. *Wednesday, Apr. 15.* After school rode to "Seaside" on my faithful horse--Edisto. Shall take up my abode here for the present. Had a delightful ride hither through the woods. Enjoyed it perfectly. House is still barely furnished, and has rather a comfortless look; but I suppose it will soon seem like home. Tis fortunate that one gets easily accustomed to these changes. Tis pleasant to have a piano, though it is a poor one.

Saturday, Apr. 18. Had a pleasant little ride to Dr. White's, a plantation a few miles from here. The grounds must once have been beautiful, but have a somewhat decayed look now. The house is rather poor looking though large. Tis painted a dull red, in which it differs from the other houses down here, most of which are white. Edisto went with great spirit to-day--quite distinguished himself-- passed the other horses with astonishing ease.

Sunday, Apr. 19. Went to church, and afterward to Oaklands where we dined. Mr. Tomlinson who is now Gen. Superintendent instead of Mr. Soule (who has resigned and gone home) dined with us. I enjoyed his society very much. He is so genial and happy. Makes sunshine wherever he goes. And is also deeply interested in the people here. Think he will make a splendid Superintendent.

Saturday, Apr. 25. All this week have ridden to school on horseback and enjoyed it very much though Edisto is rather rough.

Yesterday had a very kind letter from B.P. Hunt.

Today went on horseback with Lizzie and Mrs. B to the village which is about eight miles from here. Had a lovely ride through June woods;--the air laden with the fragrance of the locust; the birds singing merrily, the golden sunlight pouring its flood of beauty upon the delicious green of the young leaves. The village is delightfully situated on quite a large and pleasant stream of water. The ladies upon whom we went to call were not at home, but Lieut. B was there, and we dined with him, then walked around under the trees and enjoyed the water.

Had a lovely ride home through the pines just at sunset. The beauty of these wonderful days sinks deep,deep, into my soul.

The people on the place have grand "shouts." They are most inspiring. Went to one Thursday night. There is an old blind man, Maurice, who has a truly wonderful voice, so strong and clear.--It rings our like a trumpet. One song-- "Gabriel blow the Trumpet"--was the grandest thing I have yet heard. And with what fire and enthusiasm the old blind man led off. He seemed inspired.

Sunday, Apr. 26. After church dined at Oaklands and had another perfect ride home through the woods. Ah how I revel in these days. They are almost "too much, too much."

This eve. attended in the "Praise House," the grandest shout I have yet seen. Several of the soldiers who had come home on a visit joined in the shout with great spirit. The whole thing was quite inspiring. How thoroughly Mr. Ware enjoyed it, too. I like him exceedingly. He is such a thoroughly good abolitionist--a friend of Mr. Garrison's too--so *of course* I like him. He is very intelligent, gentlemanly and pleasant. He is Superintendent of our plantation and now lives with us.

Wednesday, Apr. 29. Last night Capt. Dutch and one or two others called. The Capt. came to make arrangements for our accompanying him to Edisto. He is going to take every precaution for our safety. But as Lieut. B says there are 5000 Union troops on the island I sh'ldn't think there'd be any danger. I am not afraid, at any rate, I think I sh'ld enjoy going very much. We are to go to the village early to-morrow morning, and thence take boats to the Kingfisher, Capt. Dutch's boat.

Thursday, Apr. 30. Fast Day. Started this morn. with Mrs. B and Lizzie Hunn to go to the village, but my poor horse was too sick to go. I myself felt far from well, so gave up the expedition and went to Oaklands,--thence to church, where young Mr. Ware preached. There was but a small attendance. Am housekeeper now that the others have gone--No sinecure--for it is not easy to get anything to eat. Barely escape starvation. Tis fortunate that we shall have our rations in a few days.

Friday, May 1. A lovely May Day. Sunny and bright--not unpleasantly warm. Rode...this morn. to visit Mr. Sumner's school. Found but a very small attendance. Just missed one class, and was too soon for the first, which comes in the afternoon. Am sorry to have missed it. Mr. Sumner is very witty and original. Don't know half the time, however, whether he is in jest or earnest--which is provoking....

Rode a nice little horse belonging to one of the men. It canters very fast--has a swift bounding motion which is most exhilarating. Her name is Linda. Shall hire her, and let my poor Jeanie have a good rest before I use her again.

This is a glorious moonlight night. From the window I can see the water in silver waves shining in the clear soft light. Sat a long time on the piazza listening to the low tones of the piano or the equally musical murmur of the wind in the tree tops, and thinking of some loved ones who are far, far away! How old memories crowd around one on such nights as these! And how dreamy, strange and unreal the present seems. Here on the piazza of this old southern house I sit and think of friends a thousand miles away--of scenes that have past, never, never to return again. Shall I ever see the dear ones "up North" I wonder? Something answers "never" but for to-night at least, I will not listen to that voice. Here the fleas interpose. Farewell to all reminiscences. Now for tortures unendurable! Oh the fleas!! the fleas!! The fleas!!

Sunday, May 3. Too weary and ill to go to church, which I regretted for I always like to see the people, looking so bright and cheerful in their Sunday attire, and to hear them sing....

The people, after "Praise" had one of their grandest shouts, and Lizzie and I, in a dark corner of the Praise House, amused ourselves with practicing a little. It is wonderful what perfect time the people keep with hands, feet, and indeed with every part of the body. I enjoy these "shouts" very much.

Oaks, Wednesday, May 6. Miss Murray and I spent the day in procuring flowers and decorating the church for Miss Nellie's marriage. She is to be married to-morrow. Arranged three bouquets for the pulpit and twined ivy around the little pillars supporting it; while Miss Murray arranged beautiful hanging baskets for each side of the pupit and another for the table. The church has been nicely cleaned by some of the people. To-night have been very busy arranging flowers for the house. Such exquisite roses!

At Sea--Friday, July 31. Said farewell to Seaside and its kind household, white and black, and very early this morn Lieut. Walton's boy drove me to Land's End, whence we were to take the steamboat which was to convey us to the steamer at Hilton Head. Mr. Williams and his son who were to be our companions were behind in another carriage. I was barely in time for the boat, and it was with great difficulty that the Capt. was prevailed upon to wait for Mr. Williams. Our trunks were at least two miles behind in one of the tedious mule carts, so of course, there was no hope of getting them on board. Mr. E.W. waited for them, intending to take a row boat and follow us at all speed down to Hilton Head. He was quite sanguine of getting there before the steamer left. But he did not. And here we are, homeward bound but minus our baggage. I am sorry for Mr. E.W.'s disappointment. His health is so poor, it is really important that he sh'ld go North as soon as possible.

The "Fulton" sailed from Hilton Head between eight and nine. We have quite a pleasant party on board. Several friends of mine--Mr. Pierce, Dr. Rogers, Mr. and Mrs. Harrison, Mr. and Mrs. Fairfield and Mr. Hall--all good people.

We have had a perfect day. Besides our party there are two or three ladies and many gentlemen, principally officers, whom I do not know. The waves are a rich deep green the sky a lovely blue, the sun shines brightly, it is very, very pleasant at sea. Early this afternoon we came in sight of Charleston, and stopped outside the harbor for an hour or two. Saw plainly the steeples of the hateful little rebel city. Had an excellent view of Fort Sumter, which seems to rise out of the water--bold, grim, and most formidable looking. In the distance we c'ld see the smoke from the guns on Morris Island, and through a glass caught a very indistinct view of Fort Wagner. I shudder at the thought of that place, remembering the beautiful and brave young colonel who found a grave there, and his heroic men, some dead beneath the walls--some prisoners, doomed, doubtless, to a fate far, far worse than death.

Our captain is an immense man--a perfect Falstaff indeed, but wonderfully active for such a "mountain of flesh." He informs us that he is a Cape Cod man, and had been going to sea for nearly fifty years. Surely he ought to be most thoroughly *en rapport* with Old Ocean. I cannot help envying him.

Saturday, Aug. 1. How perfect last night was. Mr. Pierce and I sat on deck late in the lovely, lovely moonlight, talking very pleasantly. This morn. after several hours of a most doleful experience in my stateroom I at last succeeded in getting dressed, and struggled up on deck. There I literally *dropped* down upon the nearest seat feeling unspeakably woebegone. My kind friend Mr. Pierce secured the best seat he c'ld for me, and afterward read Dicken's Christmas Stories to me. After a time felt better. Spent the day on deck--talking, or listening to Emerson and Tennyson, very kindly read to me by Dr. Rogers and Mr. Hall.

Another very lovely day. The sea is unusually calm, and of the most beautiful emerald hue. Am rather sorry that nothing has occurred. Think I sh'ld like a storm if I c'ld be outside and see its full grandeur. Our captain says we shall reach New York to-morrow. I have thought of the faithful ones who have gathered at Abington to celebrate this day in that lovely pine grove. I w'ld be very pleasant to be with them. God bless them!

FRANCES ANNE
ROLLIN

FRANCES ANNE ROLLIN
(1847-1901)

The collaboration which resulted in the book, *Life and Services of Martin D. Delany*, is an extraordinary one. Frances Anne Rollin was born to a prosperous free mulatto family in Charleston, South Carolina, and was the youngest of four brilliant sisters. At the beginning of the war in 1861, she was sent to school in Philadelphia to study at the famed Institute for Colored Youth. In 1865 she returned to Charleston where she secured a teaching post in one of the American Missionary Association Schools for Blacks. During the course of a civil rights action which she initiated, she made the acquaintance of Martin D. Delany, who was serving as an officer in the army and, informing him of her ambition to be a writer, the twenty-year old young woman received a commission to write the life of this quite remarkable man.

Martin R. Delany (1812-1885) had been born in Virginia, to a mother who was free and a father who was a slave. His mother, under threat of legal action for allowing her children to learn to read and write, moved the family to Chambersburg, Pennsylvania, where the children continued their studies. In 1831, in pursuit of further opportunities, the young Delany went to Pittsburgh. He continued vigorously to pursue his education privately since no colleges were open to him, and he threw himself into the anti-slavery movement.

In 1843 Delany founded and edited a weekly newspaper, *The Mystery*, for several years. In the meantime Delany studied medicine privately, having been refused admission to a number of medical colleges. Finally, he was admitted to Harvard and upon graduating in 1852 returned to Pittsburgh to practice medicine, and to lecture on medical and ethnological subjects.

The 1850s was a decade of extraordinary activity for Delany, he devoted much time to the anti-slavery cause, writing *The Condition, Elevation, Emigration and Destiny of the Colored People of the United States Politically Considered*

(1852). He moved, because of the reactionary temper of the time to Canada in 1856. While there he was visited by John Brown, travelling in pursuit of support for his own solution to the slavery question.

It is during his period in Canada that Delany wrote a complex fictional work *Blake, or the Huts of America* which appeared serially in periodicals, partially in 1859, and in 1862. In *Blake*, he presents many of his insights and opinions on the American slave system and casts an eye on Southern sentiments for the annexation of Cuba as a slave state. He clearly envisions a destiny for Cuba as a Black country.

In 1859, in pursuit of an emigration scheme deriving from his 1852 essay, he conducted in company with a Jamaican, Robert Campbell, a reconnaissance in the Niger Valley, meeting and signing a treaty with local potentates in Abeokuta. He published an account of this project in *The Official Report of the Niger Valley Exploring Party* (1861).

Upon leaving Africa in 1860, Delany had gone to London. There he appeared before the Royal Geographical Society and was invited to participate in the International Statistical Congress where his reception caused the withdrawal of A.B. Longstreet, the American delegate, a jurist and writer from Georgia.

With the coming of the Civil War, Delany agitated for the participation of Black soldiers in the Union army, and when this was conceded, actively engaged in recruiting. Ultimately, but late in the war, he was commissioned to raise a "Corps d'Afrique", as recounted in his biography.

Delany's documents and notes relating to his life up to this time were turned over to Rollin who went to Boston to undertake the project. So copiously are Delany's own materials used in the biography that he can be considered an active collaborator in the work.

Rollin labored under considerable difficulty since the support promised by Delany was not forthcoming and she had to adopt other expedients such as clerical work and sewing to maintain herself. She made a wide acquaintance in Boston, however, in abolitionist circles, and profited from many advantages such as hearing lectures by Emerson and others.

The finished biography was accepted by the publishers Lee

and Shepard, who had also published Brown's *The Negro in the American Rebellion.* The author's name was modified to the masculine form Frank A. Rollin so as not to offend the public.

Following the publication of her book, Rollin returned to South Carolina, and joined her three sisters in Columbia, South Carolina, where their home was a meeting place for Blacks active in the Reconstruction political life of the state. She served as clerk for William J. Whipper, a Black legislator and a widower, who asked her to marry him. She did so in September of 1868.

Rollin became the mother of three children, but eventually left her husband, taking her children to Washington, D.C. Her only son became the famed actor Leigh Whipper.

CHAPTER XIX
THE COUNCIL-CHAMBER--PRESIDENT LINCOLN

We give in Major Delany's own language his interview with President Lincoln.

He tells us, "On entering the executive chamber, and being introduced to his excellency, a generous grasp and shake of the hand brought me to a seat in front of him. No one could mistake the fact that an able and master spirit was before me. Serious without sadness, and pleasant withal, he was soon seated, placing himself at ease, the better to give me a patient audience. He opened the conversation first.

"'What can I do for you, sir?' he inquired.

"'Nothing, Mr. President,' I replied; 'but I've come to porpose something to you, which I think will be beneficial to the nation in this critical hour of her peril.' I shall never forget the expression of his countenance and the inquiring look which he gave me when I answered him.

"'Go on, sir,' he said, as I paused through deference to him. I continued the conversation by reminding him of the full realization of arming the blacks of the South, and the ability of the blacks of the North to defeat it by complicity with those at the South, through the medium of the Underground Railroad--a measure known only to themselves.

"I next called his attention to the fact of the heartless and almost relentless prejudice exhibited towards the blacks by the Union army, and that something ought to be done to check this growing feeling against the slave, else nothing that we could do would avail. And if such were not expedited, all might be lost. That the blacks, in every capacity in which they had been called to act, had done their part faithfully and well. To this Mr. Lincoln readily assented. I continued: 'I would call your attention to another fact of great considera- tion; that is, the position of confidence in which they have been placed, when your officers have been under obligations to them, and in many instances even the army in their power. As pickets, scouts, and guides, you have trusted them, and found them faithful to the duties assigned; and it follows that if you can find them of higher qualifications, they may, with equal credit, fill higher and more important trusts.'

"'*Certainly*,' replied the president, in his most emphatic manner. 'And what do you propose to do?' he inquired.

"I responded, 'I propose this, sir; but first permit me to say that, whatever I may desire for black men in the army, I know that there exists too much prejudice among the whites for the soldiers to serve under a black commander, or the of- ficers to be willing to associate with him. These are facts which must be admitted, and, under the circumstances, must be regarded, as they cannot be ingored. And I propose, as a most effective remedy to prevent enrolment of the blacks in the rebel service, and induce them to run to, instead of from, the Union forces--the commissioning and promotion of black men now in the army, according to merit.'

"Looking at me for a moment, earnestly yet anxiously, he demanded, 'How will you remedy the great difficulty you have just now so justly described, about the objections of white soldiers to colored commanders, and officers to colored associates?'

"I replied, 'I have the remedy, Mr. President, which has not yet been stated; and it is the most important suggestion of my visit to you. And I think it is just what is required to complete the prestige of the Union army. I propose, sir, an army of blacks, commanded entirely by black officers, except such whites as may volunteer to serve; this army to penetrate through the heart of the South, and make conquests, with the banner of Emancipation unfurled, proclaiming freedom as they go, sustaining and protecting it by arming the emancipated, taking them as fresh troops, and leaving a few veterans among the new freedmen, when occasion requires, keeping this banner unfurled until every slave is free, according to the letter of your proclamation. I would also take from those already in the service all that are competent for commission officers, and establish at once in the South a camp of instructions. By this we could have in about three months an army of forty thousands blacks in motion, the presence of which anywhere would itself be a power irresistible. You should have an army of blacks, President Lincoln, commanded entirely by blacks, the sight of which is required to give confidence to the slaves, and retain them to the Union, stop foreign intervention, and speedily bring the war to a close.'

"'This,' replied the president, 'is the very thing I have been looking and hoping for; but nobody offered it. I have thought it over and over again. I have talked about it; I hoped and prayed for it; but till now it never has been proposed. White men couldn't do this, because they are doing all in that direction now that they can; but we find, for various reasons, it does not meet the case under consideration. The blacks should go to the interior, and the whites be kept on the frontiers.'

"'Yes, sir,' I interposed; 'they would require but little, as they could subsist on the country as they went along.'

"'Certainly,' continued he; 'a few light artillery, with the cavalry, would comprise your principal advance, because all the siege work would be on the frontiers and waters, done by the white division of the army. Won't this be a grand thing?' he exclaimed, joyfully. He continued, 'When I issued my Emancipation Proclamation, I had this thing in contemplation. I then gave them a chance by prohibiting any interference on the part of the army; but they did not embrace it,' said he, rather sadly, accompanying the word with an emphatic gesture.

"'But, Mr. President,' said I, 'these poor people could not read your proclamation, nor could they know anything about it, only, when they did hear, to know that they were free.'

"'But you of the North I expected to take advantage of it,' he replied.

"'Our policy, sir,' I answered, 'was directly opposite, supposing that it met your approbation. To this end I published a letter against embarrassing or compromising the government in any manner whatever; for us to remain passive, except in case of foreign intervention, then immediately to raise the slaves to insurrection.'

"'Ah, I remember the letter,' he said, 'and thought at the time that you mistook my designs. But the effect will be better as it is, by giving character to the blacks, both North and South, as a peaceable, inoffensive people.' Suddenly turning, he said, 'Will you take command?'

"'If there be none better qualified than I am, sir, by that time I will. While it is my desire to serve, as black men we shall have to prepare ourselves, as we have had no opportunities of experience and practice in the service as officers.'

"'That matters but little, comparatively,' he replied; 'as some of the finest officers we have never studied the tactics till they entered the army as subordinates. And again,' said he, 'the tactics are easily learned, especially among your people. It is the head that we now require most--men of plans and executive ability.'

"'I thank you, Mr. President,' said I, 'for the--'

"'No--not at all,' he interrupted.

"'I will show you some letters of introduction, sir,' said I, putting my hand in my pocket to get them.

"'Not now,' he interposed; 'I know all about you. I see nothing now to be done but to give you a line of introduction to the secretary of war.'

"Just as he began writing, the cannon commenced booming.

"'Stanton is firing! listen! he is in his glory! noble man!' he exclaimed.

"'What is it about, sir,' I reiterated, ignorant of the cause.

"'Why, don't you know? Haven't you heard the news? Charleston is ours!' he answered, straightening up from the table on which he was writing for an instant, and then resuming it. He soon handed me a card, on which was written,--

'February 8, 1865.
'HON. E. M. STANTON, *Secretary of War.*
'Do not fail to have an interview with this most extraordinary and intelligent black man.
'A. LINCOLN.'

"This card showed he perfectly understood my views and feelings; hence he was not content that my color should make its own impressions, but he expressed it with emphasis, as though a point was gained. The thing desired presented itself; not simply a man that was *black*, because these had previously presented themselves, in many delegations and committees,--men of the highest intelligence,--for various objects; but that which he had wished and hoped for, their own proposed measures matured in the council-chamber had never been fully presented to them in the person of a black man."

This, then, was what was desired to complete the plans of the president and his splendid minister, the secretary of war. The "ponderous beam," being removed, to use his figurative expression, his passport was clear to every part of the mansion. He entered the war department for the purpose of seeing the minister. As he entered, a glance revealed to him the presiding genius of the situation, surrounded by his assistants. In the room was a pressing crowd of both sexes, representing nearly every condition of life, each in turn endeavoring to reach the centre of the room, where, at an elevated desk, stood one of the greatest men of the times, and the able director of the war department.

After he had sent forward his card, he was requested by the secretary in person, to whom he was not previously unknown, to call at the department again.

He had gained the interview with the president that he wished, and the indications were brighter than his most sanguine expectations had promised. The war minister's influence alone could effect the balance.

He sought Dr. William Elder, the distinguished biographer of Dr. Kane, of Arctic memory, who was then chief of the bureau of statistics, and gave him an account of his mission to the president.

After explaining everything to the doctor, his face assuming an expression peculiar to himself, of a whole-souled satisfaction, he exclaimed, "I'll be hanged if I haven't got the thing! just the thing! Will you give me that in writing?" he asked; "I mean the points touched upon, that may be written in a letter to me."

On receiving it, in the afternoon of the same day, after he had read it, he turned to the future major, and said, "*You shall* have what you want," in like manner as he replied to a speech of Louis Kossuth, when he told him if he went to war with Austria, *he shouldn't die.*

When Delaney left Dr. Elder, he was thoroughly convinced, that if the secretary of war could be influenced by any man, in regard to his mission, in none abler could he depend than upon this true and earnest advocate of his race.

The next call at the war department was made the following Monday, the 12th inst. His reception there, being equally as cordial as the first, seemed already to indicate success to his measures.

"What do you propose to do, doctor?" asked the secretary, as Dr. Delany began to explain to him as he did to the president. "I understand the whole thing, and fully comprehend your design; I have frequently gone over the whole ground, in council with the president. What do you wish? What position?" He replied,--

"In any position or place whatever, in which I may be instrumental in promoting the measures proposed, and be of service to the country, so that I am not subject and subordinate to every man who holds a commission, and, with such, chooses to assume authority."

"Will you take the field?" asked the secretary.

"I should like to do so as soon as possible, but not until I have had sufficient discipline and practice in a camp of instruction, and a sufficient number of black officers to command each regiment," was the answer given.

"Of course," said the secretary, "you must establish your camp of instruction; and as you have a general knowledge of the qualified colored men of the country, I propose to commission you at once, and send you South to commence rais-

ing troops, to be commanded by black officers, on the principles you proposed, of which I most highly approve, to prevent all clashing or jealousy,--because of no contact to arouse
prejudices. It is none of white men's business what rank a
black man holds over his own people. I shall assign you to
Charleston, with advices and instructions to Major General
Saxton. Do you know him?" he asked. Being answered, he
continued, "He is an unflinching friend of your race. You
will impart to him, in detail, that which will not be written.
The letter giving special instructions will be given to you--all
further instructions to be obtained at the department.

Assistant Adjutant General of Volunteers Colonel C.W.
Foster, at this juncture having been sent for, was instructed
by the secretary of war to take him to his department, and
make the necessary examination; there being no rejection, to
prepare and fill out a parchment, with commission of *Major
of Infantry*, the *regiment* to be left blank, to be filled by order
of Major General Saxton, according to instructions to be
given, and to report the next morning at eleven o'clock.

After the examination by the adjutant general, he remarked, "This is certainly an important and interesting feature of the war. And the secretary must expect much to be
done by you, for he certainly holds you in high esteem."

"I hope colonel," he replied, "that neither the honorable
secretary of war nor the government will expect too much
from an individual like myself. My only hope is, that I may
be able to do my duty well and satisfactorily."

"I have no fears for your success," returned the colonel;
"you have qualifications and ability, and must succeed, when
your chances are such as they will now be. This is a great
thing for you," he continued, "and you have now an opportunity of making yourself *anything that you please*, and doing for your race all that may be required at the hands of the
government." He, attempting to thank the colonel for the
encouraging as well as complimentary remarks, was stopped
by him, saying, "I speak as I think and feel about it. The
secretary has great confidence in you, and I simply wish to
indorse it for your encouragement. There is nothing now to
be done," he continued, "but to call tomorrow, and go with
me to the war department to report finally to the secretary of

war, and receive your commission from his hands." All arrangements being completed in the adjutant's department, he withdrew.

CHAPTER XX
THE GOLD LEAF

No Sabbath in wartimes, we are told, and there was no exception in this case. The following morning (Sabbath), in accordance with the appointment, Delany reported himself at the office of the adjutant general, who accompanied him to the war department. Here the secretary, making the necessary inquiries of the adjutant, received the parchment from him. History repeated itself--the Hebrew in the palaces, the Hun in high places. At that moment the great war minister of our revolution, affixing his official signature, made an epoch in the history of a hitherto unrecognized race, and a pledge in the name of the nation to them irrevocable through all time. It seemed remarkable that in two hemispheres this man should be selected from among so many others to represent marked events in the history of his race! Says Lamartine, "We should not despise any, for the finger of destiny marks in the soul, and not upon the brow."

So long had Delany fought against error and injustice towards his race, that it seemed almost hopeless to witness, in his day, the faintest semblance of recognition of their right in this land, and for him to be the first to receive that appointment seemed indeed to promise an age "of better metal."

While the interesting ceremony was being performed, a major general entered the apartment, followed soon after by Senator Ben Wade, of Ohio, now president of the Senate, before whom the new officer was addressed for the first time with a military title.

"Gentlemen," said the secretary, "I am just now creating a black field officer for the United States service." Then, addressing himself directly to the new officer, he said "Major Delany, I take great pleasure in handing you this commission of *Major* in the United States army. You are the first of your race who has been thus honored by the government; therefore much depends and will be expected of you. But I feel assured it is safe in your hands."

"Honorable Secretary," replied the major, as the secretary concluded his remarks, "I can assure you, whatever be my failure to meet the expectations concerning me, on one thing you may depend,--that this parchment will never be dishonored in my hands."

"Of this I am satisfied. God bless you! Good by." With a hearty shake of the hand, the secretary concluded, when the first black major in the history of the republic left the department.

If the war had not ended so soon after the major received his commission, there exists no doubt but that his merits would have received further recognition. It is unlikely that the government would have given an unmeaning promotion, and thus debar him from rising to the higher ranks of the army through the same medium as other officers. On returning to the office of the adjutant general, the adjutant remarked, "Major Delany, you have now a great charge intrusted to you,--a great responsibility, certainly, and much will be expected of you, both by your friends and others. You have now an opportunity, if the war continues, of rising in your position to the highest field rank--that of major general."

His reply was, that he hoped to be able to perform his duty, so as to merit the approval of his government and his superior officers, and, as a matter of course, intimated courteously that further promotion would not be unacceptable to him.

The following commission is in the usual form; but, being the first on the records of our country credited to a colored American, we reproduce it here.

The Secretary of War of the United States of America.

TO ALL WHO SHALL SEE THESE PRESENTS, GREETING:

Know ye, that reposing special trust and confidence in the patriotism, valor, fidelity, and abilities of MARTIN R. DELANY, the President does hereby appoint him Major, in the One Hundred and Fourth Regiment of United States Colored Troops, in the service of the United States, to rank as such from the day of his muster into service, by the duly appointed commissary of musters, for the command to which said regiment belongs.

He is therefore carefully and diligently to discharge the duty of Major, by doing and performing all manner of things thereunto belonging. And I do strictly charge, and require, all officers and soldiers under his command to be obedient to his orders as Major. And he is to observe and follow such orders and directions, from time to time, as he shall receive from me or the future Secretary of War, or other superior officers set over him, according to the rules and discipline of war. This appointment to continue in force during the pleasure of the President for the time being.

Given under my hand at the War Department, in the City of Washington, D.C., this twenty-sixth day of February, in the year of our Lord one thousand eight hundred and sixty-five.

By the Secretary of War.

EDWIN M. STANTON, *Secretary of War.*

C.W. FOSTER, *Assistant Adjutant General Volunteers.*

(*Indorsement.*)

Mustered into the United States Service, February 27, 1865.

HENRY KETELLAS, *Captain 15th Infantry, Chief Muster and District Officer.*

ADJUTANT GENERAL'S OFFICE,
WASHINGTON, Feb. 27, 1865.

Sir: I forward herewith your appointment of Major in the U.S. Colored Troops; your receipt and acceptance of which you will please acknowledge without delay, reporting at the same time your *age* and *residence*, when appointed, the *state* where *born*, and your full *name* correctly written. *Fill up, subscribe,* and return as soon as possible, the accompanying *oath,* duly and carefully *executed.*

You will report in person to Brevet Major General R. Saxton, Beaufort, South Carolina.

I am, sir, very respectfully,

Your obedient servant,

C.W. FOSTER,

Assistant Adjutant General Volunteers.

Major Martin R. Delany, *U.S. Colored Troops.*

WAR DEPARTMENT, A.G. OFFICE,
WASHINGTON, D.C., Feb. 27, 1865.

Captain HENRY KETELLAS, 15th U.S. Infantry,

Commissary of Musters:

I am directed by the Secretary of War to instruct you to muster Major Martin R. Delany, U.S. Colored Troops,

regiment into the service of the United States, for the period of three years, or during the war, as of this date.

Very respectfully, your obedient servant,

(Signed)   C.W. FOSTER,

Assistant Adjutant General Volunteers.

Official Copy, respectfully furnished for the information of Major Martin R. Delany, U.S. Colored Troops.

C.W. FOSTER,
Assistant Adjutant General Volunteers.

WAR DEPARTMENT, A.G. OFFICE,
WASHINGTON, Feb. 27, 1865.

Brevet Major General R. Saxton, *Supt. Recruitment and Organization of Colored Troops, Dept. of the South, Hilton Head, S.C.*

General: I am directed by the Secretary of War to inform you that the bearer, *Major M.R. Delany*, U.S. Colored Troops, has been appointed for the purpose of aiding and assisting you in recruiting and organizing colored troops, and to carry out this object you will assign him to duty in the city of Charleston, S.C.

You will observe that the regiment to which Major *Delany* is appointed is not designated, although he has been mustered into service. You will cause Major *Delany* to be assigned to, and his name placed upon the rolls of, the first regiment of colored troops you may organize, with his proper rank, not, however, with a view to his duty in such regiment.

I am also directed to say, that Major *Delany* has the entire confidence of the Department.

I have the honor to be, very respectfully,

Your obedient servant,

(Signed)   C.W. FOSTER,
Assistant Adjutant General Volunteers.
Official.   C.W. FOSTER,
Assistant Adjuntant General Volunteers.

CHAPTER XXI
IN THE FIELD

The appointment of the black officer was received, as such advanced measures are generally, with comments of all shades. By the friends of progress it was hailed with general satisfaction.

True there was, prior to his appointment, one of *like* rank, but differing in position--that of Dr. Augusta, of Canada, who was accepted after a most rigid examination, as is customary in such cases.

But in the appointment of this field officer there existed an indisputable recognition of the claims of his race to the country. With this interpretation those who formerly hesitated in accepting the policy of the administration now upheld it with confidence.   And from the golden leaf of promise, borne upon the shoulders of the first black officer, a light clear and steady seemed to shine forth, illumining with a strange, wild splendor the hitherto dark pages of his people's history, heralding the glory of the future to them.

Before he left Washington, he communicated with colored men, as far as was prudent, to make the necessary preparation in the event of a black army being organized, to be commanded by black officers.   For in the Union army there were many men, from the North especially, of fine talent and scholastic attainments, who, from their experience and knowledge gained in the military campaigns, could at once be made available.

Certain leading spirits of the *"Underground Railroad"* were invoked.   Scouts *incog.* were already "on to Richmond," and the services of the famous Harriet Tubman, having been secured to serve in the South, had received her transportation for Charleston, S.C.

These arrangements being effected, he went to Cleveland, Ohio, to meet a council of his co-laborers, in order to enforce suitable measures by which the slave enlistedment might be prevented, and to demoralize those already enrolled, as rumors had reached the North of such enlistment having been started at Richmond.

With his friend George Vosburg, Esq., in the lead, whom he likens always to "a flame alive, but unseen," the most active measures were instituted at this council, as their proceedings show.

These gave evidence that the appointment of one of their number was recognized by them as an appeal, though the day was far spent of the country's need for the aid of the colored men of the North, and at the first *certain sound* they hastened with their offerings.

A few days were spent at his home, preparing for his departure; and being delayed on the way by a freshet, he did not reach New York until the second day after the departure of the steamer for Charleston.   While it delayed the principal measures, it gave him a week in New York, in which to perfect preliminary arrangements.   Here business of importance was entered upon, and the eloquent William Howard Day,

M.A., was chosen to arrange the *military policy* of the *underground railroad* relative to the *slave enlistment.*

Mr. Day, in obedience to instructions of the plans laid down, and in anticipation of some appointment, such as his splendid talents entitled him to, performed the task with ability and earnestness. There were others among the leading colored men who showed their appreciation of this movement; among them the learned Rev. J.W.C. Pennington, D.D., as the following extract from his letter, dated March 29, will show:--

"Major: Finding that our views so nearly harmonize in reference to arming the slaves, I will give you one of the illustrations I use in my lecture on the duty of interposing our efforts to prevent the rebels from consummating the act: 'We have noticed by *their own* papers that the rebel authorities have many of their great meetings in the African church in Richmond. It was there that Benjamin, the rebel secretary of state, first publicly announced the plan of arming the slaves. Did the pastor of that colored church and his congregation have the privilege of taking part in that meeting? Not a bit of it. Did they have the privilege of holding a meeting on the subject themselves in their own place of worship? No.

"'What was the object of the rebels in holding their great meetings in the African church? Was it because it is one of the largest buildings in the city? No, they had another object. That was, to *suppress any Union feelings that exist among the hundreds of slaves and free people of color who compose that congregation, and to palm off the lie to the world that they are friendly to the colored people, and that those people are acting freely with them.*

"'Look at the devilish impudence of this scheme of holding meetings in the African church! It is to drag the slaves and colored Christians with them into all the wickedness of the rebellion. Now, it is asked, Why we do not hear a voice from the pastor of that church and his people? The answer is obvious. They are prevented by the FORCE of CIRCUMSTANCES from speaking a word.

"'If the Son of God should enter that house, as he did the temple at Jerusalem (Mark xi. 15,16), and thus give that congregation the right of free speech, you would soon hear a voice going out from that church, that would reach every slave in the South, telling them which way to fight.   And that church will speak as soon as Grant takes Richmond! And who does not long for the day when that, the largest colored church in the United States shall be free?   Who would not aid in that great forward movement of the Army of the Potomac, that will result in clearing Richmond?   But in this state of facts as to that church, *we have precisely* the position of the 200,000 slaves whom the rebels are about to arm against us!

"'Let us not forget what slavery is. It is based upon the assumption, first, that the slave has no will of his own; second, that his sole business is to obey orders. Hence they will be put into the rebel army *as slaves*, to all intents and purposes, and substantially under slave discipline; they will be surrounded by circumstances which will make if far more difficult for them to escape than many think; and of course, for the time being, they would be COMPELLED to do us untold injury. What, then, is our duty? Our duty is to *anticipate* the action of the rebels--organize, plan, and go forward, and settle the case for our brethren. We have no right to stand still, and presume that they will, when armed, turn at once on our side. And it is cruel to prejudge them in the matter. Our duty is to *carry out* the letter and spirit of the Proclamation of Freedom. It would be an awful state of things to see the 200,000 Union colored soldiers confronted by 200,000 of our own race, under the rebel banner!... No, this must not be. It shall not be. It cannot be if we do our duty. That is, to go to our brethren, and tell them what to do.'"

A romantic incident is related in connection with the Cleveland council. As Delany concluded, a moment of intense interest and silence followed, and suddenly an interesting girl of some fourteen years sprang to her feet, and rushed up to the platform where he stood, gently resting her hand upon his arm, and anxiously looking up into his face, exclaimed, "O, Major Delany, I ask one favor of you: will you spare my grandfather when you reach Charleston?" Giving the name of her grandfather in the same excited breath, she continued, "Spare him and grandma! There sits my ma: for her sake, if not mine, spare my dear grandpa's family."

He strove to calm her anxiety, assuring her of the security of her grandfather's family, even if the genuine Schemmelfening had not already had the city. His mission was not with fire and sword for indiscriminate slaughter, but rather to guide his brethren to liberty.

On his arrival in Charleston, the honored grandparents, unconscious of this incident, were among the earliest callers to give him welcome, and to offer him the generous civilities of their family; and these were ever after numbered among his most esteemed friends.

In expectation of a continuance of the war, he writes, "I was anxious to reach my destination, organize the black army, and see that elegant mulatto gentleman as field officer, hear his rich, deep-toned voice as he rode along the lines, giving command, or shouting in the deadly conflict, rallying the troops on to victory. Such a sight I desired to see in the cause of liberty and the Union. For William Howard Day, unobstrusive as he appears, is a brave, determined man: once aroused, he is as a panther, that knows no fear. But now that the war is ended, his aid in the battle-field will not be required. And the Union will be safe if reestablished on the basis of righteousness, truth, and justice."

Leaving New York, and having secured the ablest workers with whom to begin the great mission intrusted to him, he arrived at Hilton Head, and in the same afternoon at Beaufort.

This beautiful little town, facing a bay of equal beauty, but of tortuous winding, never gave promise of rivalling or imitating the cities of Charleston and Savannah on either side in commercial greatness. In fact, its population was limited almost exclusively to the planters of the adjoining islands and their slaves, a few free colored families, and a less number of poor whites. The salubrity of the climate enhanced its attractions, and made it desirable as the summer residence of many of the wealthy magnates. The town was abandoned by the entire white population at the approach of the naval force. Here were the headquarters of Brevet Major General Saxton, at which Major Delany reported himself for duty, immediately on his arrival. Some time afterwards, speaking of the noble general who led, by sealed orders, the first campaign set forth to proclaim *emancipation*, he said that in his frequent intercourse with him there, he was soon convinced that the friends of his race were not confined to the executive department at Washington. This may be considered as the general opinion uttered by him; for among the colored people and *poor whites* of South Carolina, General Rufus Saxton stood as the beloved friend and benefactor, and esteemed among his brother officers generally as a gentleman and soldier.

At the post, while every officer rode with a black orderly, General Saxton's orderly *was white!*

The post was in active preparation for the flag raising at Sumter. And on the Saturday previous to the memorable 19th of April, the general and staff, Major Delany accompanying the party, sailed for Charleston.

Prior to leaving Beaufort he received the following order:-

HEAD QRS. SUPT. RECRUITMENT AND ORGANIZATION
COLORED TROOPS, DEPARTMENT OF THE SOUTH,
BEAUFORT, S.C., April 5, 1865.

Special Orders. No. 7.

I. Major M.R. *Delany*, United States Colored Troops, in accordance with orders received from the War Department, will proceed without delay to Charleston, S.C., reporting in person to *Lieutenant Colonel R.P. Hutchins*, 94th Ohio Volunteer Infantry, Recruiting Officer at that post, for the purpose of aiding in the recruitment of troops.

II. *Major Delany* will visit the freedmen of Charleston and vicinity, and urge them to enlist in the military service of the United States, reporting by letter from time to time to these headquarters the result of his labors.

By order of   Brevet Major General R. SAXTON,
GEN. SUPT. RECT. & O. C. P. D. S.
STUART M. TAYLOR, *Asst. Adjt. Gen.*

Major M.R. DELANY, U. S. C. T.

CHAPTER XXII
AT CHARLESTON AND FORT SUMTER

The excitement attending the scenes of the evacuation of the city and its occupation by the Union forces was scarcely lulled, when it rose again on the arrival of the "black major," to whom the rumor preceding his advent had given rank of *Major General.*

Arriving in the city on the Sabbath, when most of the people were gathered at the various places of worship, the news soon became noised about. And from the early forenoon until long after nightfall, a continuous stream of visitors poured in upon him, eager to pay their respects to him. These composed the colored residents of both sexes, representing every age and condition; nor did this cease when their curiosity became satisfied, but grew with their acquaintance and increased with time. At the time of his arrival the population of the once proud city was limited, consisting only of a few regiments of Union soldiers on duty, the former free people, the new freedmen,--a greater portion of the latter being driven from the plantations around the city, and from the upper portions of the state,--and a few white families representing the old element. An air of mournful desolation seemed to brood over the conquered city. There existed no signs of traffic, except in the sutlers' stores of the regiments.

Confederate bonds and scrip were most plenteous, and but a small amount of currency was in circulation with which to purchase the common necessaries of life. For this cause thousands were thrown upon the charity of the government for daily subsistence. Nor was it confined to the colored people; it was no uncommon sight to meet daily in the streets many of the former enemies of the government, loaded with its injustice (!) to them in the form of a huge basket of subsistence received from the quartermaster's department, and in many instances assisted by some former chattel, who in several known cases, afterwards, with true negro generosity, divided their own portion with them. Such was their position after the evacuation of the city. Never before in the history of Anglo-Saxon civilization were there such manifestations of genuine charity and forbearance towards an unscrupulous and implacable foe, as indicated by the actions of the government. "I was hungry and ye gave me meat, naked and ye clothed me," were literally proven by these recipients of its immense charities. This gave promise of more converts than the sword. While the great concourse of people, gathered for rations at different places, attracted thither the curious visitor, he would turn from this to the many evidences of the unerring precision of the batteries of Morris Island, which met his gaze on every hand, suggestive of the tales of horror, and in many instances of retributive justice, through which they had so recently passed. Much property was destroyed and but few lives during the siege.

There were incidents related of marvellous escapes from the reach of these shells, and also deaths of a most appalling character on being overtaken by them,--the greater portion of the latter being colored persons, the innocent sharing a worse fate than the guilty.

One case of sad interest happened at midnight, while the siege was at its height, occurring in a family representing the wealth, culture, and refinement of the respectable colored citizens of the city. The father of this family, a man of great mechanical genius, accumulated considerable property and established for himself a well-earned reputation as a skilful machinist throughout the state. They were aroused one night by the noise which usually precedes the near approach of a shell, which was seen by a member of the family to fall within a few feet of the house, who, occupying the third story of the building, attempted to escape below with his wife; but before either could escape from the room, a second report was heard, followed almost immediately by the appearance of a shell entering the roof above them, crashing through the ceilings, which, in covering the latter with its *debris*, preserved her life, the fragments scattering, one of the pieces falling into the front room beneath, only disfiguring a bedstead, but not injuring its occupants, while another piece, more remorseless, taking another direction, entered the back room, burying itself in the side of an interesting boy of twelve years, the little grandson of the old gentleman. The child, startled from its sleep by the double shock of the explosion and terrible wound, rushed from the room, exclaiming, in his agony, "Mother! mother! I am killed!" It was eleven days of the most excruciating agony before the angel of death relieved little Weston McKenlay. Never did Christianity and true womanhood beam more beauteously than at the moment when the mother of that child, relating the wild confusion of that night, laying aside her own personal sorrow, said, "It was God's will that the deliverance of the South should cost us something." Major Delany, in speaking of this class of Charlestonians, as well as the colored people generally, says, "Their courtesy and natural kindness I have never seen equalled, while instances of their humanity to the Union prisoners at the risk of their own lives, speak in trumpet tones to their credit, of which the country is already cognizant." On Tuesday after his arrival, an immense gathering greeted him at Zion's Church, the largest in the city, indescribable in enthusiasm and numbers. In the church were supposed to be upwards of three thousand, while the yard and street leading to the church were densely packed.

The resolutions passed on this memorable occasion by them we present here, embodying a testimony of their gratitude for their signal deliverance from a conflagration which threatened to involve them in a general desolation, and of their patriotism, setting aside forever the error that the sympathies of the free colored citizens were enlisted on the side of their enemies, and not that of the Union, for many they were who participated in this meeting. We reproduce it also as expressive of the sentiments gushing from the hearts of a people for the first time in their history holding a political meeting on the soil of Carolina, with *open doors*, with none to condemn it as "an unlawful assemblage," amenable to law for the act.

Brevet Major General Saxton, and other distinguished officers were present, and freely took part in the proceedings. Here Major Delany, for the first time, introduced the subject foremost in his mind, that of raising an armee d'Afrique, which subject met the enthusiastic approval of his auditors, and the movement for its organization soon became popular.

The eventful 14th of April, which was so eagerly awaited, came, and the earliest beams of the morning found the "City of the Sea" alive with preparations for the brilliant scene at Sumter, unconscious of its fearful tragic close at Washington. The city was almost deserted during the ceremony in the harbor, for all were anxious to witness the flag in its accustomed place, with its higher, truer symbol, placed there by the same hands which were once compelled to lower it to a jubilant but now conquered foe, maddened prior to their destruction. As the old silken bunting winged itself to its long-deserted staff, thousands of shouts, and prayers fervent and deep, accompanying, greeted its reappearance.

Major Delany embarked to witness the ceremony on the historical steamer Planter, with its gallant commander, Robert Small, whose deeds will live in song and story, whose unparalleled feat and heroic courage in the harbor of Charleston, under the bristling guns of rebel batteries, bearing comparison with the proudest record of our war, will remain, commemorative of negro strategy and valor.

On the quarter-deck of the steamer the major remained an interested witness. Beside him stood one, whose father, believing and loving the doctrine that all men were born free and equal, and within sight of the emblem of freedom as it floated from the battlements of Sumter, dared to aim a blow by which to free his race. Betrayed before his plans were matured, the scaffold gave to Denmark Vesey and his twenty-two slave-hero compatriots in Charleston, South Carolina, in 1822, the like answer which Charlestown, Virginia, gave John Brown in 1859.

Virginia was free, and black soldiers were now quartered in the citadel of Charleston, and garrisoned in Fort Sumter. The matyred reformers had not died in vain.

The excitement attending the scene continued during the week, occasioned by the presence of the distinguished company who came to participate in the restoration of the flag at Fort Sumter. There were seen the veterans of the anti-slavery cause, the inspired and dauntless apostle of liberty, William Lloyd Garrison, the time-honored Joshua Leavitt, the eloquent George Thompson of England; then the glorious young editor of the Independent, the able and accomplished orator of the day, Rev. Henry Ward Beecher, Judge Kellogg, and others, all anxious to tell the truths of freedom to these hungry souls. The colored schools paraded the streets to honor these visitors, flanked by thousands of adults, marshalled by their superintendent and assistants, and led by stirring bands discoursing martial music, the citadel square densely crowded, and the great Zion's Church packed to overflowing. There were speakers on the stands erected on the square--speakers at the church. There were shouts for liberty and for the Union, shouts for their great liberator, shouts for the army, rousing cheers for the speakers, for their loved General Saxton, and for the "black major;" the people swayed to and fro like a rolling sea.

On Saturday morning, when the visitors left, an immense concourse followed to the wharf; the steamer seemed loaded with floral gifts, the graceful ovation of the colored people to their friends. Cheer after cheer resounded for a parting word from them. They were answered by Messrs. Thompson and Tilton; at last came forth the immortal Garrison in answer to an irresistible call.

Major Delany, describing this parting scene at the dock, says, "The mind was forcibly carried back to the days of the young and ardent advocate of emancipation, incarcerated in a Baltimore prison, peering through the gates and bars, hurling defiance at his cowardly opponents, exclaiming, 'No difficulty, no dangers, shall deter me: at the East or at the West, at the North or at the South, wherever Providence may call me, my voice shall be heard in behalf of the perishing slave, and against the claims of his oppresors.' Again did the mind revert to him in after years, as a man of high integrity in the city of Boston, led as a beast to the slaughter, with the lyncher's rope around his neck, only escaping death by imprisonment. When exhausted, he fell to the floor, exclaiming, 'Never was man so glad to get into prison before!' And in this his last speech he was more sublime than ever. There he stood in the harbor of Charleston, surrounded by the emancipated slave, giving his last anti-slavery advice:--

"'And now, my friends, I bid you farewell. I have always advocated non-resistance; but this much I say to you, *Come what will never do you submit again to slavery! Do anything; die first! But don't submit again to them--never again be slaves.* Farewell.

"When the steamer gracefully glided from the pier, the music struck up in stirring strains, shouts rent the air, and the masses, after gazing with tearful eyes, commenced slowly retracing their steps homeward. Never can I forget the scenes transpiring in this eventful week of my arrival at Charleston, nor on different similar occasions during my official station there."

At a meeting of the colored citizens of Charleston, South Carolina, held at Zion Presbyterian Church, March 29, 1865, the following preamble and resolutions were unanimously adopted:--

Whereas it is fitting that an expression should be given to the sentiments of deep-seated gratitude that pervade our breasts, be it

Resolved, 1. That by the timely arrival of the army of the United States in the city of Charleston, on the 18th of February, 1865, our city was saved from a vast conflagration, our houses from devastation, and our persons from those indignities that they would have been subjected to.

Resolved, 2. That our thanks are due, and are hereby freely tendered, to the district commander, Brigadier General Hatch, and through him to the officers and soldiers under his command, for the protection that they have so readily and so impartially bestowed since their occupation of this city.

Resolved, 3. That to Admiral Dahlgren, United States Navy, we do hereby return our most sincere thanks for the noble manner in which he cared for and administered to the wants of our people at Georgetown, South Carolina; and be he assured that the same shall ever be held in grateful remembrance by us.

Resolved, 4. That to his Excellency, the President of the United States, Abraham Lincoln, we return our most sincere thanks and never-dying gratitude for the noble and patriotic manner in which he promulgated the doctrines of republicanism, and for his consistency in not only promising, but invariably conforming his actions thereto; and we shall ever be pleased to acknowledge and hail him as the champion of the fights of freedom.

Resolved, 5. That a copy of these resoltuions be transmitted to Brigadier General Hatch, Admiral Dahlgren, and his Excellency, the President of the United States, and that they be published in the Charleston Courier.

MOSES B. CAMPLIN, *Chairman.*

ROBERT C. DE LARGE. *Secretary.*

The following we quote from him as descriptive of his impressions on his arrival at Charleston:--

"I entered the city, which, from earliest childhood and through life, I had learned to contemplate with feelings of the utmost abhorrence--a place of the most insufferable assumption and cruelty to the blacks; where the sound of the lash at the whipping-post, and the hammer of the auctioneer, were coordinate sounds in thrilling harmony; that place which had ever been closed against liberty by an arrogantly

assumptuous despotism, such as well might have vied with
the infamous King of Dahomey; the place from which had
been expelled the envoy of Massachusetts, for daring to present the claims of the commonwealth in behalf of her free
citizens, and into which, but a few days before, had proudly
entered in triumph the gallant Schemmelfening, leading
with wild shouts the Massachusetts Fifty-fourth Regiment,
composed of some of the best blood and finest youths of the
colored citizens of the Union. For a moment I paused--then,
impelled by the impulse of my mission, I found myself dash-
ing on in unmeasured strides through the city, as if under a
forced march to attack the already crushed and fallen enemy.
Again I halted to look upon the shattered walls of the once
stately but now deserted edifices of the proud and super-
cilious occupants. A doomed city it appeared to be, with few,
or none but soldiers and the colored inhabitants. The
haughty Carolinians, who believed their state an empire, this
city incomparable, and themselves invincible, had fled in
dismay and consternation at the approach of their con-
querors, leaving the metropolis to its fate. And but for the
vigilance and fidelity of the colored firemen, and other colored inhabitants, there would have been nothing left but a
smoldering plain of ruins in the place where Charleston once
stood, from the firebrands in the hands of the flying whites.
Reaching the upper district, in the neighborhood of the
citadel, I remained at the private residence of one of the most
respectable colored citizens (free before the war), until quarters suitable could be secured. Whatever impressions may
have previously been entertained concerning the free
colored people of Charleston, their manifestation from my
advent till my departure, gave evidence of their pride in
identity and appreciation of race that equal in extent the
proudest Caucasian."

Many were the scenes of interest there related, on the entry of the troops into Charleston, some of a most thrilling
character. It was a memorable day to the enslaved. An incident is related--that a soldier, mounted on a mule, dashed up
Meeting Street, at the head of the advancing column, bearing
in his hand, as he rode, a white flag, upon which was in-
scribed, in large black letters, LIBERTY! and loudly proclaim-

ing it as he went. An old woman, who the night before had lain down a slave, and even on that morning was uncertain of her master's movements, whether or not she should be carried into the interior of the state, as had been proposed with the evacuation, now heard the shouts of people and the cry of liberty reechoed by hundreds of voices. In the deep gratitude of her heart to God, she was seen to rush with outstretched arms, as if to clasp this herald of freedom. The soldier being in the saddle, and consequently beyond her reach, unconsciously she hugged the mule around the neck, shouting, "Thank God! thank God!" So fraught with deep emotion were the bystanders at this scene, that it drew tears from the eyes of many, instead of creating merriment, as it would have done under different circumstances.

A lady, in rehearsing to another this scene and others of that day, said, "O, had you been here, you would have felt like embracing something yourself, had it been but to grasp a flag-staff, or touch the drapery of the floating colors."

CHAPTER XXIII
ARMEE D'AFRIQUE

Immediately after the restoration of the flag, active duty was resumed by the military at Charleston, and none more heartily rejoiced at the prospect of beginning his work than did Major Delany. Without loss of time, independent quarters were assigned him, equal to those of other officers, this being by special orders from the war department; it was also ordered that he should report directly to Brevet Major General Saxton, and detailed subordinates were placed at his command.

The residence assigned him was elegant and commodious; but being an intolerable sight to the owner, a plea of loyalty was soon raised, which induced its relinquishment, and quarters equally as comfortable were secured at the south-east corner of Calhoun and St. Philip Streets. Here were to be seen daily, in beautiful contrast to bayonets and the circumstance of war, and in graceful profusion, at Major Delany's office, the choicest bouquets and other personal compliments of like delicacy indicative of the high respect in which he was held.

Before his arrival, the 102d United States Colored Troops had been completed, and the 103d had just been commenced, of which regiment, according to the spirit of the order of the war department, he was entitled to the major's command; but by request of his general he waived his right to an officer to whom the position had been promised previous to his arrival, though he had aided in its organization, and soon began to recruit his own.

As a field officer at the head of such a service, it is evident that as many of lower grade as the duties of his command required and needed, could be secured, agreeable to regulations. In order to avoid innovations and clashings, he chose instead a few non-commissioned officers from the 54th and 55th Massachusetts Volunteers, for whom he made requisition. Sergeant Frederick Johnson, of the 54th, an excellent penman and clerk, was placed in charge of the books, while Sergeant Major Abraham Shadd, from the 55th Massachusetts Volunteers, a gentleman of fine attainments, besides excellent military capability, was appointed acting captain to command recruits, and his own son, private Toussaint L. Delany, of the 54th Massachusetts Volunteers, as acting lieutenant, to act in conjuction with acting Captain Shadd.

Lieutenant Colonel R.P. Hutchins, of the 94th Ohio Volunteers, had been detailed as assistant superintendent of the recruiting and organizing of colored troops to General Saxton. Of him Major Delany says, "I found Liieutenant Colonel Hutchins an accomplished young gentleman, well adapted to his position, with a staff of fine young officers, among whom was Captain Spencer, of Sherman's army. The 104th was now rapidly increasing, and would soon require its complement of officers. The following order was then necessary to its accomplishment:--

HEADQUARTERS, SUPERINTENDENT RECRUITMENT
AND ORGANIZATION COLORED TROOPS,
DEPARTMENT OF THE SOUTH,
BEAUFORT, S.C., APRIL 11, 1865.

Special Orders. No. 13.

II. In accordance with instructions received from the war department, the following appointment is made in the 104th United States Colored

Troops; Major M.R. Delany, United States Colored Troops, to be major, and to report to Colonel Douglas Frazar, commanding regiment.
By order of   Brevet Major General R. SAXTON,
Gen. Supt. Rec. & O.C.T., D.S.
STUART M. TAYLOR, *Asst. Adjt. Gen.*

Major M.R. DELANY, *U.S.C.T.*

CHAPTER XXIV
THE NATIONAL CALAMITY

None in all the land can forget when the telegraph flashed the fearful news upon us. But if there was sorrow felt by one class more than another, we must look to the freedmen of the South, to whom the name of Lincoln and the government meant one and the same--all justice and goodness.

On the morning of the 18th of April (communications being so irregular then), the beauty of the morning and the surroundings seeming to charm the senses, happiness came upon many a hitherto scowling face, while a sense of returning forgiveness seemed to hover above the rebellious city, and the once unfrequented streets began to give evidence of returning life. The major and a friend were in King Street, when they were met by a captain, who, stepping from his buggy to the sidewalk, entered into a conversation: in the midst of it they were interrupted by a soldier, breathlessly running towards them, holding in his hand a paper, exclaiming, "My God! President Lincoln is assassinated!"

"No! no! it can't be so!" replied the captain.

"Some hoax," interposed the major, on seeing the heading of the New York Herald; but the trembling hand of the rough soldier pointed out the telegram, while tears coursed down his cheeks: before the dark message they stood for a time, gazing one upon the other in mute agony, without power to express the thoughts uppermost in their mind, while vengeance seemed written in the quivering of every feature.

Any description, however graphic, would fail to convey an idea of the feelings produced, as the fatal tidings circulated. If every man of secession proclivities had been put to the sword, every house belonging to such burnt to the ground, the Unionists would hardly have interfered, and would not have been surprised. The only cause for wonderment was, that there was not a scene of fire and slaughter. At the major's quarters, where, in his unfeigned sorrow he had sought retirement, he was forced to show himself to the excited people; for while the Unionists generally were aroused to a point of doubtful forbearance, the intense grief, excitement, and anxiety of the new freedmen knew no bounds. The white men of undefined politics, and known secessionists, wisely avoided the blacks, or kept within doors. The avenging torch at one period seemed imminent, but the outstretched hands of reason spared the city once more. There was to the casual observer nothing extraordinary in the outward demonstration, perhaps, but a strong under-current was madly coursing along, threatening destruction to every opposing barrier. Doubtless but for the presence of the black major, whom they sought instantly, and whose influence over them was powerful, there would have been a most lamentable state of confusion, so determined were they to avenge the death of their friend. Some of these were even actuated by fears of being returned

An order was issued by the military for public mourning. The famous Zion's Church was the most tastefully draped, remaining thus for one year, the military using whatever they could command in the tradeless city, the secessionist such as was required by law, while the mourning of the new freedmen presented an incongruity in many instances extremely touching. Flags made of black cloth were nailed against the dwelling-houses, or floated from their roofs. Their black flags were intended as mourning, not as defiance.

Major Delany, in these sad days, was not unemployed. Already had he devised some tangible and practical evidence by which the colored people could demonstrate their appreciation and reverence for the memory of the martyred president. The following is an extract from a letter to the Anglo-African of April 20. We doubt whether any plan for a monument was originated previous to this.

"A calamity such as the world never before witnessed--a calamity the most heart-rending, caused by the perpetration of a deed by the hands of a wretch the most infamous and atrocious--a calamity as humiliating to America as it is infamous and atrocious--has suddenly brought our country to mourning by the untimely death of the humane, the benevolent, the philanthropic, the generous, the beloved, the able, the wise, great, and good man, the President of the United States, Abraham Lincoln the Just. In his fall a mighty chieftain and statesman has passed away. God, in his inscrutable providence, has suffered this, and we bow with meek and humble resignation to his divine will, because he doeth all things well. God's will be done!

"I suggest that, as a just and appropriate tribute of respect and lasting gratitude from the colored people of the United States to the memory of President Lincoln, the Father of American Liberty, every individual of our race contribute *one cent*, as this will enable each member of every family to contribute, parents paying for every child, allowing all who are able to subscribe any sum they please above this, to such national monument as may hereafter be decided upon by the American people. I hope it may be in Illinois, near his own family residence.

"This penny or one cent contribution would amount to the handsome sum of forty thousand ($40,000) dollars, as a tribute from the black race (I use the generic term), and would not be at all felt; and I am sure that so far as the South is concerned, the millions of freedmen will hasten on their contributions."

The following design for the monument he proposed was communicated to the same journal a month later. He, also, through the same medium, suggested that a gold medal be given to Mrs. Lincoln, as a tribute from the colored people to the memory of her noble husband. He still hopes that the suggestion concerning the medal may find favor among the colored poeple, and it would be more appropriate if it could be executed by a colored artist.

MONUMENT TO PRESIDENT LINCOLN

I propose for the National Monument, to which all the colored people of the United States are to contribute each one cent, a design, as the historic representation of the humble offering of our people. On one side of the *base* of the monument (the *south* side for many reasons would be the most appropriate, it being the south from which the great Queen of Ethiopia came with great offerings to the Temple at Jerusalem, the south from which the Ethiopian Ambassador came to worship at Jerusalem, as well as the south from which the greatest part of our offerings come to contribute to this testimonial) shall be an urn, at the side of which shall be a female figure, kneeling on the right knee, the left thigh projecting horizontally, the leg perpendicular to the ground, the leg and thigh forming the angle of a square, the body erect, but little inclined over the urn, the face with eyes upturned to heaven, with distinct tear-drops passing down the face, falling into the urn, which is represented as being full; distinct tear-drops shall be so arranged as to represent the figures 4,000,000 (four million), which shall be emblematical not only of the number of contributors to the monument, but the number of those who shed tears of sorrow for the great and good deliverer of their race from bondage in the United States; the arms and hands extended--the whole figure to represent "Ethiopia stretching forth her hands unto God." A drapery is to cover the whole figure, thrown back, leaving the entire arms and shoulders bare, but drawn up *under* the arms, covering the breast just to the verge of the swell below the neck, falling down full in front, but leaving the front of the knee, leg, and foot fully exposed. The lower part of the drapery should be so arranged behind as just to expose the *sole* of the right foot in its projection. The urn should be directly in front of the female figure, so as to give the best possible effect to, or view of, it. This figure is neither to be Grecian, Caucasian, nor Anglo-Saxon, Mongolian nor Indian, but African--*very* African--an ideal representative *genius* of the race, as Europa, Britannia, America, or the Goddess of Liberty, is to the European race.

Will not our clever mutual friend, Patrick Reason, of New York, sketch the outlines of a good representation of this design? This is to be prominently carved or moulded in whatever material the monument is erected of. Let the one-cent contribution at once commence everywhere throughout the United States. I hope the Independent, and all other papers friendly, especially the religious and weeklies, will copy my article published in the Ango-African of the 13th of May; also this article on the design.

In behalf of this great nation,

M.R. DELANY,

Major 104th U.S.C.T.

JOHN MERCER LANGSTON

JOHN MERCER LANGSTON (1829-1897)

In his autobiography *From the Virginia Plantation to the National Capitol* (1894), written in the third person in a prolix and orotund style, John Mercer Langston tells of his Civil War involvement as a recruiter and politician. Indeed Langston had been born on a plantation in Virginia. The plantation, that of Captain Ralph Quarles, was an unusual one, conducted according to a code emphasizing humanity toward the slaves, and therefore one inviting social ostracism of the owner, despite his distinguished lineage. Like many slaveholders Captain Quarles had a slave mistress. Unlike most, he made her the virtual mistress of the plantation. This slave, Lucy Langston, was the daughter of an Indian mother who was also on the plantation. After the birth of her first child, Quarles legally manumitted his mistress and her daughter. John Mercer Langston, one of three subsequent children, was therefore born free on his father's plantation. Langston was only four when both parents died. Quarles left the bulk of his estate to his three sons, having already settled an estate on the oldest child, the daughter. In his will he also manumitted several slaves.

Prudently, led by the oldest son, the three brothers left slave territory and moved to Ohio. There the young John was received into the family of Colonel William Gooch, one of his father's executors. When the Gooch family left Ohio for Missouri, a slave state, Langston's half-brother initiated a court action to assure that the boy would remain in Ohio. He was returned to the Gooch farm, now owned by a stern abolitionist named Richard Long. Eventually Langston was sent to Cincinnati to attend a private school. He boarded with various well-established Black families. At the age of 15, proficient in Greek and Latin, he went to Oberlin College, where he boarded in the home of George Whipple, a professor of mathematics. During his first vacation he taught in a country school. After finishing his Oberlin course, Langston sought admission to law schools, but was denied because of his color. He returned to Oberlin and studied theology for three years, graduating in 1853; he had had, however, no intention of abandoning his quest for legal training, and he was shortly after received into the law offices and family of Judge Philemon Bliss of Elryia, Ohio.

The next year when Langston was 21, Judge Bliss nominated him to the bar. Though the three-man examining committee found him qualified on all grounds, the two Democrats on the committee stated the verbal reservation that he was colored. The court decided that since he did not "look" colored the reservation could be overlooked and he was admitted to the bar.

Within a few years, married and with several children of his own, Langston was a successful lawyer in Oberlin. The large household included a number of boarding students, the colored sons of a rich Louisiana planter, a young African, as well as girl students of Oberlin College. Inevitably Langston became involved in the defense of fugitive slaves. Politically he affiliated with the Republican Party to which he remained faithful throughout his career.

The coming of the Civil War involved Langston directly and he devotes two chapters of his autobiography to his activities in the conflict.

Langston's subsequent career was illustrious. In 1868, he organized the law department of Howard University and was subsequently acting president of the University, serving, in all, seven years. In 1877 he was appointed by President Hayes to the post of Minister and Consul General to Haiti. (It is interesting to note that Langston had given the middle name Dessalines to his first child, a son born in 1855.) Langston served there until 1885. Later in the same year he accepted the presidency of the Virginia Normal Institute, now Virginia State College of Petersburg. The return to power of the Democratic Party in Virginia led to changes in the social and intellectual climate which caused Langston to resign from this post two years later. It was then that Langston acceded to a proposal to be the Republican candidate for Congress from the Fourth Congressional District of Virginia. Amid much anti-Black vituperation and chicanery he was elected in 1888, serving in the Firty-First Congress. Democrats and some Republicans had attempted to block his assumption of his seat, charging electoral fraud before the Congress. Such challenges were not unusual at the time, since seventeen such were made to the Fifty-First Congress. By a vote of 151 to 1, the House of Representatives found Langston's election in order, even though it is clear many members avoided the vote. No Democrat was present in the House on the day that Langston took his seat in Congress. Langston did not seek a second term. Writing in 1894, he expressed a pious wish:

> It is hoped, however, and greatly to be desired that ultimately, and at a day not distant, the political elements and forces of the district as well as those of the entire state, will be so improved, reconstructed and reorganized under new and better legislation and honest management, as to insure justice and honorable dealing in all elections, local, state, and federal.

Sixty years later Virginia was the leader in "massive resistance" to the Supreme Court Desegregation Ruling of 1954. Ninety-one years later, Virginia elected a Black lieutenant-governor. So much for "a day not distant."

CHAPTER XV
HIS RECRUITMENT OF COLORED TROOPS
FOR THE NATIONAL SERVICE

ABRAHAM LINCOLN had been elected president of the United States! The circumscription, if not the overthrow of slavery, seemed to be at hand. The temper and metal of the South were now to be tested. Would secession, to be followed inevitably by war, be adopted as the only and last source of defence left to an oligarchy of slavery which sought to dominate the country and government? The feelings of the country, gathering strength and intensity under the influence of an agitation rendered serious and affecting by words as well as deeds, calculated to stir and heat the blood, even of a people ordinarily cool and deliberate, ran high as a mighty angry flood about to sweep everything before it. The sagest statesmen were staggered in the presence of the threatening events which threw their black appalling shadows across the republic. They could not speak with authority and

reliable forecast as to what of portent and calamity awaited
the nation. All could feel, however, the approach of a cruel,
deadly storm. That slavery, strong now and defiant in its
purposes and designs against the government, would make
open war-like assaults upon it, was generally feared. Although few persons in the land seemed prepared to assert the
certainity of such procedure, all felt that it must come. The
president-elect, the representative of all those republican
principles and doctrines which the South loathed and de-
tested, had hardly felt upon his election that such murderous, popular feeling existed in any part of the country as to
render his journey from Illinois to Washington city dangerous or difficult. His friends, however, found it necessary to
warn him on his arrival at Harrisburg, Pennsylvania, that it
would be well for him to move upon his guard in passing
through the city of Baltimore to the capital. Early after his
inauguration, the South seizing his advent to power as cause
for their rebellious proceedings, announced their secession in
the thunder of great guns, as they echoed and re-echoed the
attack of the insolent, mad oligarchy of despotism upon the
nation. The attack at first was treated as an insurrection of
small power which might be easily crushed. Soon however
the purpose and strength of the insurgent forces were
discovered, and instead of seventy-five thousand soldiers
called for a brief period of enlistment, the government
needed hundreds of thousands of its most valiant men, to go
out to make war in earnest and to the end to save the Union,
free institutions and the government, as the Fathers of the
Republic had bequeathed them to loyal worthy sons. The
War of the Rebellion was actually upon the nation!

At its commencement, there was the strongest possible
feeling found in all parts of the country, against taking colored men into the army of the nation as soldiers. And it was
not until after the famous meeting of loyal governors held at
Altoona, Pennsylvania, as late as the early part of 1863, that
the purpose was expressed by the late John A. Andrew, governor of Massachusetts, as permitted by his colleagues, and as
authorized by the general government, to organize regiments of such persons. His colleagues, the loyal governors
persent, gave him their consent to that proposition, allowing

enlistments from their several States as credited to his own work, and expressed the wish that he undertake such work.

There was no man in the United States, all things considered, so well adapted to inaugurate the movement in this behalf, as the man to whom Governor Andrew assigned it. Full of genuine devotion to that freedom and impartiality which knows no color in a human being; wholly alive to the deadly effects of slavery upon every interest of his country; anxious to employ every honorable means to stay its encroachments and to snatch from its bloody clutches any instrument or power which it might wield to the ruin of the government and the country; with full knowledge of the soldierly qualities of the negro troops of the Revolutionary Army and of the War of 1812; Mr. George L. Stearns, an old tried friend of John Brown, a loyal merchant of Boston, wealthy himself and able to secure all the means necessary for the early stages of such work, was the man of all others to be charged with this duty. He was well known in connection with his efforts to prevent slaveholding in Kansas, employing his means largely and his entire influence to accomplish this object. Nor, when questioned even by a committee of Congress with regard to any part he had taken in such work, or any support which he had given John Brown in his raid on Harper's Ferry, did he hesitate to speak frankly and fully on those subjects, telling what he did and what funds he furnished to advance and support either enterprise. New England could not produce a man of higher social position, antislavery fame and general influence than Mr. Stearns. He was armed too for this special task by reason of his great knowledge of the leading colored men and their chief white friends of the United States, all of whom he might employ as instruments of the largest importance in promoting the recruitment of the colored troops. It was of the first importance under the circumstances that his knowledge of the colored men of the United States be such that he would understand well how to make selections with the most desirable results in this service. It was material too that he should have knowledge of such white men in every quarter as might further by counsel and influence any movement which might be made to reach the colored citizen and to secure his enlist-

ment. Accordingly, he had no sooner accepted the responsibility of recruiting the first colored troops from the North to
be admitted to the national service, than he did select colored
men, who by their ability and influence were capable of doing
the most successful work among their own class; while he
organized such committees of white men, in different sections of the country, to aid and support the movement in
such general way as seemed to be necessary. To one well advised his efforts in such respects must be deemed of the
greatest importance. At the time that he commenced his
service, the government supplied neither means nor men
for his use. He was compelled to find and furnish both.

As his chief recruiting agent for the western part of the
country, Mr. Stearns selected and employed Mr. John M.
Langston. The duties which he enjoined upon this agent, in
whom he reposed the greatest confidence, were much beyond
that of mere recruiting. For he invited him not only to special consultations connected with the service, but expected
him to attend and address great popular assemblies, as might
seem to be necessary in the great cities and important rural
districts, explaining every feature of the national and state
laws concerning the recruitment of all troops enlisted and
sent to Massachusetts for organization in regiments and service as credited to that State. The questions of monthly pay,
allowances generally and bounties were of special importance, and required careful and proper explanation. Besides,
the feeling against taking any part as soldiers in the war so far
as the colored people were concerned, consequent upon their
rejection heretofore, whenever offering to do so, had to be
overcome by cautious, truthful statements, made with such
candor and appeal as to create after meeting their prejudices,
favorable and effective impressions. Mr. Langston's work
was largely, almost entirely in the beginning, of such character, and even when Mr. Stearns was himself present at such
public meetings he insisted that his agent should do the
speaking. He invited Mr. Langston to meet him first at Buf-
falo, New York, for consultation. Subsequently, he invited
him to meet a large company of friends interested in the
work at Philadelphia, Pennsylvania. After this last conference, Mr. Langston entered vigorously, by request of Mr.

Stearns and by arrangement made with him, upon the recruitment of the 54th Massachusetts Regiment. His success in this work, especially in the States of Ohio, Indiana and Illinois, was entirely satisfactory, and although a very large number of men--perhaps three thousand or more--was sent to Massachusetts from which to select choice ones for the regiment, its recruitment was soon accomplished. The last seventy-five men taken into Company K, were sent from Xenia, Ohio, where recruited, to Camp Meigs, Massaschusetts. Quite immediately upon their enlistment, the regiment was moved to South Carolina, and within a very short time, under its illustrious commanding officer, Colonel Shaw, made its famous charge upon Fort Wagner. Every one of these seventy-five men, young, vigorous, manly, and brave, fell in this charge. They fell with Shaw, and sleep in graves as honorable as his!

A single incident connected with the recruitment of these men is worthy of special mention. The son of an aged black woman living a mile or more out of Xenia upon the public highway, was one of their number. He was her only son, in fact her only child, and she relied upon him for support and protection. This mother called upon Mr. Langston, just after her son had bidden her farewell and left his home. Her heart was evidently moved by the deepest feeling as she thought of him, the dangers which awaited him, and realized that she might not see him again. As she entered the house, inquiring for the man who was inducing and enlisting persons to go to the war, it was feared that she had come, perhaps, to make complaint in violent and untempered language. Her bearing and manner, however, soon removed all such feeling. And, as she opened her mouth, she discovered in the midst of her sadness a temper of remarkable intelligence and good nature. She had not come to make complaint. Instead, she came to say that while she regretted the loss of her son, she wanted him, now that he had gone, to enter the service intelligently, with manly purpose, and to discharge his duty as an American soldier with courage and vigor. She asked that he be, accordingly, fully instructed and disciplined, so that such would be his course. In every word and act she manifested the spirit and devotion of an earnest and worthy

American mother. When assured that the greatest care would be taken not only to instruct and discipline, but to protect her son, consistently with the faithful discharge of his duties as a soldier, she expressed full confidence in the statement and the hope that not only all might go well with her child, but that the cause of the government and the welfare of her people might be promoted, if need be, even in his death. "For," she said, "liberty is better than life." As already stated, her son went out to die, making her offering to the country and the cause of her people a precious and costly one. The number of colored mothers who thus gave their only sons, and who might detail in sympathetic words their own similar experiences with those of this one, shall never be known. Fortunately, however, for the country, no one of them is found, even to this day, who would offer any word of complaint. They are all too proud that they were permitted to bear sons, who at last should constitute their richest gifts to the republic.

The 54th Massachusetts Regiment was one composed of selected men. Its *personnel* was of the highest character. Many of the first colored families had representatives in it, and many of the very best young colored men were numbered among its troops. The roster of its commissioned officers showed the names of the very finest representative young white men, chosen and appointed as well with reference to their social position and family connections, as to their qualifications for their several duties. For it was the purpose of the friends of the experiment which this regiment should make in connection with the national service, to wisely and thoroughly furnish it in officers, men and every appointment for the work which it was called to perform. Besides, every care was exercised to put the regiment, while in camp, in the best possible physical, moral and mental condition and discipline for the field. No regiment ever left its camp followed by more hearty anxieties and earnest prayers for its welfare than this one. And no State ever exhibited deeper interest in the success of any portion of its soldiery, than Massachusetts for the troops of its 54th Regiment. Governor Andrew and his agent, Mr. Stearns, appreciated most fully the expectations which were entertained with regard to this enterprise inaugurated by them and the experiences which must await the men of their first regiment. The men were not themselves unconscious of the dignity, responsibility and danger of their position, and yet they advanced to the full discharge of their duties with intelligent American courage. The proof of this is shown in the patriotic, shining record which this regiment made for itself in contests requiring the best soldierly elements and behavior.

Upon the completion of the 54th, Mr. Stearns, with his full force, including of course Mr. Langston, undertook the recruitment of the 55th Massachusetts Regiment. Care was still taken as to the physical condition and make of the men enlisted and forwarded to Camp Meigs, and it is to be said with truth that this was also a regiment of selected men. They were, however, mainly enlisted in and sent from Ohio. At this time denied, especially in that State, the opportunity and privilege of enlistment for the public service on common equal terms, the colored men of Ohio had very generally resolved to leave their own State, and going to Massachusetts, enter the service as citizens of that Commonwealth. More than this, Ohio had provided no bounties for such troops, while Massachusetts had, and the latter had made arrangements through state appropriation for equalizing the pay of colored troops from that State with that of white troops, and all allowances were identical in value and character. It is not difficult to understand how such considerations would operate in determining the action of the colored men. When it is added that they had already come to understand that Governor Andrew and Mr. Stearns were special friends of their race, and would see to it beyond doubt that they had fair treatment in all respects, in the camp and in the field, their action in such regard would seem to be under the circumstances, natural and inevitable. So far as the major portion of the regiment was concerned, it was composed of Ohio men; so much so that Mr. Langston, who supervised and directed its recruitment, determined to have made in his own state and at his own expense, a full stand of regimental colors for it. Accordingly, colors were purchased as ordered and made by Scheilotto & Co., Cincinnati, Ohio. To this arrangement Governor Andrew and Mr. Stearns gave their ready assent and the colors, made of the very finest materials used for such purposes, were on the completion of its recruitment, forwarded by express to Camp Meigs and formally and duly presented. They were borne in pride by the regiment from the camp to the field, in every battle in which it played a part, and returned at last, bearing all the marks of patriotic, brave service, to the capitol of the Commonwealth of Massachusetts, where they can be seen this day, as sacredly kept among the precious relics of the War of the Rebellion.

At first Mr. Langston had intended to deliver the colors in person to the 55th Massachusetts Regiment, and was on his way with them, when on reaching Columbus, Ohio, the governor of the State, the Hon. David Todd, hearing that he was in the city, invited him to call for a special interview. He did so, when to his surprise the governor asked him to engage in the recruitment of colored troops for his state. Heretofore, about one year before this call, Mr. Langston had suggested to Governor Todd that he would be glad, were it agreeable to his feelings and judgment, to recruit and locate a regiment of a thousand and one colored men in Camp Delaware, without expense of a single dollar to the state government, upon the sole condition that they be received, duly organized, officered and employed as regular soldiers in the national service; to all of which the governor made reply of most remarkable character, but what under the circumstances in his State and the country seemed to be altogether natural. This meeting occurred prior of course to the convention of loyal governors, and the answer which he made was a reflection of the general feeling obtaining in the country with respect to the status of the colored American and his relations to the government. His reply was in substance as follows: "Do you not know, Mr. Langston, that this is a *white man's* government; that white men are able to defend and protect it, and that to enlist a negro soldier would be to drive every white man out of the service? When we want you colored men we will notify you." To which Mr. Langston made respectful reply, "Governor, when you need us, send for us." But now a great change had come over the feelings and the judgment of Governor Todd, and he had actually sent for the very man to whom he had made the speech given, and who had made the promise implied in his response. However, Mr. Langston occupied another position than that in which he stood when he tendered his services in connection with the proposed Ohio regiment of the year before. So he explained to the governor and advised him that he could do now no recruiting even in Ohio, without the authority and direction of Mr. Stearns, as he might issue his orders to such effect by command of the secretary of war. He also informed the governor that he had just completed the recruitment of the 55th Massachusetts Regiment, which was composed mainly of Ohio men, and that he was then on his way to Camp Meigs with a stand of regimental colors, purchased as they had been ordered expressly for this regiment. The governor manifested such interest in the matter that he insisted that Mr. Langston allow him to send a porter to his hotel for the box containing the colors, that he might see and examine them. This was done without the least hesitation, and so soon as brought and the governor had had seen them, he pronounced them so beautiful and the purpose for which they had been secured so important and interesting, that he wanted them exhibited from the eastern steps of the capitol to a popular gathering, miscellaneous and general, which he offered to call together upon condition that Mr. Langston would make what he called "a war speech." To this proposition the governor was told that it was necessary for the colors to be delivered in Massachusetts at an early day, and that any considerable delay in such respect might work serious embarrassment. However, upon reflection and a little calculation of dates, a hurried meeting was agreed upon and subsequently held. Meantime, in a second visit to Governor Todd, and after he had communicated by telegraph both with Mr. Stearns and Secretary Stanton, it was settled that Mr. Langston should send the colors forward by express and proceed at once to the recruitment of a regiment of colored troops which should be credited to Ohio. The governor accordingly himself had the colors sent forward and he, his private secretary Judge Hoffman, and Mr. Langston made without the least delay all necessary arrangements for the recruitment of the Ohio regiment.

The 5th United States colored troops was the regiment referred to, and it was composed of young Ohio men, in the main of excellent physique, character and courage. Perhaps no braver men ever saw service among any class of people at any period in the history of the world than those who constituted its rank and file. The first three hundred men recruited were deceived by statements with respect to their monthly pay and allowances for clothing. This mistake under the circumstances, was the result of the belief and opinion that the men of Ohio would be treated precisely as those enlisted for Massachusetts, and was wholly natural. In a conference with Judge Hoffman, it was discovered that the rule of law applying to the national service in accordance with which the pay and allowances of the Ohio troops must be regulated, differed from those applied to the Massachusetts troops, in that the national regulations failing in full and equal provision for the colored troops of the last named State, that State made special provision in that behalf. Ohio did no such thing, and hence the error and mistake made as indicated. No sooner had this matter been brought to the attention of the governor than he held and ordered that the men already thus deceived and in rendezvous at Camp Delaware, must have full explanation made to them, and informed that they were all at liberty to return to their homes should they so decide to do, at the expense of the government; that no deception however made could be allowed in their case. At once full explanations were made to the men, the mistakes were pointed out with the greatest care and minuteness, and they advised that they were at liberty should they choose, to leave the camp for their homes. These men had been recruited in different parts of Ohio. About one-third of them came from Washington County, the other two-thirds from Athens and neighboring counties; all of the latter, however, in a single company, as they had been collected through the influence of their leader, who had calculated to enlist them finally for Massachusetts. Indeed, all these men at first had expected to be sent to that State for entry of the service. Their leaders were Messrs. Solomon Grimes of the first one-third mentioned, and Milton M. Holland of the other portion. These two persons, the latter but a mere boy, held their respective companies completely under their influence and control, and either, when the explanations alluded to were given, might have directed his men to leave the camp and they would have gone. However, Mr. Holland and his men were decided and manly at once in their course, thus greatly influencing Mr. Grimes and his men to remain, and so not a single man of the three hundred left the camp. All accepted the explanations as made in good faith, as they concluded the mistakes had been made without intent to do the least injury. Besides, the leaders and every man asserted that he was ready to accept the situation just as it was, and show his patriotism and devotion to his country in efforts and struggles for its defence which might cost him even his life. More beautiful, manly conduct was not exhibited in any camping ground of the American soldier during the wars of the late Rebellion, than this of these colored troops of Ohio at Camp Delaware. Thereafter, the recruitment of the regiment was conducted with reasonable rapidity and success. Such was the conduct of the men coming to camp, and their reputation for considerate behavior, aptness and attention to drill and soldierly advancement, that all over the State, young colored men were moved to the emulation of their example, and towards the close of its recruitment in many cases sought place in the regiment. On its completion it showed in its *personnel*, a fine body of excellent men, of soldierly qualities and character. Ohio, so far as the rank and file of its best regiments were concerned, could boast of no better material in its representatives collected in any camp, and called as its soldiers to the defence of the government.

Great care was taken to make wise and judicious selections of commissioned officers for these troops. The colonel of the regiment was selected from among the scholars of the State with special reference to his personal respect and consideration of the class of people whose sons he would lead and command in the face of danger. Professor G.W. Shurtliff was a young man of extraordinarily high personal and social character, of strictly Christian principles and habits, with recognized reputation and influence as an abolitionist and friend of the negro race. He was besides a white person, in every sense manly, noble and brave. Every man in the regiment upon making his acquaintance, witnessing his behavior and bearing, became heartily and thoroughly devoted to him as to a faithful, staunch friend, always ready to do whatever he might for the good of his command. The lieutenant-colonel and all the other commissioned officers were white men of great fitness for their special duties and of like high personal and social name and position. The recruitment of the regiment, with the selection and commission of every officer, was completed by the early part of November, 1863. The white inhabitants residing in the neighborhood of Camp Delaware, were at first utterly opposed to having that camp occupied by colored troops. They feared every sort of disorderly, unbecoming conduct on their part, and dreaded them as a host of petty thieves coming among them to commit manifold and frightful depredations. White troops had been in rendezvous there, and it was their bad conduct largely which had superinduced this dread of the presence of the colored ones. However, it is not recorded in the doings of the camp, or remembered by the community, that a single act of vandalism or any conduct unbecoming an American soldier, stands charged against any one of the men composing this regiment, while in camp. It remained there, from the date of the arrival of its first men to that of its departure, for a little over four months. The leading white men of the neighborhood were open and positive in expressions favoring the good conduct of the men. Such record made in camp and by the first regiment of colored men recruited in Ohio, was regarded by all friends of the race as most important and favorable.

Mr. Langston was determined that no regiment going into the service of the government should do so under richer or more beautiful colors than this one. And he was equally determined that they should not leave the camp without suitable and impressive ceremonies in connection with their presentation. He therefore made arrangements with the firm of Scheilotto & Co., of Cincinatti, to make for it a stand of first-class regimental colors. He provided for presenting them at the camp on the day before the regiment was to leave for the field. Governor Todd, ex-Governor William Dennison, with several other leading citizens, prominent in the state, had been invited and were present and took part in the exercises. The principal speech of the occasion was made to the full regiment, with every officer present, by the governor himself. He appreciated fully the real character of the circumstances, and moved in accordance therewith, he made an address of remarkable and peculiar power and effect. It was solemn, earnest, pathetic, impressive and eloquent. He reached the climax however, when in closing he said to the regiment, "My boys, sons of the State, go forth now as you are called to fight for our country and its government! Let your conduct be that of brave, intelligent devoted, American citizens! If such shall be your course, if spared and I can reach you no otherwise, on your return I will come upon my hands and knees to meet and greet you! And my words of commendation and praise shall be prompted by my pride and satisfaction in view of your behavior! But, should your conduct be that of cowards, showing your forgetfulness of the fearful responsibility which now rests upon your shoulders and the supreme dignity of the mission to which your government calls and this State sends you, as you return, I will crawl if need be, away from you, that I may never look again in your faces! I have, however, full confidence in you; and my prayer to Almighty God is that He will protect while He gives you victory in every battle in which you may be called to take part." This address was received in the spirit with which it was delivered, and accepted by the men as the parting counsel of one deeply and cordially interested in their welfare. Every circumstance and feature of this occasion was marked by the happiest, though solemn indications of prospective success. Accepting its colors from the hands of a distinguished ex-governor of the State, who above all others present could employ words befitting that service, tender, generous and affecting, the regiment discovered in its deep emotion and intelligent expression of its feelings, as shown in the response of Colonel Shurtliff, its appreciation and value of the honor done it in their presentation. The record which the regiment made in the desperate and deadly struggles in which it played important conspicuous part under those colors about Richmond and Petersburgh, shall tell whether they bore them bravely in glory to the end!

No state bounty had been provided by the government of Ohio for these troops. Massachusetts had done her duty in such behalf for her colored troops in generous provision. Mr. Langston, therefore, undertook to raise by voluntary contribution, at least money enough to make a small purse, to be presented to every man of the regiment on the day that the colors were given. He succeeded in collecting only enough to give each soldier two dollars and a half. This sum, in view of the very kind treatment which the commandant of the post, Colonel McCoy, had shown the regiment, and in view of its very great respect and love of him, was used to purchase presents for himself and his wife. The gift to him was a fine gold watch, and that to his wife a rich, costly and elegant ring. Mr. Langston presented the gifts in the name of the regiment to the commandant. This officer was so deeply moved and affected by this unexpected proceeding, that he was compelled, in the midst of his tears even, to ask ex-Governor Dennison to thank the regiment for himself and Mrs. McCoy.

The regiment leaving Camp Delaware in the early part of November, 1863, went directly to Portsmouth, Virginia, taking its place in the Army of the James, in that Department of that State. Very shortly it was ordered into active service, and figured with unsurpassed courage and brilliancy in at least ten battles about Richmond and Petersburgh, winning special distinction in its charge upon New Market Heights. Its courage, gallantry and endurance were put to the test, indeed, in this charge which gave it such note. The names of several young men connected with this regiment, especially certain of its non-commissioned officers, who, by reason of the sad havoc made among its commissioned ones in killed and wounded, were permitted to and did make honorable records in hot, deadly battle, might be mentioned. Indeed, their names shall be written here, because of the merits and deserts of those who bear them, and because they represent a great class whose highest aspiration is discovered in their desire and determination to serve, even unto death, their country and its government. Milton M. Holland, Powhatan

Beatty, Robert A. Pinn, James S. Tyler, James Bronson, not to mention others, constitute a galaxy of heroes, who by exemplary, manly, and daring conduct, as officers and men of the 5th United States colored troops, are entitled to signal fame and renown.

An incident connected with the recruitment of Milton M. Holland and the men whom he held under his command, when Mr. Langston commenced his work in connection with the enlistment of troops for his regiment, is worthy of special note here. Mr. Stearns had sent to Ohio a young white gentleman to assist in the recruitment of the regiment, who while active and energetic, was a person of unusual moderation and wisdom. He was especially successful, as a rule, in all errands of business upon which he might be sent to any given person or place. Of amiable disposition and pleasing manners, he soon won favor with men wherever found, who were inclined to enter the United States service. Such was his kindly treatment of every colored person, that he was not long, when he had opportunity, in bringing such one to clear and decided sense of his duty in the matter of his enlistment. Learning of Holland and his men as situated in a temporary unofficial camp in the Fair Grounds of Athens County, near the city of Athens, Ohio, Mr. Langston, desirous to secure their enlistment for the Ohio regiment, sent the gentleman spoken of, his assistant, Captain Dunlop, to Athens to meet, confer with, recruit and bring them at once to Camp Delaware. The men were found in camp as stated; but so determined to go to Massachusetts, there enlist and be credited to that State as the men of the 54th and 55th Regiments had been, that they would not allow him, or any other person to enter their camp grounds to talk with them of their enlistment in Ohio. Captain Dunlop was compelled to telegraph these facts to Mr. Langston, and he was compelled himself to go to Athens and seek approach to Mr. Holland and his men through special white friends in whom they had great confidence. No man could reach the men except as he did through their captain, as they called Mr. Holland. He was a young colored Texan, sent North and located as a student at that time in the Albany Colored School, prominent in that part of Ohio. He was by nature a soldier. He smelt battle from afar, and was ready at the shortest warning to engage in deadly conflict. At the time he was really a lad of about nineteen years of age, with all the fire of such youthful, daring nature as he possessed in blood and by inheritance. He was a young person of remarkable native intelligence, good name, bearing himself constantly, even among his men, so as to win the largest respect and confidence. The promise of manly life and endeavor were apparent in his case on the most casual observation and contact.

Mr. Langston took the precaution on reaching Athens, having learned somewhat of this young man and of those by whom he was regarded and treated with special consideration, to call upon the chief business man of the town, the leading banker, Mr. Moore, a person well known and of the greatest respectability, to ascertain what he might with respect to him and the men generally under his control, and whether the community favored the recruitment of the state regiment of colored men. He found that Mr. Moore was exactly the man to answer every question respecting such matters with intelligence. He was so entirely acquainted with Mr. Holland and the men controlled by him, and had such influence and entertained such feelings, that he was able and did bring Mr. Langston at once into such relations to all concerned, that the work in view was accomplished very speedily and with the least possible difficulty. He even went so far as to put his fine saddle-horse at the disposal of Mr. Langston, to ride to the camp grounds, a mile away, and to give him a note of introduction which proved wholly satisfactory in securing the attention and confidence of those to be reached. It was about five o'clock in the afternoon on a beautiful day in June, and in a section of the country famous for its richness and delightsome conditions, that Mr. Langston, armed as indicated, approached the gate of the Fair Grounds where he would find the men whom he sought. A sentinel was on guard, and it was very apparent that he must be treated with becoming consideration and respect by any one who would through him secure communication with the commanding officer. Such etiquette was duly observed, and it was not long before the visitor was confronted at the gate by the student-officer in command. The note of introduction was at once presented, when formal salutations and compliments were passed, and the two persons up to that time utter strangers, seemed to be wholly at home with each other. The errand of the visitor was made known with careful detail, and information given that no colored troops would be sent from that date to Massachusetts from Ohio, while a regiment would be at once recruited of such men and duly credited to Ohio. Upon this statement, with the request that he might bring the subject of their enlistment for the regiment to the attention of his men and take their decision in the premises, Mr. Holland replied that he would at once consult with them, and if he found them willing to do so he would make all the necessary arrangements to that end without the least delay. He retired, going to his headquarters, and within a very few minutes the fife and drum were heard and the gathering of the men near headquarters was immediately witnessed. Not tarrying in his movements, the young man returned, and inviting Mr. Langston in most polite manner to enter the camp, directed his sentinel to let him pass. Dismounting, as conducted by Mr. Holland, Mr. Langston went directly to the headquarters, where the men all drawn up in hollow-square awaited his arrival, and his statements and explanations. The manner and behavior of the young colored officer during this whole affair was that of a youthful, brave American, hopeful of an early opportunity to display any courage which he might possess in a battle the results of which would work the salvation of his country. It is enough to say here that in less than an hour and a half from the time he and Mr. Langston exchanged salutations, through his good offices he and his one hundred and forty-nine men had signed the recruitment rolls, and had promised to leave the Athens County Fair Grounds for Camp Delaware the next day at ten o'clock in the morning.

During the night the good banker, Mr. E.H. Moore, to whose great kindness so much was due for any success attending this transaction, sent in great haste to Cincinnati, to purchase a beautiful silk company flag, to be presented early on the following morning to the men as they left their camp grounds, passing through the city on the way to the depot to take the train, via Chillicothe, to Camp Delaware. The flag arrived in due season, and was formally presented with no little *eclat*. The men had left the Fair Grounds in good spirit and in fair general condition, and it is not saying too much to state that they made a fine impression in their parade and conduct, in the city and upon the community. The presentation speech was made by a young gentleman, the son of the donor of the flag, Colonel Moore. His address was full of stirring sentiments, highly ornate and affecting. The response on behalf of the men was made by Mr. Langston himself, in such spirit and manner as to gain not only the favor and applause of those in whose name he spoke, but the sympathy and good will of the vast concourse of loyal citizens who heard him. From Athens through Chillicothe and Columbus to Camp Delaware, such were the bearing and behavior of these men, that they constantly won popular admiration and applause. Throughout their camp experiences, labors and struggles, they maintained, however tried and tested, unsullied reputations.

In the charge at New Market Heights, the young Texan student who figured as described in the Athens County Fair Grounds, now become a veteran in service if not in years, the color-sergeant of the regiment, when he had discovered how his troops had lost in the early stages of the charge, well-nigh all its commissioned officers, including especially the colonel and lieutenant-colonel, under the purpose to achieve victory or die, passing his colors to another soldier of the regiment, took himself command of Company C, of which he had been made at first the orderly-sergeant, and with it led the charge, winning a victory which brought not only large favorable results to the government, but additional and signal glory to American arms. It was in this charge, requiring the best elements of the genuine brave American soldier, indifferent to danger and determined to snatch success from desperate odds, that the young colored men whose names have been recorded, won as well their distinction as their medals of bronze and silver.

In a conversation had with Gen. B.F. Butler, just after the war and his election to the House of Representatives, in speaking of the 5th United States colored troops, its colonel and its behavior during its service, especially its charge at

New Market Heights, he said in warm emphatic manner to Mr. Langston, "I had only to command and Shurtliff with his regiment would attempt and perform any feat of daring and danger. He and his men constituted the very best of the national service." Continuing, he said, "This regiment made its celebrated charge under my observation, and while every man performed his duty with courage and devotion, those to whom I awarded medals demeaned themselves with such heroism as to merit at once the commendation of their commanding officers and the praise and gratitude of the country. So far as the conduct of the color-sergeant, Holland, was concerned, in the charge at New Market Heights, had it been within my power I would have conferred upon him in view of it, a brigadier-generalship for gallantry on the field."

Recruited for three years, or until the close of the war, this regiment having gained and occupied conspicuous rank among the best that had fought to maintain the Union, preserve and sustain free institutions, with slavery everywhere abolished, returned, with victory perching on every banner of the national government, the Rebellion fully suppressed, without a blemish on name or character, distinguished for the glory which its patriotism and courage had won. It went to Camp Chase, Ohio, where with seven hundred of its original recruits, it was mustered out of the service, October 5th, 1865.

CHAPTER XVI
HIS FIRST OFFICIAL ERRAND
TO THE NATIONAL CAPITAL

ABRAHAM LINCOLN had been elected president of the United for the second time. Andrew Johnson had been elected vice-president. Both had been inaugurated and had entered upon the duties of their respective offices. Grant, the great Captain of the century, the commanding officer of the American army, still confronted the leader of the Confederate forces, and not even the matchless secretary of war, Stanton himself, could say that the close of the bloody contest was at hand, and peace must soon be declared, with victory gained by the national soldiery. To the common observer it seemed as if war must still be waged. Notwithstanding two years and more had passed, since on the first day of January, 1863, the Emancipation Proclamation had been issued, the forces of the Confederacy continued their defiance of the government, and in numbers, purpose and courage, seemed far from defeat and general surrender.

It was under such circumstances that Mr. Langston, after he had completed his services in the recruitment of colored troops for the regiments of Massachusetts and Ohio, made his first official visit to Washington city. It is to be added, that wherever opportunity had been given, all along the lines of battle, the colored troops, in whatsoever service they were engaged, had demonstrated their possession of all those elements of obedience, endurance, fortitude, loyalty, enthusiasm and devotion, always deemed necessary in the highest and best type of the reliable and worthy soldier. Up to this time, two colored men only, had been given commissions as regular officers of the national army. Martin R. Delaney and Orindatus S.B. Wall were the persons who had thus been signally honored. The first bore the commission of major, the second that of captain. Both had been given duty in connection with the recruitment of colored troops. They had not at this time been assigned to service, either in a company or regiment, according to their official designations. It is true, too, that the large number of non-commissioned officers found in the various regiments of colored troops, had not only demonstrated excellent military capacity and aptness, but great general warlike knowledge, coolness and decision in the midst of emergency and danger, as well as readiness and alacrity in the discharge of their duties, however manifold and trying. The government had discovered, certainly, that they composed a loyal military corps, worthy of every confidence, in view of their intelligence, patriotism and devotion, and that their instruction, drill and experience must have fitted them for any official position or duty to which they might be called. This, without doubt, was true of a very considerable number, at least, of such officers.

Mr. Langston's errand was indeed official; but he had not made a journey to the capital to ask for an ordinary place under the new administration. Nor was he seeking a position free from responsibility and danger. The civil service may have been inviting to persons far more intelligent, patriotic and worthy; but his attention and desires were not directed to anything connected therewith. He had come at his own expense, moved by patriotic considerations, to say to President Lincoln and Secretary Stanton that the time had arrived, in view of the intelligence, experience, loyalty and service of the colored troops, for the commission of a colored man to a colonelcy in the national service, with authority to recruit his own regiment and to officer it with colored men taken from regiments already in the service and who had given evidence of high soldierly qualities on the field of battle. Upon his visit with this mission in view, he being well acquainted with and the friend of Gen. James A. Garfield, then a member of Congress, having left the field to serve his constituents and the people generally in that capacity, Mr. Langston went directly to him to seek his good offices in introducing him properly to the secretary of war, and his counsel and advice with respect to and approval of his plan. He found the young, magnificent representative of Ohio, and the brilliant general who had won such enviable note and name through his masterly deeds upon the field, not only willing to do what he asked, but patient to hear and counsel him with respect to his novel but important proposition. He was prompt, earnest and enthusiastic in his approval, and without the least hesitation conducted his colored Ohio friend, with whom he seemed specially pleased, for introduction to the prince of military secretaries, whose frown or approval had dismayed or delighted so many aspirants for high martial position and responsibility. Indeed, such were the appearance, manner, address and bearing of this great secretary to the ordinary visitor, that even the bravest of fellow-citizens approached him with anxiety and manifestations of timidity. No so, however, with Garfield. He was a brave and fearless man; always bold, clear and positive in the advocacy of any measure or individual in whose promotion and interest he desired to exercise his judgment and efforts.

General Garfield, in the introduction which he made of his friend to Secretary Stanton, did not hesitate to speak of him in most favorable terms, dwelling in warmest approval upon his character, his ability, his loyalty, and his valuable services rendered in the recruitment of troops for the 54th and 55th Massachusetts regiments, the 5th United States colored troops; his employment of a substitute for himself for the service, when in no wise exposed to draft, or any enforced military duty, and other evidences furnished in his conduct, showing his devotion to the government and its support. He also dwelt in earnest, intelligent, patriotic words upon the wisdom, dignity, propriety and advantage which characterized and would be the natural results following the adoption of the proposition submitted for the recruitment and organization of an entirely colored regiment. He did not hesitate to affirm that the government might expect on the part of such a regiment, conduct of the highest soldierlike character, with the largest measure of advantageous signal effects. Upon this representation, in connection with such favorable introduction to the secretary, who was himself a citizen of Ohio, it was under the circumstances entirely natural that both the orginator of the proposition and the proposition itself should secure favorable consideration. The secretary even went so far as to express his own pleasure in view of what might be made, under wise direction and management, important results of the enterprise suggested, and was pleased to request General Garfield to go directly with Mr. Langston to Colonel Foster, who was at the time in charge of the recruitment of all colored troops, and explain to him upon introduction of his friend the measure proposed. He assured General Garfield that if upon thorough examination of the matter by the proper officer of his department, it was found to be feasible and probably advantageous, he should approve it. The visit to Colonel Foster was in no sense less agreeable than that to his chief officer, and his appreciation of the proposition and its author, with whom he seemed to be well acquainted by report, was not less hearty and cordial. So soon as Colonel Foster had the matter suitably explained, he promised that it should have his serious, prompt attention, and without delay he would present his conclusions and decision in due form to the secretary, so that General Garfield and Mr. Langston could hear from the department upon the subject without any unnecessary delay. Pleased with their visits and interviews with these distinguished military officials, General Garfield and Mr. Langston separated, with the belief firmly settled in their minds that this new proposition for the military advancement of the colored troops, which must give them ample opportunity for the display of any military genius and original prowess which they possessed, led and commanded by officers of their own nationality and complexion, would receive the sanction and approval of the authorities.

Mr. Langston remained in the city of Washington while this matter was held under consideration. He was in the city when Gen. Robert E. Lee made his surrender on the ninth of April, 1865, and the Rebellion was thus brought to a hurried overthrow and its armies to utter defeat. Other and additional troops were no longer needed. Those in the service must be soon mustered out and return to their homes. For this reason the department very properly concluded not to adopt the measure suggested, and accordingly communicated its decision to that effect, shortly after the surrender, to those concerned.

Perhaps no proposition of any character whatever so deeply and thoroughly interested Mr. Langston as this one. He always felt that in it he saw the complete redemption of the colored American from every proscription legal and social; as he might make, upon his own original force of character and courage, a record thereby on the field of battle and in the shedding of his own blood in defence of the government and the country, which would emancipate him from every distinction felt and made against him. It was an opportunity of rare good fortune for him to be called, to the number of one hundred and eighty thousand, to fight with his fellow-citizens the battles of the country, though commanded by officers of another nationality and color. It would have been, however, immensely more advantageous to him, redounding to his lasting good, in a more just and considerate appreciation of his character and deeds, could he have engaged in battle for the country, led and commanded by those who bore his own lineage and image. Another great fearful emergency of the government may bring him such opportunity. If so his salvation, as indicated, need not be despaired of, for it shall come, thus, certainly, even though greatly delayed. The experiences of this, like all other governments which have been established by man, are signalized throughout their existence by urgent and pressing occasions of trial and struggle, which require the devotion and service of all good citizens, and in view of duty well and thoroughly done under such circumstances, the loyal and true who demonstrate ability and worth may make sure of their reward, in equal impartial justice and fair equitable treatment.

It was during Mr. Langston's sojourn in the capital at this time, that the horror of horrors took place. Two nights before, he had stood with the multitude looking into the face and listening to the words of the president, who while he spoke like a prophet, reminding one of the ancient Samuel as he called the people to witness his integrity, little dreamed that any man in the whole land could be found base and cowardly enough to do him harm. His words seem now in view of his assassination so soon to follow, those of warning, admonition and counsel, grave and thrilling to his countrymen. How, without the least suspicion of danger to her husband, sat his good wife near him, apparently conscious in highest and profoundest sense of the estimate and value put by the people upon his services. For he was now a statesman without an equal; a leader, as grand in the immense proportions of his individuality as Moses himself; an emancipator of a race redeemed through the wise and sagacious adjustment of those moral and legal forces which constitute the glory of American Christian civilization, and the savior of a country which shall be at last the theater where shall be displayed the golden precious drama of man's truest and noblest life and triumphs in freedom as conserved, promoted and sustained by impartial law. But the evil hour made haste, and the great city of his presidential residence, as well as the whole country, was startled and shocked with the announcement of the assassination of the immortal Abraham Lincoln.

Mr. Wade Hickman of Nashville, Tennessee, in

Washington city at the time as the body-servant of Vice-president Andrew Johnson, brought the sad tidings of the occurence to Mr. Langston. Coming to his hotel he called upon him, not only to bring that information, but to declare his purpose to allow no human being inimical to, or having designs upon, his life, to reach the vice-president, except as he did so over his dead body. The night of the terrible tragedy in Washington city was full of awful terrors, well-calculated to inspire one of the natural courage and devotion of Hickman to make this resolution and express it in his emphatic, positive terms. Besides, there was danger, as it seemed to him, that he might that night, in his attempt to protect and defend the vice-president, lose his own life. Hence he expressed the earnest request to Mr. Langston that should he fall in this work, which was to him serious and imperative, that he would make known to his family and his friends in Tennessee that he had fallen in meeting attack against a man who was then regarded as the friend of every negro in his State. Mr. Langston made faithful promise to his friend that he would discharge the duty enjoined, should there come necessity for so doing, with fidelity and truth. Fortunately however for the country, the vice-president was spared, and the brave negro who was at once his servant and his friend, though faithful as devoted, was not called to die in defence of the successor of the murdered president.

FREDERICK
DOUGLASS

FREDERICK DOUGLASS
(1817-1895)

Few Americans of his epoch possessed the natural gifts, the commitment to humanity, and the political idealism of Frederick Douglass. The comparison and coupling of him with Lincoln, which has been traditional in Black American thought, does honor to them both and to the land they both loved. The resemblances are surprisingly great. They each rose from deprivation, achieved a broad knowledge of man and his history, and used that knowledge in the service of their country, clothing their thoughts in English prose of the highest quality.

Douglass was born on the eastern shore of Maryland on a plantation. It was a stroke of fortune that sent him to Baltimore at the age of eight, providing him during the seven years he spent there with the opportunity of seeing and observing life, albeit as a slave, in a major city. He was subsequently forced back into rural slavery and was the subject of particularly cruel treatment. Eventually he was allowed to return to Baltimore, and to work in a shipyard. From there he managed his escape to the North.

Douglass became the most famous of fugitive slaves upon the publication of his *Narrative of the Life of Frederick Douglass* (1845). Following his escape, he had settled in New Bedford, Massachusetts where he worked in a whale-oil refinery. An avid reader, he made an impressive speech before an antislavery rally and was shortly after employed by the Massachusetts Anti-Slavery Society as a lecturer. His *Narrative* was a natural consequence of this activity. Douglass went to England, after the publication of the *Narrative*, and remained there a year and a half lecturing throughout the British Isles with great success.

On his return Douglass moved his family to Rochester, New York and in the fall of 1847, aided by funds that had been entrusted to him in England, began the publication of *The North Star*, a weekly abolitionist journal, with himself and Martin R. Delany as editors. The enterprise endured until 1860, the name having been changed to *Frederick Dou-glass' Paper* in 1851. In 1850 Douglass began to publish *Dou-glass' Monthly* which he continued to write and edit until 1863.

By the end of the reactionary 1850's, even the strongly anti-emigrationist Douglass was moved to consider the prospects for Black American colonization in Haiti and had booked passage for an inspection tour. The election of Lincoln and the triumph of the Republican Party had done nothing to counter his gloom. In *Douglass' Monthly* for May, 1861, we read:

> At this writing, we are on the eve of starting for a visit of a few weeks to Haiti...
>
> The steamer secured for the voyage is to sail from New Haven, Connecticut, about the 25th of April, and will, if all be well, reach Port-au-Prince by the first of May.
>
> Though never formally solicited by an organized body of our people to acquire information which may be useful to those who are looking to that country for a home, we had been repeatedly urged to do so by individuals of the highest character and respectability. Without at all discrediting the statements of others, we have desired to see for ourselves.
>
> . . . .
>
> Since this article upon Haiti was put in type, we find ourselves in circumstances which induce us to forego our much desired trip to Haiti, for the present. The last ten days have made a tremendous revolution in all things pertaining to the possible future of the colored people in the United States. We shall stay here and watch the current of events, and serve the cause of freedom and humanity in any way that shall be open to us during the struggle now going on between the slave power and the government.

Douglass immediately turned his pen to the composing of two masterly pieces which appear also in the same issue of *Douglass' Monthly*, the "Fall of Sumter" and "Nemesis".

Douglass in his prescience saw that the Civil War would ultimately mean the end of American slavery, but he was impatient with the apparent slow pace of Lincoln in articulating this. He found himself frequently in opposition to Lincoln's policies and actions, but the logic of events placed him among the martyred President's sincerest mourners at the end of the war.

Douglass's writings during the war are among the most eloquent in the literature of the Civil War and illuminate its fundamental issues. His later career in politics and diplomacy, as statesman and race leader, is much less well-known than it should be. Benjamin Quarles' biography, *Frederick Douglass* (1948; 1968) is the best survey. *The Life and Writings of Frederick Douglass* (1952) by Philip S. Foner is invaluable.

1861
THE NEW PRESIDENT

Of one satisfaction, one ray of hope amid the darkness of the passing hour, and the reign of doubt and distraction, we may now safely begin to assure ourselves. Before we can again speak to our respected readers through this channel, the long desired 4th of March will have come, Lincoln will be inaugurated at Washington, and his policy declared. Whatever that policy may be towards the seceded and confederated States, whatever it may be towards Slavery, the ruling cause of our nation's troubles, it will at least be a great relief to know it, to rejoice in and defend it, if right, and to make war upon it if wrong. To know what it is, is now the main thing. If he is going to abandon the principles upon which he was elected, compliment the South for being wrong, and censure himself and friends for being right, court treason and curse loyalty, desert his friends and cleave to his enemies, turn his back on the cause of Freedom and give new guarantees to the system of Slavery--whatever policy, whether of peace or war, or neither, it will be a vast gain at least to know what it is. Much of the present trouble is owing to the doubt and suspense caused by the shuffling, do-nothing policy of Mr. Buchanan.--No man has been able to tell an hour before hand what to expect from that source. However well disposed he may have been, the slaveholding thieves and traitors about him have had him under their thumb from the beginning until now. Every man who wishes well to the country will rejoice at his outgoing, and feel that though he leaves the body politic weakened, and the nation's Constitution shattered, his out going, like the subsidence of some pestilence walking in darkness, is a cause for devout thanksgiving. A month longer in power, and perhaps, the epitaph of the American Republic might, if it may not now, be written, and its death consigned to the mouldy tombs of once great, but now extinct, nations.

While not at all too confident of the incorruptible purity of the new President, (for we remember the atmosphere of Washington, and the subtle devices of the enemies of Liberty, among whom he has now gone,) still we hope something from him. His stately silence during these last tumultuous and stormy three months, his stern refusal thus far to commit himself to any of the much advocated schemes of compromise, his refusal to have concessions extorted from him under the terror instituted by thievish conspirators and traitors, the cool and circumspect character of his replies to the various speeches, some delicate, appropriate, and sensible, and some rudely curious and prying, made to him during his circuitous route to Washington, the modesty with which he has pushed aside the various compliments bestowed upon him, all prove that he has not won deceitfully the title of Honest Old Abe. True, indeed, he has made no immoderate promises to the cause of freedom. His party has made none. But what were small in Chicago, will be found large at Washington, and what were moderate in the canvass, have become much augmented by the frowning difficulties since flung in the way of their accomplishment by the movement for disunion. It was a small thing six months ago to say, as the Republican party did say, that the Union shall be preserved, but events have now transpired, which make this a very solemn matter to reduce to practice. Most things are easier said than done, and this thing belongs to the general rule. That declaration in the Chicago platform implied that those who uttered it, believed that this Government possesses ample power for its own preservation, and that those powers should be in their hands, faithfully wielded for that purpose. This, then, is the first question: Will Mr. Lincoln boldly grapple with the monster of Disunion, and bring down his proud looks?

Will he call upon the haughty slave masters, who have risen in arms, to break up the Government, to lay down those arms, and return to loyalty, or meet the doom of traitors and rebels? He must do this, or do worse.--He must do this, or consent to be the despised representative of a defied and humbled Government. He must do this, or own that party platforms are the merest devices of scheming politicians to cheat the people, and to enable them to crawl up to place and power. He must do this, or compromise the fundamental principle upon which he was elected, to wit, the right and duty of Congress to prohibit the farther extension of Slavery. Will he compromise? Time and events will soon answer this question. For the present, there is much reason to believe that he will not consent to any compromise which will violate the principle upon which he was elected; and since none which does not utterly trample upon that principle can be accepted by the South, we have a double assurance that there will be no compromise, and that the contest must now be decided, and decided forever, which of the two, Freedom or Slavery, shall give law to this Republic, Let the conflict come, and God speed the Right, must be the wish of every true-hearted American, as well as of that of an onlooking world.

THE FALL OF SUMTER

As a friend of freedom, earnestly laboring for the abolition of slavery, we have no tears to shed, no lamentations to make over the fall of Fort Sumter. By that event, one danger which threatened the cause of the American slave has been greatly diminished. Through many long and weary months, the American people have been on the mountain with the wily tempter, and have been liable at any moment of weakness to grant a new lease of life to slavery. The whole power of the Northern pro-slavery press, combined with the commercial and manufacturing interests of the country, has been earnestly endeavoring to purchase peace and prosperity for the North by granting the most demoralizing concessions to the insatiate Slave Power. This has been our greatest danger. The attack upon Fort Sumter bids fair to put an end to this cowardly, base and unprincipled truckling. To our thinking, the damage done to Fort Sumter is nothing in comparison with that done to the secession cause. The hail and fire of its terrible batteries has killed its friends and spared its enemies. Anderson lives, but where are the champions of concession at the North? The traitor lips are pale and silent.

While secession confined its war operation to braggart threats, pompous declarations, exciting telegrams, stealing arms, planting liberty poles, wearing cockades, and displaying palmetto and rattlesnake flags, it exercised a potent influence over the public mind, and held the arm of the Government paralyzed. It commanded the artillery of a thousand cannon. But the secessionists themselves have now "smashed" up these magnificent machines, and have spiked their own most efficient guns. They have completely shot off the legs of all trimmers and compromisers, and compelled everybody to elect between patriotic fidelity and pro-slavery treason.

For this consummation we have watched and wished with fear and trembling. God be praised! that it has come at last. We should have been glad if the North, of its own proper virtue, had given this *quietus* to doubt and vacillation. She did not do it, and perhaps it is best that she did not. What her negative wisdom withheld has now come to us through the vengeance and rashness of slaveholders. Another instance of the wrath of man working out the purposes and praise of eternal goodness!

Had Mr. Jefferson Davis continued to allow Major Anderson, with his harmless garrison, to receive his daily bread from the markets of Charleston, or even permitted the Government at Washington to feed his men, the arm of the nation might have slept on, and the South might have got the most extravagant concessions to its pet monster, slavery. Every Personal Liberty Bill might have been swept from the statute books of the North, and every trembling fugitive hunted by Northern bloodhounds from his hiding place to save the Union. Already the hateful reaction had begun. Chicago and Cleveland, headquarters of Republicanism, had both betrayed innocent blood, while "down with Abolition" was fast becoming the cry of the mob on the one hand, and clergy on the other. The color of the Negro, always hated, was fast becoming more hated, and the few rights and liberties enjoyed by the free colored citizen were threatened. But now, thanks to the reckless impetuosity of the dealers in the bodies and souls of men, their attack upon Sumter has done much to arrest this retrograde and cowardly movement, and has raised the question as to the wisdom of thus pampering treason. Our rulers were ready enough to sacrifice the Negro to the Union so long as there was any hope of saving the Union by that means. The attack upon Sumter, and other movements on the part of the cotton lords of the lash, have about convinced them that the insatiate slaveholders not only mean the peace and safety of slavery, but to make themselves masters of the Republic. It is not merely a war for slavery, but it is a war for slavery dominion. There are points in which different nations excel.--England is mighty on the land, but mightier on the water. The slaveholders have always surpassed the North in the matter of party politics. In the arts of persuasion, the management of men, in tact and address, they have ever been remarkably successful. Accustomed to rule over slaves, and to assume the airs of vaunted superiority, they easily intimidate the timid, over-awe the servile, while they artfully cultivate the respect and regard of the brave and fearless.

It remains to be seen whether they have acted wisely in transferring the controversy with the North from the halls of diplomacy, to the field of battle. They were not forced to the measure. The Government at Washington stood waiting to be gracious. It treated treason in its embryo form, merely as an *"eccentricity,"* which a few months would probably cure. They had no purpose to resort to the straight jacket. To some of us there was far too little importance attached to the slaveholding movement by the Government at Washington. But all is changed now. The Government is active, and the people aroused. Again, we say, out of a full heart, and on behalf of our enslaved and bleeding brothers and sisters, thank God! The slaveholders themselves have saved our cause from ruin! They have exposed the throat of slavery to the keen knife of liberty, and have given a chance to all the righteous forces of the nation to deal a death-blow to the monster evil of the nineteenth century--FRIENDS OF FREEDOM! BE UP AND DOING--NOW IS YOUR TIME. The tyrant's extremity is your opportunity! Let the long crushed bondman arise and in this auspicious moment, snatch back the liberty of which he has been so long robbed and despoiled. Now is the day, and now is the hour!

Is it said that we exult in rebellion? We repel the allegation as a slander. Every pulsation of our heart is with the legitimate American Government, in its determination to suppress and put down this slaveholding rebellion. The *Stars and Stripes* are now the symbols of liberty. The Eagle that we left last month something like as good as dead, has revived again, and screams terror in the ears of the slaveholding rebels. None but the worst of traitors can now desire victory for any flag but that of the old Confederacy. He who faithfully works to put down a rebellion undertaken and carried out for the extension and perpetuity of slavery, performs an anti-slavery work. Even disunion Abolitionists, who have believed that the dissolution of the Union would be the dissolution of slavery, will, we have no doubt, rejoice in the success of the Government at Washington, in suppressing and putting down this slave holding rebellion.

NEMESIS

At last our proud Republic is overtaken. Our National Sin has found us out. The National Head is bowed down, and our face is mantled with shame and confusion. No foreign arm is made bare for our chastisement. No distant monarch, offended at our freedom and prosperity, has plotted our destruction; no envious tyrant has prepared for our necks his oppressive yoke. Slavery has done it all. Our enemies are those of our own household. It is civil war, the worst of all wars, that has unveiled its savage and wrinkled front amongst us. During the last twenty years and more, we have as a nation been forging a bolt for our own national destruction, collecting and augmenting the fuel that now threatens to wrap the nation in its malignant and furious flames. We have sown the wind, only to reap the whirlwind. Against argument, against all manner of appeal and remonstrances coming up from the warm and merciful heart of humanity, we have gone on like the oppressors of Egypt, hardening our hearts and increasing the burdens of the American slave, and strengthening the arm of his guilty master, till now, in the pride of his giant power, that master is emboldened to lift rebellious arms against the very majesty of the law, and defy the power of the Government itself. In vain have we plunged our souls into new and unfathomed depths of sin, to conciliate the favor and secure the loyalty of the slaveholding class. We have hated and persecuted the negro; we have scourged him out of the temple of justice by the Dred Scott decision, we have shot and hanged his friends at Harper's Ferry; we have enacted laws for his further degradation, and even to expel him from the borders of some of our States; we have joined in the infernal chase to hunt him down like a beast, and fling him into the hell of slavery; we have repealed and trampled upon laws designed to prevent the spread of slavery, and in a thousand ways given our strength, our moral and political influence to increase the power and ascendency of slavery over all departments of Government; and now, as our reward, this slaveholding power comes with sword, gun and cannon to take the life of the nation and overthrow the great American Government. Verily, they have their reward. The power given to crush the negro now overwhelms the white man. The Republic has put one end of the chain upon the ankle of the bondman, and the other end about its own neck. They have been planting tyrants, and are now getting a harvest of civil war and anarchy. The land is now to weep and howl, amid ten thousand desolations brought upon it by the sins of two centuries against millions on both sides of eternity. Could we write as with lightning, and speak as with the voice of thunder, we should write and cry to the nation, REPENT, BREAK EVERY YOKE, LET THE OPPRESSED GO FREE, FOR HEREIN ALONE IS DELIVERANCE AND SAFETY! It is not too late. The moment is propitious, and we may even yet escape the complete vengeance of the threatened wrath and fury, whose balls of fire are already dropping to consume us. Now is the time to put an end to the source of all our present national calamities. Now is the time to change the cry of vengeance long sent up from the tasked and toiling bondman, into a grateful prayer for the peace and safety of the Government. Slaveholders have in their madness invited armed abolition to march to the deliverance of the slave. They have furnished the occasion, and bound up the fate of the Republic and that of the slave in the same bundle, and the one and the other must survive or perish together. Any attempt now to separate the freedom of the slave from the victory of the Government over slaveholding rebels and traitors; any attempt to secure peace to the whites while leaving the blacks in chains; any attempt to heal the wounds of the Republic, while the deadly virus of slavery is left to poison the blood, will be labor lost. The American people and the Government at Washington may refuse to recognize it for a time; but the "inexorable logic of events" will force it upon them in the end; that the war now being waged in this land is a war for and against slavery; and that it can never be effectually put down till one or the other of these vital forces is completely destroyed. The irrepressible conflict, long confined to words and votes, is now to be carried by bayonets and bullets, and may God defend the right!

A BLACK HERO

While our Government still refuses to acknowledge the just claims of the negro, and takes all possible pains to assure "our Southern brethren" that it does not intend to interfere in any way with this kind of property; while the assistance of colored citizens in suppressing the slaveholders' rebellion is peremptorily and insultingly declined; while even Republicans still deny and reject their natural allies and unite with pro-slavery Democrats in recognizing their alleged inferiority--it has happened that one of the most daring and heroic deeds--one which will be likely to inflict the heaviest blow upon the piratical enterprizes of Jeff. Davis--has been struck by an obscure negro. All know the story of this achievement: The schooner "S.J. Waring," bound to Montevideo, having on board a valuable cargo, when scarcely beyond the waters of New York, was captured by the privateer "JEFF. DAVIS". The captain and the mate of the Waring were sent home, and a prize crew, consisting of five men, were put on board of her. Three of the original crew, two seamen and William Tillman, the colored steward, besides a passenger, were retained. Tillman, our hero, very soon ascertained from conversations which he was not intended to hear, that the vessel was to be taken to Charleston, and that he himself was to be sold as a slave. The pirates had chuckled over their last item of their good luck; but, unfortunately for them, they had a man to deal with, one whose brave heart and nerves of steel stood athwart their infernal purposes.

Tillman took an early occasion to make known to his fellow prisoners the devilish purpose of the pirates, and declared that they should never succeed in getting him to Charleston alive. Only one of his fellow prisoners, a German named Stedding, consented to take part in the dangerous task of recapturing the vessel. He watched anxiously for a favorable moment to slay the pirates and gain his freedom. So vigilant, however, were the prize captain and crew, that it was not until they had nearly reached the waters of Charleston, in the very jaws of a fate which he dreaded more than death, that an opportunity offered. They were within fifty miles of Charleston; night and sleep had come down upon them--for even pirates have to sleep. Stedding, the German, discovered that now was the time, and passing the word to Tillman, the latter began his fearful work--killing the pirate captain, mate and second mate, and thus making himself master of the ship with no other weapon, than a common hatchet, and doing his work so well that the whole was accomplished in seven minutes, including the giving the bodies of the pirates to the sharks. The other two men were secured, but afterwards released on condition that they would help to work the ship back to New York. Here was a grand difficulty, even after the essential had been accomplished, one before which a man less hopeful and brave than Tillman would have faltered. Neither himself nor his companions possessed any knowledge of navigation, and they might have fallen upon shores quite as unfriendly as those from which they were escaping, or they might have been overtaken by pirates as savage as those whose bodies they had given to the waves. But, despite possible shipwreck and death, they managed safely to reach New York, Tillman humorously remarking that he came home as captain of the vessel in which he went out as steward.

When we consider all the circumstances of this transaction, we cannot fail to perceive in Tillman a degree of personal valor and presence of mind equal to those displayed by the boldest deeds recorded in history. The soldier who marches to the battle field with all inspirations of numbers, music, popular applause, "the pomp and circumstance of glorious war," is brave; but he who, like Tillman, has no one to share danger with him, in whose surroundings there is nothing to steel his arm or fire his heart, who has to draw from his own bosom the stern confidence required for the performance of the task of man-slaying, is braver. The soldier knows that even in case of defeat there are stronger probabilities in his favor than against him. Tillman, on the other side, was almost alone against five, and well knew that if he failed, an excruciating death would be the consequence. He was on the perilous ocean, at the mercy of the winds and waves, with whose powers he was as well acquainted as he was conscious of his inability by skill and knowledge to defy them. How much nerve, moreover, does it not require in a man unaccustomed to bloodshed, a stranger to the sights and scenes of the battle field, to strike thus for liberty! Tillman is described as anything but a saguinary man. His whole conduct in sparing the lives of part of the pirate crew proves that the description of his good-natured and gentle disposition is no exaggeration of his virtures. Love of liberty alone inspired him and supported him, as it had inspired Denmark Vesey, Nathaniel Turner, Madison Washington, Toussaint L'Ouverture, Shields Green, Copeland, and other negro heroes before him, and he walked to his work of self-deliverance with a step as firm and dauntless as the noblest Roman of them all. Well done for Tillman! The N.Y. *Tribune* well says of him, that the nation is indebted to him for the first vindication of its honor on the sea. When will this nation cease to disparage the negro race? When will they become sensible of the force of this irresistible Tillman argument?

CAST OFF THE MILL STONE

We are determined that our readers shall have line upon line and precept upon precept. Ours is only one humble voice; but such as it is, we give it freely to our country, and to the cause of humanity. That honesty is the best policy, we all profess to believe, though our practice may often contradict the proverb. The present policy of our Government is evidently to put down the slaveholding rebellion, and at the same time protect and preserve slavery. This policy hangs like a millstone about the neck of our people. It carries disorder to the very sources of our national activities. Weakness, faint heartedness and inefficiency is the natural result. The mental and moral machinery of mankind cannot long withstand such disorder without serious damage. This policy offends reason, wounds the sensibilities, and shocks the moral sentiments of men. It forces upon us inconsequent conclusions and painful contradictions, while the plain path of duty is obscured and thronged with multiplying difficulties. Let us look this slavery-preserving policy squarely in the face, and search it thoroughly.

Can the friends of that policy tell us why this should not be an abolition war? Is not abolition plainly forced upon the nation as a necessity of national existence? Are not the rebels determined to make the war on their part a war for the utter destruction of liberty and the complete mastery of slavery over every other right and interest in the land?--And is not an abolition war on our part the natural and logical answer to be made to the rebels? We all know it is. But it is said that for the Governbment to adopt the abolition policy, would involve the loss of the support of the Union men of the Border Slave States. Grant it, and what is such friendship worth? We are stronger without than with such friendship. It arms the enemy, while it disarms its friends. The fact is indisputable, that so long as slavery is respected and protected by our Government, the slaveholders can carry on the rebellion, and no longer.--Slavery is the stomach of the rebellion. The bread that feeds the rebel army, the cotton that clothes them, and the money that arms them and keeps them supplied with powder and bullets, come from the slaves, who, if consulted as to the use which should be made of their hard earnings, would say, give it to the bottom of the sea rather than do with it this mischief. Strike here, cut off the connection between the fighting master and the working slave, and you at once put an end to this rebellion, because you destroy that which feeds, clothes and arms it. Shall this not be done, because we shall offend the Union men in the border states?

But we have good reasons for believing that it would not offend them. The great mass of Union men in all those Border States are intelligently so. They are men who set a higher value upon the Union than upon slavery. In many instances, they recognize slavery as the thing of all others the most degrading to labor and oppressive towards them. They dare not say so now; but let the government say the word, and even they would unite in sending the vile thing to its grave, and rejoice at the opportunity. Such of them as love slavery better than their country are not now, and have never been, friends of the Union. They belong to the destestable class who do the work of enemies in the garb of friendship, and it would be a real gain to get rid of them. Then look at slavery itself--what good thing has it done that it should be allowed to survive a rebellion of its own creation? Why should the nation pour out its blood and lavish its treasure by the million, consent to protect and preserve the guilty cause of all its troubles? The answer returned to these questions is, that the Constitution does not allow of the exercise of such power. As if this were a time to talk of constitutional power! When a man is well, it would be mayhem to cut off his arm. It would be unconstitutional to do so. But if the arm were shattered and mortifying, it would be quite unconstitutional and criminal not to cut it off. The case is precisely so with Governments. The grand object, end and aim of Government is the preservation of society, and from nothing worse than anarchy. When Governments, through the ordinary channels of civil law, are unable to secure this end, they are thrown back upon military law, and for the time may set aside the civil law precisely to the extent which it may be necessary to do so in order to accomplish the grand object for which Governments are instituted among men. The power, therefore, to abolish slavery is within the objects sought by the Constitution. But if every letter and syllable of the Constitution were a prohibition of abolition, yet if the life of the nation required it, we should be bound by the Constitution to abolish it, because there can be no interest superior to existence and preservation.

A very palpable evil involved in the policy of leaving slavery untouched, is that it holds out the idea that we are, in the end, to be treated to another compromise, and the old virus left to heal over, only to fester deeper, and break out more violently again some time not far distant, perhaps, to the utter destruction of the Government for which the people are now spilling their blood and spending their money. If we are to have a compromise and a settlement, why protract the war and prolong the bloodshed? Is it said that no compromise is contemplated? It may be so; but while slavery is admitted to have any right to be protected by our army, it will be impossible not to recognize its right to be protected by Congress; and already we see a leading Republican journal in this State urging the acceptance of the Crittenden Compromise, by which the system of slavery shall be established in all territory south of 36º 30 min. of north latitude. The way to put an end to any farther sham compromises is to put an end to the hateful thing itself, which is the subject of them; and whatever the slave-driving rebels may say, the plain people of the country will accept the proposition of emancipation with the utmost satisfaction.

Another evil of the policy of protecting and preserving slavery, is that it deprives us of the important aid which might be rendered to the Govenment by the four million slaves. These people are repelled by our slaveholding policy. They have their hopes of deliverance from bondage destroyed. They hesitate now; but if our policy is pursued, they will not need to be compelled by Jefferson Davis to fight against us. They will do it from choice, and with a will--deeming it better

"To endure those ills they have,
Than fly to others they know not of."

If they must remain slaves, they would rather fight for than against the masters which we of the North mean to compel them to serve. Who can blame them? They are men, and like men governed by their interests. They are capable of love and hate. They can be friends, and they can be foes. The policy of our Government serves to make them our foes, when it should endeavor by all means to make them our friends and allies.

A third evil of this policy, is the chilling effect it exerts upon the moral sentiment of mankind. Vast is the power of the sympathy of the civilized world. Daniel Webster once said that it was more powerful than "lightning, whirlwind or earthquake."--This vast and invisible power is now evidently not with us. On the briny wing of every eastern gale there comes a depressing chill to the North, while to the South it brings encouragement and hope. Our policy gives the rebels the advantage of seeming to be merely fighting for the right to govern themselves. We divest the war on our part of all those grand elements of progress and philanthropy that naturally win the hearts and command the reverence of all men, and allow it to assume the form of a meaningless display of brute force. The idea that people have a right to govern themselves, whether true or false, has a very strong hold upon the minds of men throughout the world. They naturally side with those who assert this right by force in any part of the world. The example of America has done much to impress this idea upon mankind, and the growing sympathy of the world seems now far more likely to bring some Lafayette with an army of twenty thousand men to aid the rebels, then some Garibaldi to aid the Government in suppressing the rebels. Our slaveholding, slave-catching and slave insurrection policy gives to the South the sympathy which would naturally and certainly flow towards us, and which would be mightier than lightning, whirlwind or earthquake in extinguishing the flames of this momentous slaveholding war.

Another evil arising from this mischievous slaveholding policy, is that it invites the interference of other Governments with our blockade. Break up the blockade, and the war is ended, and the rebels are victorious, and the South is independent. It is already evident that France and England will not long endure a war whose only effect is to starve thousands of their people, slaughter thousands of our own, and sink millions of money. If they are to suffer with us, they will demand--and they have a perfect right to demand--that something shall be gained to the cause of humanity and civilization. Let the war be made an abolition war, and no statesman in England or France would dare even, if inclined, to propose any disturbance of the blockade. Make this an abolition war, and you at once unite the world against the rebels, and in favor of the Government.

1862
WHAT SHALL BE DONE WITH THE SLAVES IF EMANCIPATED?

It is curious to observe, at this juncture, when the existence of slavery is threatened by an aroused nation, when national necessity is combining with an enlightened sense of justice to put away the huge abomination forever, that the enemies of human liberty are resorting to all the old and ten thousand times refuted objections to emancipation with which they confronted the abolition movement twenty-five years ago. Like the one stated above, these pro-slavery objections have their power mainly in the slavery-engendered prejudice, which every where pervades the country. Like all other great transgressions of the law of eternal rectitude, slavery thus produces an element in the popular and depraved moral sentiment favorable to its own existence. These objections are often urged with a show of sincere solicitude for the welfare of the slaves themselves. It is said, what will you do with them? they can't take care of themselves; they would all come to the North; they would not work; they would become a burden upon the State, and a blot upon society; they'd cut their masters' throats; they would cheapen labor, and crowd out the poor white laborer from employment; their former masters would not employ them, and they would necessarily become vagrants, paupers and criminals, over-running all our alms houses, jails and prisons. The laboring classes among the whites would come in bitter conflict with them in all the avenues of labor, and regarding them as occupying places and filling positions which should be occupied and filled by white men; a fierce war of races would be the inevitable consequene, and the black race would, of course, (being the weaker,) be exterminated. In view of this frightful, though happily somewhat contradictory picture, the question is asked, and pressed with a great show of earnestness at this momentous crisis of our nation's history, What shall be done with the four million slaves if they are emancipated?

This question has been answered, and can be answered in many ways. Primarily, it is a question less for man than for God--less for human intellect than for the laws of nature to solve. It assumes that nature has erred; that the law of liberty is a mistake; that freedom, though a natural want of the human soul, can only be enjoyed at the expense of human welfare, and that men are better off in slavery than they would or could be in freedom; that slavery is the natural order of human relations, and that liberty is an experiment. What shall be done with them?

Our answer is, do nothing with them; mind your business, and let them mind theirs. Your *doing* with them is their greatest misfortune. They have been undone by your doings, and all they now ask, and really have need of at your hands, is just to let them alone. They suffer by every interference, and succeed best by being let alone. The Negro should have been let alone in Africa-- let alone when the pirates and robbers offered him for sale in our Christian slave markets--(more cruel and inhuman than the Mohammedan slave markets)--let alone by courts, judges, politicians, legislators and slave-drivers--let alone altogether, and assured that they were thus to be let alone forever, and that they must now make their own way in the world, just the same as any and every other variety of the human family. As colored men, we only ask to be allowed to *do* with ourseves, subject only to the same great laws for the welfare of human society which apply to other men, Jews, Gentiles, Barbarian, Sythian. Let us stand upon our own legs, work with our own hands, and eat bread in the sweat of our own brows. When you, our white fellow-countrymen, have attempted to do anything for us, it has generally been to deprive us of some right, power or privilege which you yourselves would die before you would submit to have taken from you. When the planters of the West Indies used to attempt to puzzle the pure-minded Wilberforce with the question, How shall we get rid of slavery? his simple answer was, "quit stealing." In like manner, we answer those who are perpetually puzzling their brains with questions as to what shall be done with the negro, "let him alone and mind your own business." If you see him plowing in the open field leveling the forest, at work with a spade, a rake, a hoe, a pick-axe or a bill--let him alone; he has a right to work. If you see him on his way to school, with spelling book, geography and arithmetic in his hands--let him alone. Don't shut the door in his face, nor bolt your gates against him; he has a right to learn--let him alone. Don't pass laws to degrade him. If he has a ballot in his hand, and is on his way to the ballot-box to deposit his vote for the man whom he thinks will most justly and wisely administer the Government which has the power of life and death over him, as well as others--let him *alone*; his right of choice as much deserves respect and protection as your own. If you see him on his way to church, exercising religious liberty in accordance with this or that religious persuasion--let him alone.--Don't meddle with him, nor trouble yourselves with any questions as to what shall be

The great majority of human duties are of this negative character. If men were born in need of crutches, instead of having legs, the fact would be otherwise. We should then be in need of help, and would require outside aid; but according to the wiser and better arrangement of nature, our duty is done better by not hindering than by helping our fellowmen; or, in other words, the best way to help them is just to let them help themselves.

We would not for one moment check the outgrowth of any benevolent concern for the future welfare of the colored race in America or elsewhere; but in the name of reason and religion, we earnestly plead for justice before all else. Benevolence with justice is harmonious and beautiful; but benevolence without justice is a mockery. Let the American people, who have thus far only kept the colored race staggering between partial philanthropy and cruel force, be induced to try what virtue there is in justice. First pure, then peaceable--first just, then generous.--The sum of the black man's misfortunes and calamities are just here: He is everywhere treated as an exception to all the general rules which should operate in the relations of other men. He is literally scourged beyond the beneficent range of truth and justice.--With all the purifying and liberalizing power of the Christian religion, teaching, as it does, meekness, gentleness, brotherly kindness, those who profess it have not yet even approached the position of treating the black man as an equal man and a brother. The few who have thus far risen to this requirement, both of reason and religion, are stigmatized as fanatics and enthusiasts.

What shall be done with the negro if emancipated? Deal justly with him. He is a human being, capable of judging between good and evil, right and wrong, liberty and slavery, and is as much a subject of law as any other man; therefore, deal justly with him. He is, like other men, sensible of the motives of reward and punishment. Give him wages for his work, and let hunger pinch him if he don't work. He knows the difference between fullness and famine, plenty and scarcity. "But will he work?" Why should he not? He is used to it, and is not afraid of it. His hands are already hardened by toil, and he has no dreams of ever getting a living by any other means than by hard work. But would you turn them all loose? Certainly! We are no better than our Creator. He has turned them loose, and why should not we?

But would you let them all stay here?--Why not? What better is *here* than *there*? Will they occupy more room as freemen than as slaves? Is the presence of a black freeman less agreeable than that of a black slave? Is an object of your injustice and cruelty a more ungrateful sight than one of your justice and benevolence? You have borne the one more than two hundred years--can't you bear the other long enough to try the experiment? "But would it be safe?" No good reason can be given why it would not be. There is much more reason for apprehensions from slavery than from freedom. Slavery provokes and justifies incendiarism, murder, robbery, assassination, and all manner of violence.-- But why not let them go off by themselves? That is a matter we would leave exclusively to themselves. Besides, when you, the American people, shall once do justice to the enslaved colored people, you will not want to get rid of them. Take away the motive which slavery supplies for getting rid of the free black people of the South, and there is not a single State, from Maryland to Texas, which would desire to be rid of its black people. Even with the obvious disadvantage to slavery, which such contact is, there is scarcely a slave State which could be carried for the unqualified expulsion of the free colored people. Efforts at such expulsion have been made in Maryland, Virginia, and South Carolina, and all have failed, just because the black man as a freeman is a useful member of society. To drive him away, and thus deprive the South of his labor, would be as absurd and monstrous as for a man to cut off his right arm, the better to enable himself to work.

There is one cheering aspect of this revival of the old and thread-bare objections to emancipation--it implies at least the presence of danger to the slave system. When slavery was assailed twenty-five years ago, the whole land took the alarm, and every species of argument and subterfuge was resorted to by the defenders of slavery. The mental activity was amazing; all sorts of excuses, political, economical, social, ethical, theological and ethnological, were coined into barricades against the advancing march of anti-slavery sentiment. The same activity now shows itself, but has added nothing new to the argument for slavery or against emancipation.-- When the accursed slave system shall once be abolished, and the negro, long cast out from the human family, and governed like a beast of burden, shall be gathered under the divine government of justice, liberty and humanity, men will be ashamed to remember that they were ever deluded by the flimsy nonsense which they have allowed themselves to urge against the freedom of the long enslaved millons of our land. That day is not far off.

"O hasten it in mercy, gracious Heaven!"

SERVICES OF COLORED MEN

The negro is the veritable Mark Tapley of this country. That most obliging good tempered character in "Martin Chuzzlewit," was not more determined to be jolly under severely unfavorable circumstances, than the negro is to "come out strong" in patriotism under every possible discouragement. The Government and people have both repelled with insult his offers of assistance, and have tried hard to convince him that they can get along without him; but he treats their coldness as ill judged, the result of ill temper, and owing to a feeling of false pride, which a considerable friend

is bound to disregard. The true history of this war will show
that the loyal army found no friends at the South so faithful,
active, and daring in their efforts to sustain the Government
as the negroes. It will be shown that they have been the
safest guides to our army and the best pilots to our navy, and
the most dutiful laborers on our fortifications, where they
have been permitted thus to serve. It is already known that
the tremendous slaughter of loyal soldiers at Pittsburgh
Landing, where our army was surprised and cut to pieces,
would have been prevented had the alarm given by a negro,
who had risked his life to give it, been taken. The same is
true of the destruction of the Maryland Regiment the other
day at Port Royal. Gen. Burnside, in the difficult task committed to him of feeling his way into the intricate rivers and
creeks of Virginia and North Carolina, has found no assistance among the so called loyal whites comparable in value
to that obtained from intelligent black men. The folly and
expense of marching an army to Manassas, after it had been
evacuated more than a week, would have been prevented
but for the contemptuous disregard of information conveyed
by the despised men of color. Negroes have repeatedly
threaded their way through the lines of the rebels exposing
themselves to bullets to convey important information to
the loyal army of the Potomac. Thousands of lives and millions of treasure might have been saved to the Government
if these services had been appreciated by Commanding Generals. It was a negro who struck the first terrible blow at rebel
privateering by killing the pirates and capturing the vessel,
and to-day there is no man of the same opportunity so ser-
viceable to the loyal army in South Carolina, as Robert
Smalls, the colored pilot. The whites of the South, rich and
poor, receive the loyal soldiers with sullen aversion, while
the blacks deem it their highest privilege to do them a service, although for doing so they have been delivered up by
ungrateful officers to their rebel masters to suffer stripes and
death.--They seem determined to deserve credit whether
they get it or not. Repeatedly have the colored people of the
north, by resolutions, and through the press, expressed their
desire to assist in the nation's extreme need, but they have
been rejected and their friends humbled. Nevertheless, they

have occasionally been permitted to load and fire a gun against the rebels, and when thus permitted they have performed their part with a will. They did so at Hatteras Inlet, and have done so in Col. Jennison's regiment in Missouri, and elsewhere.

Gen. Hunter is said to have organized a black brigade in South Carolina, but this terrible iron arm, more dreaded by the rebels than ten thousand men of any other color, is said to be disbanded by order from Washington just at the moment when the blow was most needed, and when it was about to be struck. Though thus repelled, and insulted, the Negro persists in his devotion to the Government, and will serve it with a pickaxe if he cannot with a pistol, a spade if he cannot with sword.

In all this the Negro is wise. He can see what wise men have failed to see, that however tortuous and dark may be the present conduct of the Government, by the essential nature of things, this war is a war between slavery and freedom, that whether our rulers know it or not, wish it not, they are striking a blow for the destruction of slavery. They know that the Rebel States are the slave States, and that the loyal States are the free States; from these broad premises, they are able to draw wise conclusions. They know that they have no friends at home, and that they may have them abroad. When a slave, we could discern at a glance, in a crowd of a thousand, the single man whose soul revolted at the deeds of slavery, and so can most slaves. The voice and manner of the northern soldier, despite all his efforts, it may be to disguise his true sentiment, tells the contrabands that he is their friend and that he recognizes their manhood. Thus it is that colored men flock, and will continue to flock to the loyal army, glad to serve that army in any and every way possible.

THE SLAVEHOLDERS' REBELLION.
A speech delivered on the 4th day of July, 1862, at Himrods Corners, Yates Co., N.Y.
Fellow Citizens:

Eighty-six years ago the fourth of July was consecrated and distinguished among all the days of the year as the birthday of American liberty and Independence. The fathers of the Republic recommended that this day be celebrated with joy and gladness by the whole American people, to their latest posterity. Probably not one of those fathers ever dreamed that this hallowed day could possibly be made to witness the strange and portentous Events now transpiring before our eyes, and which even now cast a cloud of more than midnight blackness over the face of the whole country. We are the observers of strange and fearful transactions.

Never was this national anniversary celebrated in circumstances more trying, more momentous, more solemn and perilous, than those by which this nation is now so strongly environed. We present to the world at this moment, the painful spectacle of a great nation, undergoing all the bitter pangs of a gigantic and bloody revolution. We are torn and rent asunder, we are desolated by large and powerful armies of our own kith and kin, converted into desperate and infuriated rebels and traitors, more savage, more fierce and brutal in their modes of warfare, than any recognized barbarians making no pretentions to civilization.

In the presence of this troubled and terrible state of the country, in the appalling jar and rumbling of this social Earthquake, when sorrow and sighing are heard throughout our widely extended borders, when the wise and brave men of the land are everywhere deeply and sadly contemplating this solemn crisis as one which may permanently decide the fate of the nation, I should greatly transgress the law of fitness, and violate my own feelings and yours, if I should on this occasion attempt to entertain you by delivering anything of the usual type of our 4th of July orations.

The hour is one for sobriety, thoughtfulness and stern truthfulness. When the house is on fire, when destruction is spreading its baleful wings everywhere, when helpless women and children are to be rescued from devouring flames, a true man can neither have ear nor heart for anything but the thrilling and heart-rending cry for help. Our country is now on fire. No man can now tell what the future will bring forth. The question now is whether this great Republic before it has reached a century from its birth, is to fall in the wake of unhappy Mexico, and become the constant theatre of civil war, or whether it shall become like old Spain, the mother of Mexico, and by folly and cruelty part with its renown among the nations of the earth, and spend the next seventy years in vainly attempting to regain what it has lost in the space of this one slaveholding rebellion.

Looking thus at the state of the country, I know of no better use to which I can put this sacred day, I know of no higher duty resting upon men, than to enforce my views and convictions, and especially to hold out to reprobation, the short sighted and ill judged, and inefficient modes adopted to suppress the rebels. The past may be dismissed with a single word. The claims of our fathers upon our memory, admiration and gratitude, are founded in the fact that they wisely, and bravely, and successfully met the crisis of their day. And if the men of this generation would deserve well of posterity they must like their fathers, discharge the duties and responsibilities of their age.

Men have strange notions nowadays as to the manner of showing their respect for the heroes of the past. They every where prefer the form to the substance, the seeming to the real.--One of our Generals, and some of our editors, seem to think that the fathers are honored by guarding a well, from which those fathers may have taken water, or the house in which they may have passed a single night, while our sick soldiers need pure water, and are dying in the open fields for water and shelter. This is not honoring, but dishonoring your noble dead. Nevertheless, I would not even in words do violence to the grand events, and thrilling associations, that gloriously cluster around the birth of our national independence. There is no need of any such violence. The thought of to-day and the work of to-day, are alike linked, and interlinked with the thought and work of the past. The conflict between liberty and slavery, between civilization and barbarism, between enlightened progress, and stolid indifference and inactivity is the same in all countries, in all ages, and among all peoples. Your fathers drew the sword for free and independent Government, Republican in its form, Democratic in its spirit; to be administered by officers duly elected by the free and unbought suffrages of the people, and the war of to-day on the part of the loyal north, the east and the west, is waged for the same grand and all commanding objects. We are only continuing the tremendous struggle, which your fathers and my fathers began eighty-six years ago. Thus identifying the present with the past, I propose to consider the great present question, uppermost and all absorbing in all minds and hearts throughout the land.

I shall speak to you of the origin, the nature, the objects of this war, the manner of conducting, and its possible and probable results.

ORIGIN OF THE WAR

It is hardly necessary at this very late day of this war, and in view of all the discussion through the press and on the platform which has transpired concerning it, to enter now upon any elaborate enquiry or explanation as to whence came this foul and guilty attempt to break up and destroy the national Government. All but the willfully blind or the malignantly traitorous, know and confess that this whole movement which now so largely distracts the country, and threatens ruin to the nation, has its root and its sap, its trunk and its branches, and the bloody fruit it bears only from the one source of all abounding abomination, and this is slavery. It has sprung out of a malign selfishness and a haughty and imperious pride which only the practice of the most hateful oppression and cruelty could generate and develop. No ordinary love of gain, no ordinary love of power, could have stirred up this terrible revolt.--The legitimate objects of property, such as houses, land, fruits of the earth, the products of art, science and invention, powerful as they are, could never have stirred and kindled this malignant flame, and set on fire this rebellious fury. The monster was brought to its birth by pride, lust and cruelty which could not brook the sober restraints of law, order and justice. The monster publishes its own parentage. Grim and hideous as this rebellion is, its shocking practices, digging up the bones of our dead soldiers slain in battle, making drinking vessels out of their skulls, drumsticks out of their arm bones, slaying our wounded soldiers on the field of carnage, when their gaping wounds appealed piteously for mercy, poisoning wells, firing upon unarmed men stamp it with all the horrid characteristics of the bloody and barbarous sytem and society from which it derived its life.

Of course you know, and I know that there have been and still are, in certain out of the way places here at the north, where rebels, in the smooth disguise of loyal men, do meet and promulgate a very opposite explanation of the origin of this war, and that grave attempts have been made to refute their absurd theories. I once heard Hon. Edward Everett entertain a large audience by a lengthy and altogether unnecessary argument to prove that the south did not revolt on account of the fishing bounty paid to northern fishermen, nor because of any inequalities or discrimination in the revenue laws. It was the Irishman's gun aimed at nothing and hitting it every time. Yet the audiene seemed pleased with the learning and skill or the orator, and I among the number, though I hope to avoid his bad example in the use of time.

There is however one false theory of the origin of the war to which a moment's reply may be properly given here. It is this. The abolitionists by their insane and unconstitutional attempt to abolish slavery have brought on the war. All that class of men who opposed what they were pleased to call coercion at the first, and a vigorous prosecution of the war at the present, charge the war directly to the abolitionists. In answer to this charge, I lay down this rule as a basis to which all candid men will assent. Whatever is said or done by any class of citizens, strictly in accordance with rights guaranteed by the Constitution, cannot be fairly charged as against the Union, or as inciting to a dissolution of the Union.

Now the slaveholders came into the Union with their eyes wide open, subject to a Constitution wherein the right to be abolitionists was sacredly guaranteed to all the people. They knew that slavery was to take its chance with all other evils against the power of free speech and national enlightenment. They came on board the national ship subject to these conditions, they signed the articles after having duly read them, and the fact that those rights, plainly written, have been exercised is no apology whatever for the slaveholder's mutiny and their attempt to lay piratical hands on the ship and its officers. When therefore I hear a man denouncing abolitionsts on account of the war, I know that I am listening to a man who either does not know what he is talking about, or to one who is a traitor in disguise.

THE NATURE OF THE REBELLION

There is something quite distinct and quite individual in the nature and character of this rebellion. In its motives and objects it stands entirely alone, in the annals of great social disturbances. Rebellion is no new thing under the sun. The best governments in the world are liable to these terrible social disorders. All countries have experienced them. Generally however, rebellions are quite respectable in the eyes of the world, and very properly so. They naturally command the sympathy of mankind, for generally they are on the side of progress. They would overthrow and remove some old and festering abuse not to be otherwise disposed of, and introduce a higher civilization, and a larger measure of liberty among men. But this rebellion is in no wise analogous to such.--The pronounced and damning peculiarity of the present rebellion, is found in the fact, that it was conceived, undertaken, planned, and perservered in, for the guilty purpose of handing down to the latest generations the accursed system of human bondage. Its leaders have plainly told us by words as well as by deeds, that they are fighting for slavery. They have been stirred to this perfidious revolt, by a certain deep and deadly hate, which they warmly cherish toward every possible contradiction of slavery whether found in theory or in practice. For this cause they hate free society, free schools, free states, free speech, the freedom asserted in the Declaration of Independence, and guaranteed in the Constitution.--Herein is the whole secret of the rebellion.--The plan is and was to withdraw the slave system from the hated light of liberty, and from the natural operations of free principles. While the slaveholders could hold the reins of government they could and did pervert the free principles of the Constitution to slavery, and could afford to continue in the union, but when they saw that they could no longer control the union as they had done for sixty years before, they appealed to the sword and struck for a government which should forever shut out all light from the southern conscience, and all hope of Emancipation from the southern slave. This rebellion therefore, has no point of comparison with that which has brought liberty to America, or with those of Europe, which have been undertaken from time to time, to throw off the galling yoke of despotism. It stands alone in its infamy.

Our slaveholding rebels with an impudence only belonging to themselves, have sometimes compared themselves to Washington, Jefferson, and the long list of worthies who led in the revolution of 1776, when in fact they would hang either of these men if they were now living, as traitors to slavery, because they each and all considered the system an evil.

THE CONFLICT UNAVOIDABLE

I hold that this conflict is the logical and inevitable result of a long and persistent course of national transgression. Once in a while you will meet with men who will tell you that this war ought to have been avoided. In telling you this, they only make the truth serve the place and perform the office of a lie. I too say that this war ought never to have taken place. The combustible material which has produced this terrible explosion ought long ago to have been destroyed.— For thirty years the abolitionists have earnestly sought to remove this guilty cause of our troubles. There was a time when this might have been done, and the nation set in permanent safety. Opportunities have not been wanting. They have passed by unimproved. They have sometimes been of a character to suggest the very work which might have saved us from all the dreadful calamities, the horrors and bloodshed, of this war. Events, powerful operators, have eloquently pleaded with the American people to put away the hateful slave system. For doing this great work we have had opportunities innumerable. One of these was presented upon the close of the war for Independence, the moral sentiment of the country was purified by that great struggle for national life. At that time slavery was young and small, the nation might have easily abolished it, and thus relieved itself forever of this alien element, the only disturbing and destructive force in our republican system of Government. Again there was another opportunity for putting away this evil in 1789, when we assembled to form the Consitution of the United States. At that time the anti-slavery sentiment was strong both in church and state, and many believed that by giving slavery no positive recognition in the Constitution and providing for the abolition of the slave trade, they had given slavery its death blow already. They made the great mistake of supposing that the existence of the slave trade was necessary to the existence of slavery, and having provided that the slave trade should cease, they flattered themselves that slavery itself must also speedily cease. They did not comprehend the radical character of the evil. Then again in 1819 the Missouri question gave us another opportunity to seal the doom of the slave system, by simply adhering to the early policy of the fathers and sternly refusing the admission of another State into the Union with a Constitution tolerating slavery. Had this been done in the case of Missouri, we should not now be cursed with this terrible rebellion. Slavery would have fallen into gradual decay. The moral sentiment of the country, instead of being vitiated as it is, would have been healthy and strong against the slave system. Political parties and politicians would not, as they have done since, courted the slave power for votes and thus increased the importance of slavery.

THE FIRST PALPABLE DEPARTURE FROM RIGHT POLICY

The date of the Missouri Compromise forms the beginning of that political current which has swept us on to this rebellion, and made the conflict unavoidable. From this dark date in our nation's history, there started forth a new political and social power. Until now slavery had been on its knees, only asking time to die in peace. But the Missouri Compromise gave it a new lease of life. It became at once a tremendous power. The line of thirty-six degrees, thirty minutes, at once stamped itself upon our national politics, our morals, manners, character and religion.--From this time there was a south side to everything American, and the country was at once subjected to the slave power, a power as restless and vigilant as the eye of an escaping murderer. We became under its sway an illogical nation. Pure and simple truth lost its attraction for us. We became a nation of Compromisers.

It is curious to remark the similarity of national to individual demoralization. A man sets out in life with honest principles and with high purposes inspired at the family hearthstone, and for a time steadily and scrupulously keeps them in view. But at last under the influence of some powerful temptation he is induced to violate his principles and push aside his sense of right. The water for the first moment is smooth footing. The broad flood, resistless as the power of fate, sweeps him onward, from bad to worse, he becomes more hardened, blind and shameless in his crimes till he is overtaken by dire calamity, and at last sinks to ruin. Precisely this has been the case with the American people. No people ever entered upon the pathway of nations, with higher and grander ideas of justice, liberty and humanity than ourselves. There are principles in the Declaration of Independence which would release every slave in the world and prepare the earth for a millenium of righteousness and peace.--But alas! we have seen that declaration intended to be viewed like some colossal statue at the loftiest altitude, by the broad eye of the whole world, meanly subjected to a microscopic examination and its glorious universal truths craftily perverted into seeming falsehoods. Instead of treating it, as it was intended to be treated, as a full and comprehensive declaration of the equal and sacred rights of mankind, our contemptible negro-hating and slaveholding critics have endeavored to turn it into absurdity by treating it as a declaration of the equality of man in his physical proportions and mental endowments. This gross and scandalous perversion of the true intents and meaning of the declaration did not long stand alone. It was soon followed by the heartless dogma, that the rights declared in that instrument did not apply to any but white men. The slave power at last succeeded, in getting this doctrine proclaimed from the bench of the Supreme Court of the United States. It was there decided that "all men" only means some men, and those white men. And all this in face of the fact, that white people only form one fifth of the whole human family--and that some who pass for white are nearly as black as your humble speaker. While all this was going on, lawyers, priests and politicians were at work upon national prejudice against the colored man.--They raised the cry and put it into the mouth of the ignorant, and vulgar and narrow minded, that "this is the white man's country," and other cries which readily catch the ear of the crowd. This popular method of dealing with an oppressed people has, while crushing the blacks, corrupted and demoralized the whites. It has cheered on the slave power, increased its pride and pretension, till ripe for the foulest treason against the life of the nation. Slavery, that was before the Missouri Compromise couchant, on its knees, asking meekly to be let alone within its own limits to die, became in a few years after rampant, throttling free speech, fighting friendly Indians, annexing Texas, warring with Mexico, kindling with malicious hand the fires of war and bloodshed on the virgin soil of Kansas, and finally threatening to pull down the pillars of the Republic, if you Northern men should dare vote in accordance with your constitutional and political convictions. You know the history; I will not dwell upon it. What I have said, will suffice to indicate the point at which began the downward career of the Republic. It will be seen that it began by bartering away an eternal principle of right for present peace. We undertook to make slavery the full equal of Liberty, and to place it on the same footing of political right with Liberty. It was by permitting the dishonor of the Declaration of Independence, denying the rights of human nature to the man of color, and by yielding to the extravagant pretensions set up by the slaveholder under the plausible color of State rights. In a word it was by reversing the wise and early policy of the nation, which was to confine slavery to its original limits, and thus leave the system to die out under the gradual operation of the principles of the Constitution and the spirit of the age. Ten years had not elapsed, after this compromise, when the demon disunion lifted its ugly front, in the shape of nullification. The plotters of this treason undertook the work of disunion at that time as an experiment. They took the tariff as the basis of action. The tariff was selected, not that it was the real object, but on the wisdom of the barber, who trains his green hands on wooden heads before allowing them to handle the razor on the faces of living men.

You know the rest. The experiment did not succeed. Those who attempted it were thirty years before their time. There was no Buchanan in the Presidential chair, and no Cobbs and Floyds in the Cabinet. Calhoun and his treasonable associates were promptly assured, on the highest authority, that their exit out of the Union was possible only by one way and that by way of the Gallows.--They were defeated, but not permanently.--They dropped the tariff and openly adopted slavery as the ostensible, as well as the real ground of disunion. After thirty years of persistent preparatory effort, they have been able under the fostering care of a traitorous Democratic President, to inaugurate at last this enormous rebellion. I will not stop here to pour out loyal indignation on that arch traitor, who while he could find power in the Constitution to hunt down innocent men all over the North for violating the thrice accursed fugitive slave Bill, could find no power in the Constitution to punish slaveholding traitors and rebels, bent upon the destruction of the Government. That bad old man is already receiving a taste of the punishment due to his crimes. To live amid all the horrors resulting from his treachery is of itself a terrible punishment. He lives without his country's respect. He lives a despised old man. He is no doubt still a traitor, but a traitor without power, a serpent without fangs, and in the agony of his torture and helplessness will probably welcome the moment which shall remove him from the fiery vision of a betrayed and half ruined country.

THE CONDUCT OF WAR

To-day we have to deal not with dead traitors, such as James Buchanan, Howell Cobb, Floyd, Thompson and others, but with a class of men incomparably more dangerous to the country. They are our weak, paltering and incompetent rulers in the Cabinet at Washington and our rebel worshipping Generals in the field, the men who sacrifice the brave loyal soldiers of the North by thousands, while refusing to employ the black man's arm in suppressing the rebels, for fear of exasperating these rebels; men who never interfere with the orders of Generals, unless those orders strike at slavery, the heart of the Rebellion. These are the men to whom we have a duty to discharge to-day, when the country is bleeding at every pore, and when disasters thick and terrible convert this national festal day, into a day of alarm and mourning. I do not underrate the power of the rebels, nor the vastness of the work required for suppressing them. Jefferson Davis is a powerful man, but Jefferson Davis has no such power to blast the hope and break down the strong heart of this nation, as that possessed and exercised by Abraham Lincoln. With twenty millions of men behind him, with wealth and resources at his command such as might pride the heart of the mightiest monarch of Europe, and with a cause which kindles in every true heart the fires of valor and patriotism, we have a right to hold Abraham Lincoln sternly responsible for any disaster or failure attending the suppression of this rebellion. I hold that the rebels can do us no serious harm, unless it is done through the culpable weakness, inbecility or unfaithfulness of those who are charged with the high duty of seeing that the Supreme Law of the land is everywhere enforced and obeyed. Common sense will confess that five millions ought not to be a match for twenty millions. I know of nothing in the mettle of the slaveholder which should make him superior in any of the elements of a warrior to an honest Northern man. One slaveholder ought not longer to be allowed to maintain the boast that he is equal to three Northern men; and yet that boast will not be entirely empty, if we allow those five millions much longer to thwart all our efforts to put them down. It will be most mortifyingly shown that after all our appliances, our inventive genius, our superior mechanical skill, our great industry, our muscular energy, our fertility in strategy, our vast powers of endurance, our overwhelming numbers, and admitted bravery, that the eight or ten rebel slave States, sparsely populated, and shut out from the world by our possession of the sea, are invincible to the arms of the densely populated and every way powerful twenty free States. I repeat, these rebels can do nothing against us, cannot harm a single hair of the national head, if the men at Washington, the President and Cabinet, and the commanding Generals in the field will but earnestly do their most obvious duty.--I repeat Jeff. Davis and his malignant slaveholding Republic, can do this union no harm except by the permission of the reigning powers at Washington.

I am quite aware that some who hear me will question the wisdom of any criticisms upon the conduct of this war at this time and will censure me for making them. I do not dread those censures. I have on many occasions, since the war began, held my breath when even the stones of the street would seem to cry out. I can do so no longer. I believe in the absence of martial law, a citizen may properly express an opinion as to the manner in which our Government has conducted, and is still conducting this war. I hold that it becomes this country, the men who have to shed their blood and pour out their wealth to sustain the Government at this crisis, to look very sharply into the movements of the men who have our destiny in their hands.

Theoretically this is a responsible Government. Practically it can be made the very reverse. Experience demonstrates that our safety as a nation depends upon holding every officer of the nation strictly responsible to the people for the faithful performance of duty. This war has developed among other bad tendencies, a tendency to shut our eyes to the mistakes and blunders of those in power. When the President has avowed a policy, sanctioned a measure, or commended a general, we have been told that his action must be treated as final. I scout this assumption. A doctrine more slavish and abject than this does not obtain under the walls of St. Peter. Even in the Rebel States, the Confederate Government is sharply critical, and Jefferson Davis is held to a rigid responsibility.--There is no reason of right or of sound policy for a different course towards the Federal Government. Our rulers are the agents of the people. They are fallible men. They need instruction from the people, and it is no evidence of a factious disposition that any man presumes to condemn a public measure if in his judgment that measure is opposed to the public good.

This is already an old war. The statesmanship at Washington with all its admitted wisdom and sagacity, utterly failed for a long time to comprehend the nature and extent of this rebellion. Mr. Lincoln and his Cabinet will have by and by to confess with many bitter regrets, that they have been equally blind and mistaken as to the true method of dealing with the rebels.--They have fought the rebels with the Olive branch. The people must teach them to fight them with the sword. They have sought to conciliate obedience. The people must teach them to compel obedience.

There are many men connected with the stupendous work of suppressing this slaveholding rebellion, and it is the right of the American people to keep a friendly and vigilant eye upon them all, but there are three men in the nation, from whose conduct the attention of the people should never be withdrawn: The first is President Lincoln, the Commander-in-chief of the army and navy. The single word of this man can set a million of armed men in motion: He can make and unmake generals, can lift up or cast down at will. The other two men are McClellan and Halleck.   Between these two men nearly a half a million of your brave and loyal sons are divided, the one on the Potomac and the other on the Mississippi. They are the two extended arms of the nation, stretched out to save the Union.

Are those two men loyal? are they in earnest? are they competent? We have a right, and it is our duty to make these inquiries, and report and act in reference to them according to the truth.

Whatever may be said of the loyalty or competency of Mc-Clellan, I am fully persuaded by his whole course that he is not in earnest against the rebels, that he is to-day, as heretofore, in war as in peace a real pro-slavery Democrat. His whole course proves that his sympathies are with the rebels, and that his ideas of the crisis make him unfit for the place he holds. He kept the army of the Potomac standing still on that river, marching and countermarching, giving show parades during six months. He checked and prevented every movement which was during that time proposed against the rebels East and West.

Bear in mind that fact that this is a slave-holding rebellion, bear in mind that slavery is the very soul and life of all the vigor which the rebels have thus far been able to throw into their daring attempt to overthrow and ruin this country. Bear in mind that in time of war, it is the right and duty of each belligerent to adopt that course which will strengthen himself and weaken his enemy.

Bear in mind also that nothing could more directly and powerfully tend to break down the rebels, and put an end to the struggle than the Insurrection or the running away of a large body of their slaves, and then, read General McClellan's proclamation, declaring that any attempt at a rising of the slaves against their rebel masters would be put down, and put down with an iron hand. Let it be observed too, that it has required the intervention of Congress, by repeated resolutions to prevent this General from converting the army of the Potomac from acting as the slave dogs of the rebels, and that even now while our army are compelled to drink water from the muddy swamps, and from the Pamunky river, forbidden by George B. McClellan to take pure water from the Rebel General Lee's well. Let it be understood that Northern loyal soldiers have been compelled by the orders of this same General, to keep guard over the property of a leading rebel, because of a previous understanding between the loyal, and the traitor General. Bear in mind the fact that this General has in deference to the slave-holding rebels forbidden the singing of anti-slavery songs in his camp, and you will learn that this General's ideas of the demands of the hour are most miserably below the mark, and unfit him for the place he fills. Take another fact into account, General McClellan is at this moment the favorite General of the Richardsons, the Ben Woods, the Vallandighams, and the whole school of pro-slavery Buchanan politicians of the North, and that he is reported in the Richmond Dispatch to have said that he hated to war upon Virginia, and that he would far rather war against Massachusetts. This statement of the Richmond Dispatch in itself is not worth much, but if we find as I think we do find, in General McClellan's every movement an apparent reluctance to strike at Virginia rebels, we may well fear that his words have been no better than his deeds. Again, take the battles fought by him and under his order, and in every instance the rebels have been able to claim a victory, and to show as many prisoners and spoils taken as we. At Ball's Bluff, McClellan's first battle of the Potomac, it is now settled, that our troops were marched up only to be slaugh-

tered. Nine hundred and thirty of our brave northern soldiers were deliberately murdered, as much so as if they had
each been stabbed, bayonnetted, shot, or otherwise killed
when asleep by some midnight assassin, for they were so ordered and handled, that they were perfectly harmless to their
deadly foes, and helpless in their own defense. Then the battle of Seven Pines, where General Casey's Division was
pushed out like an extended finger four miles beyond the
lines of our army, towards the rebels, as if for no other purpose than to be cut to pieces or captured by the rebels, and
then the haste with which this same Division was censured
by Gen. McClellan, are facts looking all the same way. This is
only one class of facts. They are not the only facts, nor the
chief ones that shake my faith in the General of the Army of
the Potomac.

Unquestionably time is the mightiest ally that the rebels
can rely on. Every month they can hold out against the
Government gives them power at home, and prestige abroad,
and increases the probabilities of final success.--Time favors
foreign intervention, time favors heavy taxation upon the
loyal people, time favors reaction, and a clamor for peace.
Time favors fevers, and pestilence, wasting and destroying
our army. Therefore *time, time* is the great ally of the rebels.

Now I undertake to say that General McClellan has from
the beginning so handled the army of the Potomac as to give
the rebels the grand advantage of time. From the time he
took command of the Potomac army in August 1861 until
now, he has been the constant cause of delay, and probably
would not have moved when he did, but that he was compelled to move or be removed. Then behold his movement.
He moved upon Manassas when the enemy had been gone
from there seven long days. When he gets there he is within
sixty miles of Richmond. Does he go on? Oh! no, but he
just says hush, to the press and the people, I am going to do
something transcendentally brilliant in strategy. Three
weeks pass away, and knowing ones wink and smile as much
as to say you will see something wonderful soon. And so indeed we do, at the end of three weeks we find that General
McClellan has actually marched back from Manassas to the
Potomac, gotten together an endless number of vessels at a

cost of untold millions, to transport his troops to Yorktown, where he is just as near to Richmond and not a bit nearer than he was just three weeks before, and where he is opposed by an army every way as strongly posted as any he could have met with by marching straight to Richmond from Manassas. Here we have two hundred and thirty thousand men moved to attack empty fortifications, and moved back again.

Now what is the state of facts concerning the nearly four months of campaign between the James and the York Rivers? The first is that Richmond is not taken, and in all the battles yet fought, the rebels have claimed them as victories, we have lost between thirty and forty thousand men, and the general impression is that there is an equal chance that our army will be again repulsed before Richmond and driven away.

You may not go the length that I do, in regard to Gen. McClellan, at this time, but I feel quite sure that this country will yet come to the conclusion that Geo. B. McClellan is either a cold blooded Traitor, or that he is an unmitigated military Imposter. He has shown no heart in his conduct, except when doing something directly in favor of the rebels, such as guarding their persons and property and offering his services to suppress with an iron hand any attempt on the part of the slaves against their rebel masters.

THE POLICY OF THE ADMINISTRATION

I come now to the policy of President Lincoln in reference to slavery. An administration without a policy is confessedly an administration without brains, since while a thing is to be done, it implies a known way to do it and he who professes his ability to do it, but cannot show how it is to be done, confesses his own imbecility. I do not undertake to say that the present administration has no policy, but if it has, the people have a right to know what it is, and to approve or disapprove of it as they shall deem it wise or unwise.

Now the policy of an administration can be learned in two ways. The first by what it says, and the second by what it does, and the last is far more certain and reliable than the first. It is by what President Lincoln had done in reference to slavery, since he assumed the reins of goverment, that we are to know what he is likely to do, and deems best to do in the premises. We all know how he came into power. He was elected and inaugurated as the representative of the anti-slavery policy of the Republican party. He had laid down and maintained the doctrine that Liberty and Slavery were the great antagonistic political elements in this country. That Union of these States could not long continue half free and half slave, that they must in the end be all free or all slave.

In the conflict between these two elements he arrayed himself on the side of freedom, and was elected with a view to the ascendancy of free principles. Now what has been the tendency of his acts since he became Commander in chief of the army and navy? I do not hesitate to say, that whatever may have been his intentions, the action of President Lincoln has been calculated in a marked and decided way to shield and protect slavery from the very blows which its horrible crimes have loudly and persistently invited. He has scornfully rejected the policy of arming the slaves, a policy naturally suggested and enforced by the nature and necessities of the war. He has steadily refused to proclaim, as he had the constitutional and moral right to proclaim, complete emancipation to all the slaves of rebels who should make their way into the lines of our army. He has repeatedly interfered with and arrested the anti-slavery policy of some of his most earnest and reliable generals. He has assigned to the most important positions, generals who are notoriously pro-slavery, and hostile to the party and principles which raised him to power.--He has permitted rebels to recapture their runaway slaves in sight of the capital. He has allowed General Halleck to openly violate the spirit of a solemn resolution by Congress forbidding the army of the United States to return the fugitive slaves to their cruel masters, and has evidently from the first submitted himself to the guidance of the half loyal slave States, rather than to the wise and loyal suggestions of those States upon which must fall, and have fallen, the chief expense and danger involved in the prosecution of the war. It is from such action as this, that we must infer the policy of the Administration. To my mind that policy is simply and solely to reconstruct the union on the old and corrupting basis of compromise, by which slavery shall retain all the power that it ever had, with the full assurance of gaining more, according to its future necessities.

The question now arises, "Is such a reconstruction possible or desirable?" To this I answer from the depth of my soul, no. Mr. Lincoln is powerful, Mr. Lincoln can do many things, but Mr. Lincoln will never see the day when he can bring back or charm back, the scattered fragments of the Union into the shape and form they stood when they were shattered by this slaveholding rebellion.

What does this policy of bringing back the union imply? It implies first of all, that the slave States will promptly and cordially, and without the presence of compulsory and extraneous force, co-operate with the free States under the very constitution which they have openly repudiated, and attempted to destroy. It implies that they will allow and protect the collection of the revenue in all their ports.--It implies the security and safety of our postal arrangements within their border. It implies the regular election of the members of the Senate and the House of Representatives and the prompt and complete execution of all the Federal laws within their limits. It implies that the rebel States will repudiate the rebel leaders, and that they shall be punished with perpetual political degradation. So much it implies on the part of the rebel States.--And the bare statement, with what we know of the men engaged in the war, is sufficient to prove the impossibility of their fulfilment while slavery remains.

What is implied by a reconstruction of the union on the old basis so far as concerns the northern and loyal States? It implies that after all we have lost and suffered by this war to protect and preserve slavery, the crime and scandal of the nation, that we will as formerly act the disgusting part of the watch dogs of the slave plantation, that we will hunt down the slaves at the North, and submit to all the arrogance, bluster, and pretension of the very men who have imperilled our liberties and baptized our soil with the blood of our best and bravest citizens. Now I hold that both parties will reject these terms with scorn and indignation. Having thus condemned as impossible and undesirable the policy which seems to be that of the administration you will naturally want to know what I consider to be the true policy to be pursued by the Government and people in relation to slavery and the war. I will tell you: Recognise the fact, for it is the great fact, and never more palpable than at the present moment, that the only choice left to this nation, is abolition or destruction. You must abolish slavery or abandon the union. It is plain that there can never be any union between the north and the south, while the south values slavery more than nationality. A union of interest is essential to a union of ideas, and without this union of ideas, the outward form of the union will be but as a rope of sand. Now it is quite clear that while slavery lasts at the south, it will remain hereafter as heretofore, the great dominating interest, over-topping all others, and shaping the sentiments and opinions of the people in accordance with itself. We are not to flatter ourselves that because slavery has brought great troubles upon the South by this war, that therefore the people of the South will be stirred up against it. If we can bear with slavery after the calamities it has brought upon us, we may expect that the South will be no less patient. Indeed we may rationally expect that the South will be more devoted to slavery than ever. The blood and treasure poured out in its defense will tend to increase its sacredness in the eyes of southern people, and if slavery comes out of this struggle, and is re-taken under the forms of old compromises, the country will witness a greater amount of insolence and bluster in favor of the slave system, than was ever shown before in or out of Congress.--But it is asked how will you abolish slavery. You have no power over the system before the rebellion is suppressed, and you will have no right or power when it is suppressed. I will answer this argument when I have stated how the thing may be done. The fact is there would be no trouble about the way, if the government only possessed the will. But several ways have been suggested. One is a stringent Confiscation Bill by Congress. Another is by a proclamation by the President at the head of the nation. Another is by the commanders of each division of the army. Slavery can be abolished in any or all these ways. There is plausibility in the argument that we cannot reach slavery until we have suppressed the rebellion. Yet it is far more true to say that we cannot reach the rebellion until we have suppressed slavery.

For slavery is the life of the rebellion. Let the loyal army but inscribe upon its banner, Emancipation and protection to all who will rally under it, and no power could prevent a stampede from slavery, such as the world has not witnessed since the Hebrews crossed the Red Sea. I am convinced that this rebellion and slavery are twin monsters, and that they must fall or flourish together, and that all attempts at upholding one while putting down the other, will be followed by continued trains of darkening calamities, such as make this anniversary of our national Independence, a day of mourning instead of a day of transcendant joy and gladness.

But a proclamation of Emancipation, says one, would only be a paper order. I answer, so is any order emanating from our Government. The President's proclamation calling his countrymen to arms, was a paper order. The proposition to retake the property of the Federal Government in the southern States, was a paper order. Laws fixing the punishment of traitors are paper orders. All laws, all written rules for the Government of the army and navy and people, are "paper orders," and would remain only such were they not backed up by force, still we do not object to them as useless, but admit their wisdom and necessity. Then these paper orders carry with them a certain moral force which makes them in a large measure self-executing. I know of none which would possess this self-executing power in lager measure than a proclamation of Emancipation. It would act on the rebel masters, and even more powerfully upon their slaves. It would lead the slaves to run away, and the masters to emancipate, and thus put an end to slavery. The conclusion of the whole matter is this: The end of slavery and only the end of slavery, is the end of the war, the end of secession, the end of disunion, and the return of peace, prosperity and unity to the nation. Whether Emancipation comes from the North or from the South, from Jeff Davis or from Abraham Lincoln, it will come alike for the healing of the nation, for slavery is the only mountain interposed to make enemies of the North and South.

Fellow Citizens: let me say in conclusion. This slavery begotten and slavery sustained, and slavery animated war, has now cost this nation more than a hundred thousand lives, and more than five hundred millions of treasure. It has weighed down the national heart with sorrow and heaviness, such as no speech can portray. It has cast a doubt upon the possibility of liberty and self Government which it will require a century to remove.--The question is, shall this stupendous and most outrageous war be finally and forever ended? Or shall it be merely suspended for a time, and again revived with increased and aggravated fury in the future? Can you afford a repetition of this costly luxury? Do you wish to transmit to your children the calamities and sorrows of to-day? The way to either class of these results is open to you. By urging upon the nation the necessity and duty of putting an end to slavery, you put an end to the war, and put an end to the cause of the war, and make any repetition of it impossible. But just take back the pet monster again into the bosom of the nation, proclaim an amnesty to the slaveholders, let them have their slaves, and command your services in helping to catch and hold them, and so sure as like causes will ever produce like effects, you will hand down to your children here, and hereafter, born and to be born all the horrors through which you are now passing. I have told you of great national opportunities in the past, a greater than any in the past is the opportunity of the present. If now we omit the duty it imposes, steel our hearts against its teachings, or shrink in cowardice from the work of to-day, your fathers will have fought and bled in vain to establish free Institutions, and American Republicanism will become a hissing and a byword to a mocking earth.

JANUARY FIRST, 1863

The first of January, which is now separated from us only by a few days and hours, is properly looked forward to with an intense and all surpassing interest, by all classes of the American people and from the most opposite reasons and motives. The slave hopes to gain his liberty, the slaveholders fear the loss of Slaves, and northern doughfaces fear the loss of political power. It is a pivotal period in our national history--the great day which is to determine the destiny not only of the American Republic, but that of the American

Continent. Far off in the after coming centuries, some Gibbon with truthful pen, will fix upon that date, as the beginning of a glorious rise, or of a shamefull fall of the great American Republic. Unquestionable, for weal or for woe, the first of January is to be the most memorable day in American Annals. The fourth of July was great, but the first of January, when we consider it in all its relations and bearings, is incomparably greater. The one had respect to the mere political birth of a nation, the last concerns the national life and character, and is to determine whether that life and character shall be radiantly glorious with all high and noble virtues, or infamously blackened, forevermore, with all the hell darkened crimes and horrors which attach to Slavery--it is whether our national life shall be to ourselves and the world, a withering curse or a benediciton of all national blessedness for ages to come. We may well stay before it and amplify it. It is an occasion which can happen but seldom in the life of any nation. It is not the creation of individual design and calculation, but the grand result of stupendous, all controlling, wide sweeping national events. Powerful as Mr. Lincoln is, he is but the hands of the clock. He cannot change the pivotal character of the day. The world has gone forth-- and no system of balancing of props here, or weight there, can possibly anchor the national ship in anything like a stationary position after the first day of January. From that day her ample form will swing round, her towering rails will be swelled by the trade winds of the Almighty and she will either be wafted off gloriously to the open sea, on a prosperous voyage, or furiously driven by rebellious gales upon the sharp and flinty rocks only to mark the place of danger to other and aftercoming voyagers. We repeat, there is no escape. The tide is reached which must be taken at the flood.-- For the present the Angel of Liberty has one ear of the nation and the demon of Slavery the other. One or the other must prevail on the first of January. The national head swings, pendulum like, now to the one side and now to the other. Alas, no man can tell which will prevail--and we are compelled to wait, hope, labor and pray.

It is of but little use to speculate as to probabilities, when events are at the door which will dispel all doubt and make

all certain--yet we may even now glance at the probable effects which may be looked for as certain to follow any one of
the three courses--open to the President of the United States
on the first of January. We say *three courses* although in a
radical point of view there are but *two*. One is the issuing,
according to promise, of his proclamation abolishing slavery
in all the States and parts of States which shall be in rebellion
on the first of January and the second is, not to issue it at all.
Any postponement, any apology--any plan of compromise
which saves the guilty neck of slavery one hour beyond the
first of January, will be in effect a suppression of the proclamation altogether. And now supposing that Mr. Lincoln
shall fail, supposing that the hour comes and the man is
missing, what will be the effect upon him? Thus far the loyal
north has trusted him, less for his ability than his honesty.
They have supported him with patience rather than enthusiasm. His word though clumsily uttered has been esteemed his bond, good for all, and more than all it has
promised. But what, as we have already said, if the President
fails in this trial hour, what if he now listens to the demon
slavery--and rejects the entreaties of the Angel of Liberty?
Suppose he cowers at last before the half loyal border Slave
States, which have already nearly ruined his administration,
and have been of more service to Richmond than to Washington from the beginning--withholds his proclamation of
freedom--disappoints the just hopes of his true friends, dis-
pels the fear and dismay of his enemies--and thus gives a
new lease of life to the slaveholder's rebellion? Where then
will stand Mr. Abraham Lincoln? We know not what will
become of him. The North has been so often betrayed and
trifled with that it has become unsafe to predicate anything
spirited, resolute and decided on her part. But this we will
say, if Mr. Lincoln shall trifle with the wounds of his bleeding
country--thus fiddle, while the cold earth around Fredericksburg is wet with the warm blood of our patriot soldiers--ev-
ery one of whom was slain by slaveholding rebels, he will be
covered with execrations as bitter and as deep as any that ever
settled upon the head of any perjured tyrant ancient or modern. His name would go down in history scarcely less loathsome than that of Nero. Such a course on the part of Mr.

Lincoln would justly make him the distrust and scandal of his friends, the scorn of the world and the contempt of his enemies. Henceforth none but fools will believe in him and his protestations of honesty and partriotism will be hailed but as the deceitful utterances of another Iago.

To the country, a failure to issue the Emancipation proclamation would prove the most stunning and disastrous blow received during the war. It would well nigh break the loyal heart of the nation, and fill its enemies North and South, with a demoniacal enthusiasm--Missouri, with its noble German population and Western Virginia, both sternly endeavoring, against terrible odds of treachery and danger, to throw off the system of bondage would fall paralysed in the presence of their exulting foes, while the loyal North and West would feel that they had fought and bled in vain. The most hopeful of all our prophets would wilt in despair. For who could trust to presidential promises or in any arm or department of Government when the central pillar had fallen? Who but a fool can believe that any grace shown the rebels at this moment after nearly two years of patience will not be construed into conscious weakness, into a base and cowardly spirit, as another proof of the unfitness of the Northern round heads to rule, and of the necessity of rebel dominion? The natural and inevitable effect of the suppression or postponement of the proclamation will be to cheer the hopes and intensify the determination and efforts of the rebels to break up and destroy the Union. Mr. Lincoln might threaten in the event of continued resistance, to send out another decree on the fourth of July 1863, but the North would gain no hope from it and the South would be caused no fear by it for the moral constitution of the Government more solemn than all paper ones would be broken down beyond repair.

But on the other hand let the President promptly on the morning of the first of January, with the truthful steadiness and certainty of the movement of the heavenly bodies send forth his glorious proclamation of Liberty, and a shout like the voice of many waters will rise to heaven from three millions of robbed and plundered bondmen, while a groan of despair will be heard in every rebel hall South of Mason and

Dixon's line. It will add: four millions to the strength of the
Union with a single dash of the pen, establish the moral
power of the Government, kindle anew the enthusiasm of
the friends of freedom, number the days of Northern dough-
faceism, strengthen the hearts of our brave troops in the
field, convince the world of our sincerity, give a fuller meaning to the declaration of Independence, and put peace forever
between the conscience and the patriotism of the people.

*"When a deed is done for freedom, through the broad earth's
aching breast
Runs a thrill of joy prophetic trembling on from East to
West."*

But will that deed be done? Oh! that is the question.
There is reason both for hope and fear. The promise is yet
unretracted, the rebels are still in arms, bold, active, unyield-
ing, strong and defiant. There is not a sign of weakness on all
the Southern horizon, at this writing. Their army is said to
be shoeless, coatless, hatless, tentless, blanketless, half starved
and deserting, but this is on paper. On the field they tell a
different story, especially in all the Great Battles of Virginia,
and we hope for Emancipation none the less, because this is
so. The being in rebellion was the ground for the promised
proclamation. This ground within nine days of the first of
January holds good. Not a single rebel State has grounded its
weapons since the twenty second of September. Thus far the
President is dared to do his worst, thus far the villainy of the
South is a spur to the virtue of the North, and affords reason
to hope that we shall have the promised proclamation of
freedom to all the Inhabitants of the rebel States.

On the 22d of September, as we have said the President
declared that he would issue, on the first of January 1863, a
proclamation of Emancipation abolishing Slavery in all the
Slave States which should then be in rebellion. But alas, he
made these a burden of what should have been a joy. He
reached that point like an ox under the yoke, or a Slave under the lash, not like the uncaged eagle spurning his bondage
and soaring in freedom to the skies. His words kindled no
enthusiasm. They touched neither justice nor mercy. Had
there been one expression of sound moral feeling against

Slavery, one word of regret and shame that this accursed system had remained so long the disgrace and scandal of the
Republic, one word of satisfaction in the hope of burying
slavery and the rebellion in one common grave, a thrill of
joy would have run round the world, but no such word was
said, and no such joy was kindled. He moved, but was
moved by necessity.--Emancipation--is put off--it was made
future and conditional--not present and absolute.

While however, there are strong grounds for supposing
that President Lincoln will duly issue his proclamation on
the morning of the first of January, the absence of all mention of his purpose to do so, in his recent message, his reported saying that the rebellion is already substantially suppressed, his parleying with the border State men, his avowed
readiness to change his opinion, whenever he should be
convinced, the tremendous pressure likely to be brought to
bear upon him, by the conservators of Slavery, the apparent
lack in him of any vital hostility towards slavery, the delcared
motives for the measure being only military, not moral or
political necessity, the democratic pro-slavery gains obtained
at the North since the 22d of September, the space given in
his late message to compensated Emancipation, all served to
cast a doubt upon the promised and hoped for proclamation,
which only the event can remove or confirm. So stands the
case within one week of the first of January. The suspense is
painful, but will soon be over. Our paper shall wait for the
day and the deed, that it may carry especially to our transat-
lantic readers the result whatever it may be.

1863
"MEN OF COLOR, TO ARMS!"

When first the rebel cannon shattered the walls of Sumter
and drove away its starving garrison, I predicted that the war
then and there inaugurated would not be fought out entirely
by white men. Every month's experience during these dreary
years has confirmed that opinion. A war undertaken and
brazenly carried on for the perpetual enslavement of colored
men, calls logically and loudly for colored men to help

suppress it. Only a moderate share of sagacity was needed to see that the arm of the slave was the best defense against the arm of the slaveholder. Hence with every reverse to the national arms, with every exulting shout of victory raised by the slaveholding rebels, I have implored the imperiled nation to unchain against her foes, her powerful black hand. Slowly and reluctantly that appeal is beginning to be heeded. Stop not now to complain that it was not heeded sooner. It may or it may not have been best that it should not. This is not the time to discuss that question. Leave it to the future. When the war is over, the country is saved, peace is established, and the black man's rights are secured, as they will be, history with an impartial hand will dispose of that and sundry other questions. Action! Action! not criticism, is the plain duty of this hour. Words are now useful only as they stimulate to blows. The office of speech now is only to point out when, where, and how to strike to the best advantage. There is no time to delay. The tide is at its flood that leads on to fortune. From East to West, from North to South, the sky is written all over, "Now or never." Liberty won by white men would lose half its luster. "Who would be free themselves must strike the blow." "Better even die free, than to live slaves." This is the sentiment of every brave colored man amongst us. There are weak and cowardly men in all nations. We have them amongst us. They tell you this is the "white man's war"; that you will be "no better off after than before the war"; that the getting of you into the army is to "sacrifice you on the first opportunity." Believe them not; cowards themselves, they do not wish to have their cowardice shamed by your brave example. Leave them to their timidity, or to whatever motive may hold them back. I have not thought lightly of the words I am now addressing you. The counsel I give comes of close observation of the great struggle now in progress, and of the deep conviction that this is your hour and mine. In good earnest then, and after the best deliberation, I now for the first time during this war feel at liberty to call and counsel you to arms. By every consideration which binds you to your enslaved fellow-countrymen, and the peace and welfare of your country; by every aspiration which you cherish for the freedom and equality of yourselves and your children; by all the ties of blood and identity which make us one with the brave black men now fighting our battles in Louisiana and in South Carolina, I urge you to fly to arms, and smite with death the power that would bury the government and your liberty in the same hopeless grave. I wish I could tell you that the State of New York calls you to this high honor. For the moment her constituted authorities are silent on the subject. They will speak by and by, and doubtless on the right side; but we are not compelled to wait for her. We can get at the throat of treason and slavery through the State of Massachusetts. She was first in the War of Independence; first to break the chains of her slaves; first to make the black man equal before the law; first to admit colored children to her common schools, and she was first to answer with her blood the alarm cry of the nation, when its capital was menaced by rebels. You know her patriotic governor, and you know Charles Sumner. I need not add more.

Massachusetts now welcomes you to arms as soldiers. She has but a small colored population from which to recruit. She has full leave of the general government to send one regiment to the war, and she has undertaken to to it. Go quickly and help fill up the first colored regiment from the North. I am authorized to assure you that you will receive the same wages, the same rations, the same equipments, the same protection, the same treatment, and the same bounty, secured to the white soldiers. You will be led by able and skillful officers, men who will take especial pride in your efficiency and success. They will be quick to accord to you all the honor you shall merit by your valor, and see that your rights and feelings are respected by other soldiers. I have assured myself on these points, and can speak with authority. More than twenty years of unswerving devotion to our common cause may give me some humble claim to be trusted at this momentous crisis. I will not argue. To do so implies hesitation and doubt, and you do not hesitate. You do not doubt. The day dawns; the morning star is bright upon the horizon! The iron gate of our prison stands half open. One gallant rush from the North will fling it wide open, while four millions of our brothers and sisters shall march out into liberty. The chance is now given you to end in a day the bondage of centuries, and to rise in one bound from social degradation to the plane of common equality with all other varieties of men. Remember Denmark Vesey of Charleston; remember Nathaniel Turner of Southampton; remember Shields Green and Copeland, who followed noble John Brown, and fell as glorious martyrs for the cause of the slave. Remember that in a contest with oppression, the Almighty has no attribute which can take sides with oppressors. The case is before you. This is our golden opportunity. Let us accept it, and forever wipe out the dark reproaches unsparingly hurled against us by our enemies. Let us win for ourselves the gratitude of our country, and the best blessings of our posterity through all time. The nucleus of this first regiment is now in camp at Readville, a short distance from Boston. I will undertake to forward to Boston all persons adjudged fit to be mustered into the regiment, who shall apply to me at any time within the next two weeks.

THE COMMANDER-IN-CHIEF AND HIS BLACK SOLDIERS

Whatever else may be said of President Lincoln, the most malignant Copperhead in the country cannot reproach him with any undue solicitude for the lives and liberties of the brave black men, who are now giving their arms and hearts to the support of his Government. When a boy, on a slave plantation the saying was common: "Half a cent to kill a Negro and half a cent to bury him."--The luxury of killing and burying could be enjoyed by the poorest members of Southern society, and no strong temptation was required to induce white men thus to kill and bury the black victims of their lust and cruelty.--With a Bible and pulpit affirming that the Negro is accursed of God, it is not strange that men should curse him, and that all over the South there should be manifested for the life and liberty of this description of man, the utterest indifference and contempt. Unhappily the same indifference and contempt for the lives of colored men is found wherever slavery has an advocate or treason an apologist. In the late terrible mobs in New York and elsewhere, the grim features of this malice towards colored men was everywhere present. Beat, shoot, hang, stab, kill, burn and destroy the Negro, was the cry of the crowd. Religion has cursed him and the law has enslaved him, and why may not the mob kill him?--Such has been our national education on this subject, and that it still has power over Mr. Lincoln seems evident from the fact, that no measures have been openly taken by him to cause the laws of civilized warfare to be observed towards his colored soldiers. The slaughter of blacks taken as captives, seems to affect him as little as the slaughter of beeves for the use of his army. More than six months ago Mr. Jefferson Davis told Mr. Lincoln and the world that he meant to treat blacks not as soldiers but as felons. The threat was openly made, and has been faithfully executed by the rebel chief. At Murfreesboro twenty colored teamsters in the Federal service, were taken by the rebels, and though not soldiers, and only servants, they were in cold blood--every man of them--shot down. At Milliken's Bend, the same black flag with its death's head and cross-bones was raised. When Banks entered Port Hudson he found white federal prisoners, but no black ones. Those of the latter taken, were no doubt, in cold blood put to the sword. Today, news from Charleston tells us that Negro soldiers taken as prisoners will not be exchanged, but sold into slavery--that some twenty of such prisoners are now in their hands. Thousands of Negros are now being enrolled in the service of the Federal Government. The Government calls them, and they come. They freely and joyously rally around the flag of the Union, and take all the risks, ordinary and extraordinary, involved in this war. They do it not for office, for thus far, they get none; they do it not for money, for thus far, their pay is less than that of white men. They go into this war to affirm their manhood, to strike for liberty and country.--If any class of men in this war can claim the honor of fighting for principle, and not from passion, for ideas, not from brutal malice, the colored soldier can make that claim preeminently. He strikes for manhood and freedom, under the forms of law and the usages of civilized warfare. He does not go forth as a savage with tomahawk and scalping knife, but in strict accordance with the rules of honorable warfare. Yet he is now openly threatened with

slavery and assassination by the rebel Government--and the
threat has been savagely executed.

What has Mr. Lincoln to say about this slavery and murder? What has he said?--Not one word. In the hearing of the
nation he is as silent as an oyster on the whole subject. If two
white men are threatened with assassination, the Richmond
Rebels are promptly informed that the Federal Government
will retailiate sternly and severely. But when colored soldiers are so threatened, no word comes from the Capitol.
What does this silence mean? Is there any explanation short
of base and scandalous contempt for the just rights of colored
soldiers?

For a time we tried to think that there might be solid reasons of state against answering the threats of Jefferson Davis--
but the Government has knocked this favorable judgment
from under us, by its prompt threat of retaliation in the case
of the two white officers at Richmond who are under sen-
tence of death. Men will ask, the world will ask, why interference should be made for those young white officers thus
selected for murder, and not for the brave black soldiers who
may be flung by the fortunes of war into the hands of the
rebels? Is the right to "life, liberty and the pursuit of happiness" less sacred in the case of the one than the other?

It may be said that the black soldiers have enlisted with
the threat of Jefferson Davis before them, and they have assumed their position intelligently, with a full knowledge of
the consequences incurred. If they have, they have by that act
shown themselves all the more worthy of protection. It is
noble in the Negro to brave unusual danger for the life of the
Republic, but it is mean and base in the Republic if it rewards
such generous and unselfish devotion by assassination,
when a word would suffice to make the laws of war respected, and to prevent the crime. Shocking enough are the
ordinary horrors of war, but the war of the rebels toward the
colored men is marked by deeds which well might "shame
extremest hell." And until Mr. Lincoln shall interpose his
power to prevent these atrocious assassinations of Negro soldiers, the civilized world will hold him equally with Jefferson Davis responsible for them. The question is already
being asked: Why is it that colored soldiers which were first

enlisted with a view to "garrison forts and arsenals, on the Southern coast"--where white men suffer from climate, should never be heard of in any such forts and arsenals? Was that a trick? Why is it that they who were enlisted to fight the fevers of the South, while white soldiers fight the rebels are now only heard of in "forlorn hopes," in desperate charges always in the van, as at Port Hudson, Milliken's Bend, James Island and Fort Wagner? Green colored recruits are called upon to assume the position of veterans. They have performed their part gallantly and gloriously, but by all the proofs they have given of their patriotism and bravery we protest against the meanness, ingratitude and cruelty of the Government, in whose behalf they fight, if that Government remains longer a silent witness of their enslavement and assassination. Having had patience and forbearance with the silence of Mr. Lincoln a few months ago, we could at least imagine some excuses for his silence as to the fate of colored troops falling by the fortunes of war into the hands of the rebels, but the time for this is past. It is now for every man who has any sense of right and decency, to say nothing of gratitude, to speak out trumpet-tongued in the ears of Mr. Lincoln and his Government and demand from him a declaration of purpose, to hold the rebels to a strict account for every black federal soldier taken as a prisoner. For every black prisoner slain in cold blood, Mr. Jefferson Davis should be made to understand that one rebel officer shall suffer death, and for every colored soldier sold into slavery, a rebel shall be held as a hostage. For our Government to do less than this, is to deserve the indignation and the execration of mankind.

DUTY OF COLORED MEN

Gov. Seward, having been inquired of by J.M. Langston as to the duty of colored men in view of the fact that the wages offered to them as soldiers are less than those offered to whites, sends a reply as follows:

"The duty of the colored man to defend his country wherever, whenever, and in whatever form, is the same with that of the white man. It does not depend on, nor is it affected by, what the country pays us, or what position she assigns us; but it depends on her need alone, and of that she, not we, are to judge. The true way to secure her rewards and win her confidence is not to stipulate for them, but to deserve them. Factious disputes among patriots, about compensations and honors invariably betray any people, of whatever race, into bondage. If you wish your race to be delivered from that course, this is the time to secure their freedom in every land and for all generations. It is no time for any American citizen to be hesitating about pay or place." I am your obedient servant,

Wm. H. Seward"

We know not what answer--if any--Mr. Langston has made to this remarkable sophistical statement of the relations and duties of colored citizens to the American Government. We regret that the National Anti-Slavery Standard should have sent it out without a word of condemnation. To us the whole statement is an illustration of the cunning of the white hunter to the simple Indian: "you the crow and I the turkey, or I the turkey, and you the crow." "Heads I win, tails you lose." The Honorable Secretary of State has a very clear perception of the rights of Government, but in the citizen he sees only duties. We have in our simplicity always supposed that the relation of the citizen to the State is one of reciprocal rights and duties that the citizen is bound to render true allegiance to the State, and the State is equally bound to render that which is just and equal to the citizen. Mr. Seward's reasoning is a revival of the detestable doctrine now happily scouted with contempt, even through Europe, that "a subject is a person having duties but no rights." This happy piece of kingly coinage comes very properly from Lewis, King of Bavaria, but certainly is hardly fit to be echoed by the highest officer in the Cabinet of the United States. Not a word from Mr. Seward against the injustice and unfairness of asking the black citizen, to fight the battles of his country upon terms which would be scouted by white men. But with all-amazing coolness the Honorable Secretary of State from his position in the Government ridicules such contemptible little springs as pay and place. For these the citizen is not to stipulate, but to deserve. He is further not to trouble his brain about either pay or place; the government alone will attend to those little matters. Now we doubt very much if Mr. Seward's political practice corresponds with his political preaching at this point. There is scarcely a place in the Government filled by a man who did not make some representation of his qualification for the place without waiting for the Government to discover his merits. Mr. Seward's lecture to colored men would be considered everywhere as twaddle if applied to white men, but popular prejudice imparts a visage of wisdom to what would otherwise pass for political nonsense. Colored men have a right not only to ask for equal pay for equal work, but that merit, not color, should be the criterion observed by Government in the distribution of places.

ADDRESS OF THE COLORED NATIONAL CONVENTION TO THE PEOPLE OF THE UNITED STATES

Fellow-Citizens:

The members of the Colored National Convention, assembled in Syracuse, State of New York, October the 4th, 1864, to confer with each other as to the complete emancipation, enfranchisement, and elevation of our race, in essaying to address you on these subjects, warmly embrace the occasion to congratulate you upon the sucess of your arms, and upon the prospect of the speedy suppression of the slaveholders' rebellion. Baptized in the best blood of your noblest sons, torn and rent by a strife full of horrors,--a strife undertaken and prosecuted for aims and objects the guiltiest that can enter the wicked hearts of men long in the practice of crime,--we ardently hope with you that our country will come out of this tremendous conflict, purer, stronger, nobler, and happier than ever before. Having shared with you, in some measure, the hardships, perils, and sacrifices of this war for the maintenance of the Union and Government, we rejoice with you also in every sign which gives promise of its approaching termination, and of the return of our common country again to those peaceful, progressive, and humanizing activities of true national life, from which she has been so wantonly diverted by the insurrection of slaveholders.

In view of the general cheerfulness of the national situation, growing brighter every day; the rapid dispersement of the heavy clouds of dismal terror, which only a few weeks ago mantled our land with the gloomiest forebodings of national disaster and ruin,--we venture to hope that the present is a favorable moment to commend to your consideration the subject of our wrongs, and to obtain your earnest and hearty co-operation in all wise and just measures for their full redress.

When great and terrible calamities are abroad in the land, men are said to learn righteousness. It would be a mark of unspeakable national depravity, if neither the horrors of this war, nor the dawning prospect of peace, should soften the heart, and dispose the American people to renounce and forsake their evil policy towards the colored race. Assuming the contrary, we deem this a happily chosen hour for calling your attention to our cause. We know that the human mind is so constituted, that all postponement of duty, all refusal to go forward when the right path is once made plain, is dangerous.

After such neglect of, and disobedience to, the voice of reason and conscience, a nation becomes harder and less alive than before to high moral considerations. If won to the path of rectitude at all, thereafter, it must be by means of a purer light than that which first brought right convictions and inclinations to the national mind and heart. We speak, then, fellow citizens, at an auspicious moment. Conviction has already seized the public mind. Little argument is needed. We shall appeal rather than argue; and we may well implore an attentive hearing for our appeal. The nation is still in tears. The warm blood of your brave and patriotic sons is still fresh upon the green fields of the Shenandoah. Mourning mingles everywhere with the national shout of victory; and though the smoke and noise of battle are rolling away behind the southern horizon, our brave armies are still confronted in Georgia and Virginia by a stern foe, whose haughtiness and cruelty have sprung naturally from his long and undisputed mastery over men. The point attained in the progress of this war is one from which you can if you will view to advantage the calamities which inevitably follow upon long and persistent violation of manifest duty; and on the other hand, the signs of final triumph enable you to anticipate the happy results which must always flow from just and honorable conduct. The fear of continued war, and the hope of speedy peace, alike mark this as the time for America to choose her destiny. Another such opportunity as is now furnished in the state of the country, and in the state of the national heart, may not come again in a century. Come, then, and let us reason together.

We shall speak, it is true, for our race,--a race long oppressed, enslaved, ignored, despised, slandered, and degraded; but we speak not the less for our country, whose welfare and permanent peace can only result from the adoption of wise and just measures towards our whole race, North and South.

Considering the number and the grievous character of the wrongs and disabilities endured by our race in this country, you will bear witness that we have borne with patience our lot, and have seldom troubled the national ear with the burden of complaint. It is true that individuals among us have constantly testified their abhorrence of this injustice; but as a people, we have seldom uttered, as we do this day, our protest and remonstrance against the manifold and needless injustice with which we are upon all sides afflicted. We have suffered in silence, trusting that, though long delayed, and perhaps through terrible commotions, the hour would come when justice, honor, and magnanimity would assert their power over the mind and heart of the American people, and restore us to the full exercise and enjoyment of the rights inseparable from human nature. Never having despaired of this consummation so devoutly wished, even in the darkest hours of our history, we are farther than ever from despairing now. Nowhere in the annals of mankind is there recorded an instance of an oppressed people rising more rapidly than ourselves in the favorable estimation of their oppressors. The change is great, and increasing, and is viewed with astonishment and dread by all those who had hoped to stand forever with their heels upon our necks.

Nevertheless, while joyfully recognizing the vast advances made by our people in popular consideration, and the apparent tendency of events in our favor, we cannot conceal from ourselves, and would not conceal from you, the fact that there are many and powerful influences, constantly operating, intended and calculated to defeat our just hopes, prolong the existence of the source of all our ills,--the system of slavery,--strengthen the slave power, darken the conscience of the North, intensify popular prejudice against color, multiply unequal and discriminating laws, augment the burdens long borne by our race, consign to oblivion the deeds of heroism which have distinguished the colored soldiers, deny and despise his claims to the gratitude of his country, scout his pretensions to American citizenship, establish the selfish idea that this is exclusively the white man's country, pass unheeded all the lessons taught by these four years of fire and sword, undo all that has been done towards our freedom and elevation, take the musket from the shoulders of our brave black soldiers, deny them the constitutional right to keep and bear arms, exclude them from the ballot-box where they now possess that right, prohibit the extension of it to those who do not possess it, overawe free speech in and out of Congress, obstruct the right of peaceable assembling, reenact the Fugitive-slave Bill, revive the internal slave-trade, break up all diplomatic relations with Haiti and Liberia, reopen our broad territories to the introduction of slavery, reverse the entire order and tendency of the events of the last three years, and postpone indefinitely that glorious deliverance from bondage, which for our sake, and for the sake of the future unity, permanent peace, and highest welfare of all concerned, we had fondly hoped and believed was even now at the door.

In surveying our possible future, so full of interest at this moment, since it may bring to us all the blessings of equal liberty, or all the woes of slavery and continued social degradation, you will not blame us if we manifest anxiety in regard to the position of our recognized friends, as well as that of our open and declared enemies; for our cause may suffer even more from the injudicious concessions and weakness of our friends, than from the machinations and power of our enemies. The weakness of our friends is strength to our foes. When the "Anti-slavery Standard," representing the American Anti-slavery Society, denies that the society asks for the enfranchisement of colored men, and the "Liberator" apologizes for excluding the colored men of Louisiana from the ballot-box, they injure us more vitally than all the ribald jests of the whole proslavery press.

Again: had, for instance, the present Administration, at the beginning of the war, boldly planted itself upon the doctrine of human equality as taught in the Declaration of Independence; proclaimed liberty to all the slaves in all the Slave States; armed every colored man, previously a slave or a freeman, who would or could fight under the loyal flag; recognized black men as soldiers of the Republic; avenged the first act of violence upon colored prisoners, in contravention of the laws of war; sided with the radical emancipation party in Maryland and Missouri; stood by its anti-slavery generals, instead of casting them aside,--history would never have had to record the scandalous platform adopted at Chicago, nor the immeasurable horrors of Fort Pillow. The weakness and hesitation of our friends, where promptness and vigor were required, have invited the contempt and rigor of our enemies. See that, while perilling everything for the protection and security of our country, our country did not think itself bound to protect and secure us, the rebels felt a license to treat us as outlaws. Seeing that our Government did not treat us as men, they did not feel bound to treat us as soldiers. It is, therefore, not the malignity of enemies alone we have to fear, but the deflection from the straight line of principle by those who are known throughout the world as our special friends. We may survive the arrows of the known Negro-haters of our country; but woe to the colored race when their champions fail to demand, from any reason, equal liberty in every respect!

We have spoken of the existence of powerful reactionary forces arrayed against us, and of the objects to which they tend. What are these mighty forces? And through what agencies do they operate and reach us? They are many; but we shall detain by no tedious enumeration. The first and most powerful is slavery; and the second, which may be said to be the shadow of slavery, is prejudice against men on account of their color. The one controls the South, and the other controls the North. Both are original sources of power, and generate peculiar sentiments, ideas, and laws concerning us. The agents of these two evil influences are various; but the chief are, first, the Democratic party; and second, the Republican party. the Democratic party belongs to slavery; and the Republican party is largely under the power of prejudice against color. While gratefully recognizing a vast difference in our favor in the character and composition of the Republican party, and regarding the accession to power of the Democratic party as the heaviest calamity that could befall us in the present juncture of affairs, it cannot be disguised, that, while that party is our bitterest enemy, and is positively and actively reactionary, the Republican party is negatively and passively so in its tendency. What we have to fear from these two parties,--looking to the future, and especially to the settlement of our present national troubles,--is alas! only too obvious. The intentions, principles, and policy of both organizations, through their platforms, and the antecedents and the recorded utterances of the men who stand upon their respective platforms, teach us what to expect at their hands, and what kind of a future they are carving out for us, and for the country which they propose to govern. Without using the word *"slavery,"* or *"slaves,"* or *"slaveholders,"* the Democratic party has none the less declared, in its platform, its purpose to be the endless perpetuation of slavery. Under the apparently harmless verbiage, *"private rights," "basis of the Federal Union,"* and under the language employed in denouncing the Federal Administration for *"disregarding the Constitution in every part," "pretence of military necessity,"* we see the purpose of the Democratic party to restore slavery to all its ancient power, and to make this Government just what it was before the rebellion,--simply an instrument of the slave-power. "The basis of the Federal Union" only means the alleged compromises and stipulations, as interpreted by Judge Taney, by which black men are supposed to have no rights which white men are bound to respect; and by which the whole Northern people are bound to protect the cruel masters against the justly deserved violence of the slave, and to do the fiendish work of hellhounds when slaves make their escape from thraldom. The candidates of that party take their stand upon its platform; and will, if elected,--which Heaven forbid!--carry it out to the letter. From this party we must look only for fierce, malignant, and unmitigated hostility. Our continued oppression and degradation is the law of its life, and its sure passport to power. In the ranks of the Democratic party, all the worst elements of American society fraternize; and we need not expect a single voice from that quarter for justice, mercy, or even decency. To it we are nothing: the slave-holders everything. We have but to consult its press to know that it would willingly enslave the free colored people in the South; and also that it would gladly stir up against us mob-violence at the North,-- re-enacting the sanguinary scenes of one year ago in New York and other large cities. We therefore pray, that whatever wrath, curse, or calamity, the future may have in store for us, the accession of the Democratic party to the reins of power may not be one of them; for this to us would comprise the sum of all social woes.

How stands the case with the great Republican party in question? We have already alluded to it as being largely under the influence of the prevailing contempt for the character and rights of the colored race. This is seen by the slowness of our Government to employ the strong arm of the black man in the work of putting down the rebellion; and in its unwillingness, after thus employing him, to invest him with the same incitements to deeds of daring, as white soldiers; neither giving him the same pay, rations, and protection, nor any hope of rising in the service by meritorious conduct. It is also seen in the fact, that in neither of the plans emanating from this party for reconstructing the institutions of the Southern States, are colored men, not even those who had *fought* for the country, recognized has having any political existence or rights whatever.

Even in the matter of the abolition of slavery,--to which, by its platform, the Republican party is strongly committed, as well by President Lincoln's celebrated Proclamation of the first of January, 1863, and by his recent letter, "To whom it may concern,"--there is still room for painful doubt and apprehension. It is very evident, that the Republican party, though a party composed of the best men of the country, is not prepared to make the abolition of slavery, in all the Rebel

States, a consideration precedent to the re-establishment of the Union. However anti-slavery in sentiment the President may be, and however disposed he may be to continue the war till slavery is abolished, it is plain that in this he would not be sustained by his party. A single reverse to our arms, in such a war, would raise the hands of the party in opposition to their chief. The hope of the speedy and complete abolition of slavery, hangs, therefore, not upon the disposition of the Republican party, not upon the disposition of President Lincoln; but upon the slender thread of Rebel power, pride, and persistence. In returning to the Union, slavery has a fair chance to live; out of the Union, it has a still better chance to live; but, fighting against the Union, it has no chance for anything but destruction. Thus the freedom of our race and the welfare of our country tremble together in the balance of events.

This somewhat gloomy view of the condition of affairs-- which to the enthusiastic, who have already convinced themselves that slavery is dead, may not only seem gloomy, but untruthful--is nevertheless amply supported, not only by the well-known sentiment of the country, the controlling pressure of which is seriously felt by the Administration; but it is sustained by the many attempts lately made by the Republican press to explain away the natural import of the President's recent address "To whom it may concern," in which he makes the abolition of Slavery a primary condition to the restoration of the Union; and especially is this gloomy view supported by the remarkable speech delivered only a few weeks ago at Auburn, by Hon. William H. Seward, Secretary of State. Standing next to the President in the administration of the government, and fully in the confidence of the Chief Magistrate, no member of the National Cabinet is better qualified than Mr. Seward to utter the mind and policy of the Administration upon this momentous subject, when it shall come up at the close of the war. Just what it will do in the matter of slavery, Mr. Seward says,--

"When the insurgents shall have disbanded their armies, and laid down their arms, the war will instantly cease; and all the war measures then existing, including those which affect slavery, will cease also; and all the moral, economical, and political questions, as well affecting slavery as others, which slall then be existing between individuals and States and the Federal Government, whether they arose before the civil war began, or whether they grew out of it, will, by force of the Consitution, pass over to the arbitrament of courts of law, and the counsels of legislation."

These, fellow-citizens, are studied words, full of solemn and fearful import. They mean that our Republican Administration is not only ready to make peace with the Rebels, but to make peace with slavery also; that all executive and legislative action launched against the slave-system, whether of proclamation or confiscation, will cease the instant the Rebels shall disband their armies, and lay down their arms. The hope that the war will put an end to slavery, has, according to this exposition, only one foundation; and that is, that the courts and Congress will so decree. But what ground have we here? Congress has already spoken, and has refused to alter the Consitution so as to abolish Slavery. The Supreme Court has yet to speak; but what it will say, if this question shall come before it, is very easily divined. We will not assert positively what it will say; but indications of its judgment are clearly against us. What then have we? Only this, as our surest and best ground of hope; namely, that the Rebels, in their madness, will continue to make war upon the Government, until they shall not only become destitute of men, money, and the munitions of war, but utterly divested of their slaves also.

But, fellow-citizens, the object of this Address is not merely to state facts, and point out sources of danger. We would distinctly place our whole cause before you, and earnestly appeal to you to make that cause practically your cause; as we believe it is the cause of justice and of our whole country. We come before you altogether in new relations. Hitherto we have addressed you in the generic character of a common humanity, only as men; but to-day, owing to the events of the last three years, we bring with us an additional claim to consideration. By the qualities displayed, by the hardships endured, and by the services rendered the country, during these years of war and peril, we can now speak with the confidence of men who have deserved well of their country. While conscious of your power and of our comparative weakness, we may still claim for our race those rights which are not less ours by our services to the country than by the laws of human nature. All, therefore, that justice can demand, and honor grant, we can now ask, without presumption and without arrogance, of the American people.

Do you, then, ask us to state, in plain terms, just what we want of you, and just what we think we ought to receive at your hands? We answer: First of all, the complete abolition of the slavery of our race in the United States. We shall not stop to argue. We feel the terrible sting of this stupendous wrong, and that we cannot be free while our brothers are slaves. The enslavement of a vast majority of our people extends its baleful influence over every member of our race; and makes freedom, even to the free, a mockery and a delusion; we therefore, in our own name, and in the name of the whipped and branded millions, whose silent suffering has pleaded to the humane sentiment of mankind, but in vain, during more than two hundred years for deliverance, we implore you to abolish slavery. In the name of your country, torn, distracted, bleeding, and while you are weeping over the bloody graves of more than two hundred thousand of your noblest sons, many of whom have been cut down, in the midst of youthful vigor and beauty, we implore you to abolish slavery. In the name of peace, which experience has shown cannot be other than false and delusive while the rebellious spirit of Slavery has an existence in the land, we implore you to abolish slavery. In the name of universal justice, to whose laws great States not less than individuals are bound to conform, and the terrible consequences of whose violation are as fixed and certain as the universe itself, we implore you to abolish slavery; and thus place your peace and national welfare upon immutable and everlasting foundations.

Why would you let slavery continue? What good thing has it done, what evil thing has it left undone, that you should allow it to survive this dreadful war, the natural fruit of its existence? Can you want a second war from the same cause? Are you so rich in men, money, and material, that you must provide for future depletion? Or do you hope to escape the consequences of wrong doing? Can you expect any better results from compromises in the future, than from compromises with slavery in the past? If the South fights desperately and savagely to-day for the possession of four millions of slaves, will she fight less savagely and desperately when the prize for which she fights shall become eight instead of four millions? and when her ability to war upon freedom and free institutions shall have increased twofold?

Do you answer, that you have no longer anything to fear? that slavery has already received its death-blow? that it can only have a transient existence, even if permitted to live after the termination of the war? We answer, So thought your Revolutionary fathers when they framed the Federal Consitituion; and to-day, the bloody fruits of their mistake are all around us. Shall we avoid or shall we repeat their stupendous error? Be not deceived. Slavery is still the vital and animating breath of Southern society. The men who have fought for it on the battle-field will not love it less for having shed their blood in its defence. Once let them get Slavery safely under the protection of the Federal Government, and ally themselves, as they will be sure to do, to the Democratic party of the North; let Jefferson Davis and his Confederate associates, either in person or by their representatives, return once more to their seats in the halls of Congress,--and you will then see your dead slavery the most living and powerful thing in the country. To make peace, therefore, on such a basis as shall admit slavery back again into the Union, would only be sowing the seeds of war; sure to bring at last a bitter harvest of blood! The sun in the heavens at noonday is not more manifest, than the fact that slavery is the prolific source of war and division among you; and that its abolition is essential to your national peace and unity. Once more, then, we entreat you--for you have the power--to put away this monstrous abomination. You have repeatedly during this wanton slaveholding and wicked Rebellion, in the darkest hours of the struggle, appealed to the Supreme Ruler of the universe to smile upon your armies, and give them victory; surely you will not now stain your souls with the crime of ingratitude by making a wicked compact and a deceitful peace with your enemies. You have called mankind to witness that the struggle on your part was not for empire merely; that the charge that it was such was a gross slander; will you now make a peace which will justify what you have repeatedly denounced as a calumny? Your anti-slavery professions have drawn to you the sympathy of liberal and generous minded men throughout the world, and have restrained all Europe from recognizing the Southern Confederacy, and breaking up your blockade of Southern ports. Will you now proclaim your own baseness and hypocrisy by making a peace which shall give the lie to all such professions? You have over and over again, and very justly, branded slavery as the inciting cause of this Rebellion; denounced it as the fruitful source of pride and selfishness and mad ambition; you have blushed before all Europe for its existence among you; and have shielded yourselves from the execrations of mankind, by denying your constitutional ability to interfere with it. Will you now, when the evil in question has placed itself within your constitutional grasp, and invited its own destruction by its persistent attempts to destroy the Government, relax your grasp, release your hold, and to the disappointment of the slaves deceived by your proclamations, to the sacrifice of the Union white men of the South who have sided with you in this contest with slavery, and to the dishonor of yourselves and the amazement of mankind, give new and stronger lease of life to slavery? We will not and cannot believe it.

There is still one other subject, fellow-citizens,--one other want,--looking to the peace and welfare of our common country, as well as to the interests of our race; and that is, political equality. We want the elective franchise in all the States now in the Union, and the same in all such States as may come into the Union hereafter. We believe that the highest welfare of this great country will be found in erasing from its statute-books all enactments discriminating in favor or against any class of its people, and by establishing one law for the white and colored people alike. Whatever prejudice and taste may be innocently allowed to do or to dictate in social and domestic relations, it is plain, that in the matter of government, the object of which is the protection and security of human rights, prejudice should be allowed no voice whatever. In this department of human relations, no notice should be taken of the color of men; but justice, wisdom, and humanity should weigh alone, and be all-controlling.

Formerly our petitions for the elective franchise were met and denied upon the ground, that, while colored men were protected in person and property, they were not required to perform military duty. Of course this was only a plausible excuse; for we were subject to any call the Government was pleased to make upon us, and we could not properly be made to suffer because the Government did not see fit to impose military duty upon us. The fault was with the Government, not with us.

But now even this frivolous though somewhat decent apology for excluding us from the ballot-box is entirely swept away. Two hundred thousand colored men, according to a recent statement of President Lincoln, are now in the service, upon field and flood, in the army and the navy of the United States; and every day adds to their number. They are there as volunteers, coming forward with other patriotic men at the call of their imperilled country; they are there also as substitutes filling up the quotas which would otherwise have to be filled up by white men who now remain at home; they are also there as drafted men, by a certain law of Congress, which, for once, makes no difference on account of color: and whether they are there as volunteers, as substitutes, or as drafted men, neither ourselves, our cause, nor our country, need be ashamed of their appearance or their action upon the battle-field. Friends and enemies, rebels and loyal men,-- each, after their kind,--have borne conscious and unconscious testimony to the gallantry and other noble qualities of the colored troops.

Your fathers laid down the principle, long ago, that universal suffrage is the best foundation of Government. We believe as your fathers believed, and as they practised; for, in eleven States out of the original thirteen, colored men exercised the right to vote at the time of the adoption of the Federal Constitution. The Divine-right Governments of Europe, with their aristocratic and privileged classes of *priests* and *nobles*, are little better than cunningly devised conspiracies against the natural rights of the people to govern themselves.

Whether the right to vote is a natural right or not, we are not here to determine. Natural or conventional, in either case we are amply supported in our appeal for its extension to us. If it is, as all the teachings of your Declaration of Independence imply, a *natural right*, to deny to us its exercise is a wrong done to our human nature. If, on the other hand, the right to vote is simply a conventional right, having no other foundation or significance than a mere conventional arrangement, which may be extended or contracted, given or taken away, upon reasonable grounds, we insist, that, even basing the right upon this uncertain foundation, we may reasonably claim a right to a voice in the election of the men who are to have at their command our time, our services, our property, our persons, and our lives. This command of our persons and lives is no longer theory, but now the positive practice of our Government. We say, therefore, that having required, demanded, and in some instances compelled, us to serve with our time, our property, and our lives, coupling us in all the obligations and duties imposed upon the more highly favored of our fellow-citizens in this war to protect and defend your country from threatened destruction, and having fully established the precedent by which, in all similar and dissimilar cases of need, we may be compelled to respond to a like requisition,--we claim to have fully earned the elective franchise; and that you, the American people, have virtually contracted an obligation to grant it, which has all the sanctions of justice, honor, and magnanimity, in favor of its prompt fulfilment. Are we good enough to use bullets, and not good enough to use ballots? May we defend rights in time of war, and yet be denied the exercise of those rights in time of peace? Are we citizens when the nation is in peril, and aliens when the nation is in safety? May we shed our blood under the star-spangled banner on the battle-field, and yet be debarred from marching under it to the ballot-box? Will the brave white soldiers, bronzed by the hardships and exposures of repeated campaigns, men who have fought by the side of black men, be ashamed to cast their ballots by the side of their companions-in-arms? May we give our lives, but not our votes, for the good of the republic? Shall we toil with you to win the prize of free government, while you alone shall monopolize all its valued privileges? Against such a conclusion, every sentiment of honor and manly fraternity utters an indignant protest.

It is quite true, that some part of the American people may, with a show of plausibility, evade the force of this appeal and deny this claim. There are men in all countries who can evade any duty or obligation which is not enforced by the strong arm of the law. Our country is no exception to the rule. They can say in this case, "Colored men, we have done you no wrong. From first to last, we have objected to the measure of employing you to help put down this rebellion, foreseeing the very claim you now set up. Were we to-day invested with the power and authority of this Government, we would instantly disband every colored regiment now in front of Richmond, and everywhere else in the Southern States. We do not believe in making soldiers of black men" To all that, we reply, There need be no doubt whatever. No doubt they would disband the black troops if they had the power; and equally plain is it that they would disband the white troops also if they had the power.

They do not believe in making black men soldiers; but they equally do not believe in making white men soldiers to fight slaveholding rebels. But we do not address ourselves here to particular parties and classes of our countrymen; we would appeal directly to the moral sense, honor, and magnanimity of the whole nation; and, with a cause so good, cannot believe that we shall appeal in vain. Parties and classes rise and fall, combine and dissolve; but the national conscience remains forever; and it is that to which our cause is addressed. It may, however, be said that the colored people enlisted in the service of the country without any promise or stipulation that they would be rewarded with political equality at the end of the war; but all the more, on this very account, do we hold the American people bound in honor thus to reward them. By the measure of confidence reposed in the national honor and generosity, we have the right to measure the obligation of fulfilment. The fact, that when called into the service of the country, we went forward without exacting terms or conditions, to the mind of the generous man enhances our claims.

But, again, why are we so urgent for the possession of this particular right? We are asked, even by some Abolitionists, why we cannot be satisfied, for the present at least, with personal freedom; the right to testify in courts of law; the right to own, buy, and sell real estate; the right to sue and be sued. We answer, Because in a republican country, where general suffrage is the rule, personal liberty, the right to testify in courts of law, the right to hold, buy, and sell property, and all other rights, become mere privileges, held at the option of others, where we are excepted from the general political liberty. What gives to the newly arrived emigrants, fresh from lands governed by kingcraft and priestcraft, special consequence in the eyes of the American people? It is not their virtue, for they are often depraved; it is not their knowledge, for they are often ignorant; it is not their wealth, for they are often very poor; why, then, are they courted by the leaders of all parties? The answer is, that our institutions clothe them with the elective franchise, and they have a voice in making the laws of the country. Give the colored men of this country the elective franchise, and you will see no violent mobs driving the black laborer from the wharves of large cities, and from toil elsewhere by which he honestly gains his bread. You will see no influential priest, like the late Bishop Hughes, addressing mobocrats and murderers as "gentlemen"; and no influential politician, like Governor Seymour, addressing the "misguided" rowdies of New York as his "friends." The possession of that right is the keystone to the arch of human liberty; and, without that, the whole may at any moment fall to the ground; while, with it, that liberty may stand forever,--a blessing to us, and no possible injury to you. If you still ask why we want to vote, we answer, Because we don't want to be mobbed from our work, or insulted with impunity at every corner. We are men, and want to be as free in our native country as other men.

Fellow-citizens, let us entreat you, have faith in your own principles. If freedom is good for any, it is good for all. If you need the elective franchise, we need it even more. You are strong, we are weak; you are many, we are few; you are protected, we are exposed. Clothe us with this safeguard of our liberty, and give us an interest in the country to which, in common with you, we have given our lives and poured out our best blood. You cannot need special protection. Our degradation is not essential to your elevation, nor our peril essential to your safety. You are not likely to be outstripped in the race of improvement by persons of African descent; and hence you have no need of superior advantages, nor to burden them with disabilities of any kind. Let your Government be what all governments should be,--a copy of the eternal laws of the universe; before which all men stand equal as to rewards and punishments, life and death, without regard to country, kindred, tongue, or people.

But what we have now said, in appeal for the elective franchise, applies to our people generally. A special reason may be urged in favor of granting colored men the right in all the rebellious States.

Whatever may be the case with monarchial governments; however they may despise the crowd, and rely upon their *prestige*, armaments, and standing armies, to support them,-- a republican government like ours depends largely upon the friendship of the people over whom it is established, for its harmonious and happy operation. This kind of government must have its foundation in the affections of the people; otherwise the people will hinder, circumvent, and destroy it. Up to a few years of the rebellion, our government lived in the friendship of the masses of the Southern people. Its enemies were, however, numerous and active; and these at last prevailed, poisoned the minds of the masses, broke up the government, brought on the war. Now, whoever lives to see this rebellion suppressed at the South, as we believe we all shall, will also see the South characterized by a sullen hatred towards the National Government. It will be transmitted from father to son, and will be held by them "as sacred animosity." The treason, mowed down by the armies of Grant and Sherman, will be followed by a strong undergrowth of treason which will go far to disturb and peaceful operation of the hated Government.

Every United States mail-carrier, every custom-house officer, every Northern man, and every representative of the United States Government, in the Southern States, will be held in abhorrence; and for a long time that country is to be governed with difficulty. We may conquer Southern armies by the sword; but it is another thing to conquer Southern hate. Now what is the natural counterpoise against this Southern malign hostility? This it is: give the elective franchise to every colored man of the South who is of sane mind, and has arrived at the age of twenty-one years, and you have at once four millions of friends who will guard with their vigilance, and, if need be, defend with their arms, the ark of Federal Liberty from the treason and pollution of her enemies. You are sure of the enmity of the masters,--make sure of the friendship of the slaves; for, depend upon it, your Government cannot afford to encounter the enmity of both.

If the arguments addressed to your sense of honor, in these pages, in favor of extending the elective franchise to the colored people of the whole country, be strong, that which we are prepared to present to you in behalf of the colored people of rebellious States can be made tenfold stronger. By calling them to take part with you in the war to subdue their rebellious masters, and the fact that thousands of them have done so, and thousands more would gladly do so, you have exposed them to special resentment and wrath; which, without the elective franchise, will descend upon them in unmitigated fury. To break with your friends, and make peace with your enemies; to weaken your friends, and strengthen your enemies; to abase your friends, and exalt your enemies; to disarm your friends, and arm your enemies; to disfranchise your loyal friends, and enfranchise your disloyal enemies,--is not the policy of honor, but of infamy.

But we will not weary you. Our cause is in some measure before you. The power to redress our wrongs, and to grant us our just rights, is in your hands. You can determine our destiny,--blast us by continued degradation, or bless us with the means of gradual elevation. We are among you, and must remain among you; and it is for you to say, whether our presence shall conduce to the general peace and welfare of the country, or be a constant cause of discussion and of irritation,--troubles in the State, troubles in the Church, troubles everywhere.

To avert these troubles, and to place your great country in

safety from them, only one word from you, the American people, is needed, and that is JUSTICE: let that magic word once be sounded, and become all-controlling in all your courts of law subordinate and supreme; let the halls of legislation, state and national, spurn all statesmanship as mischievous and ruinous that has not justice for its foundation; let justice without compromise, without curtailment, and without partiality, be observed with respect to all men, no class of men claiming for themselves any right which they will not grant to another,--then strife and discord will cease; peace will be placed upon enduring foundations; and the American people, now divided and hostile, will dwell together in power and unity.

1865

WHAT THE BLACK MAN WANTS
(Annual Meeting of the Massachusetts Anti-slavery Society)

Mr. President:

I came here, as I come always to the meetings in New England, as a listener, and not as a speaker; and one of the reasons why I have not been more frequently to the meetings of this society, has been because of the disposition on the part of some of my friends to call me out upon the platform, even when they knew that there was some difference of opinion and of feeling between those who rightfully belong to this platform and myself; and for fear of being misconstrued, as desiring to interrupt or disturb the proceedings of these meetings, I have usually kept away, and have thus been deprived of that educating influence, which I am always free to confess is of the highest order, descending from this platform. I have felt, since I have lived out West, that in going there I parted from a great deal that was valuable; and I feel, every time I come to these meetings, that I have lost a great deal by making my home west of Boston, west of Massachusetts; for, if anywhere in the country there is to be found the highest sense of justice, or the truest demands for my race, I look for it in the East, I look for it here. The ablest discussions of the whole question of our rights occur here, and to be deprived of the privilege of listening to those discussions is a great deprivation.

I do not know, from what has been said, that there is any difference of opinion as to the duty of abolitionists, at the present moment. How can we get up any difference at this point, or any point, where we are so united, so agreed? I went especially, however, with that word of Mr. Phillips, which is the criticism of Gen. Banks and Gen. Banks' policy. I hold that that policy is our chief danger at the present moment; that it practically enslaves the Negro, and makes the Proclamation of 1863 a mockery and delusion. What is freedom? It is the right to choose one's own employment. Certainly it means that, if it means anything; and when any individual or combination of individuals undertakes to decide for any man when he shall work, where he shall work, at what he shall work, and for what he shall work, he or they practically reduce him to slavery. [Applause.] He is a slave. That I understand Gen. Banks to do--to determine for the so-called freedman, when, and where, and at what, and for how much he shall work, when he shall be punished, and by whom punished. It is absolute slavery. It defeats the beneficent intention of the Government, if it has beneficent intentions, in regards to the freedom of our people.

I have had but one idea for the last three years to present to the American people, and the phraseology in which I clothe it is the old abolition phraseology. I am for the "immediate, unconditional, and universal" enfranchisement of the black man, in every State in the Union. [Loud applause.] Without this, his liberty is a mockery; without this, you might as well almost retain the old name of slavery for his condition; for in fact, if he is not the slave of the individual master, he is the slave of society, and holds his liberty as a privilege, not as a right. He is at the mercy of the mob, and has no means of protecting himself.

It may be objected, however, that this pressing of the Negro's right to suffrage is premature. Let us have slavery abolished, it may be said, let us have labor organized, and then, in the natural course of events, the right of suffrage will be extended to the Negro. I do not agree with this. The constitution of the human mind is such, that if it once disregards the conviction forced upon it by a revelation of truth, it requires the exercise of a higher power to produce the same conviction afterwards. The American people are now in tears. The Shenandoah has run blood--the best blood of the North. All around Richmond, the blood of New England and of the North has been shed--of your sons, your brothers and your fathers. We all feel, in the existence of this Rebellion, that judgments terrible, wide-spread, far-reaching, overwhelming, are abroad in the land; and we feel, in view of these judgments, just now, a disposition to learn righteousness. This is the hour. Our streets are in mourning, tears are falling at every fireside, and under the chastisement of this Rebellion we have almost come up to the point of conceding this great, this all important right of suffrage. I fear that if we fail to do it now, if abolitionists fail to press it now, we may not see, for centuries to come, the same disposition that exists at this moment. [Applause.] Hence, I say, now is the time to press this right.

It may be asked, "Why do you want it? Some men have got along very well without it. Women have not this right." Shall we justify one wrong by another? This is a sufficient answer. Shall we at this moment justify the deprivation of the Negro of the right to vote, because some one else is deprived of that privilege? I hold that women, as well as men, have the right to vote [applause], and my heart and my voice go with the movement to extend suffrage to woman; but that question rests upon another basis than that on which our right rests. We may be asked, I say, why we want it. I will tell you why we want it. We want it because it is our *right*, first of all. No class of men can, without insulting their own nature, be content with any deprivation of their rights. We want it again, as a means for educating our race. Men are so constituted that they derive their conviction of their own possibilities largely from the estimate formed of them by others. If nothing is expected of a people, that people will find it difficult to contradict that expectation. By depriving us of suffrage, you affirm our incapacity to form an intelligent judgment respecting public men and public measures; you declare before the world that we are unfit to exercise the elective franchise, and by this means lead us to undervalue ourselves, to put a low estimate upon ourselves, and to feel that we have no possibilities like other men. Again, I want the elective franchise, for one, as a colored man, because ours is a peculiar government, based upon a peculiar idea, and that idea is universal suffrage. If I were in a monarchial government, or an autocratic or aristocratic government, where the few bore rule and the many were subject, there would be no special stigma resting upon me, because I did not exercise the elective franchise. It would do me no great violence. Mingling with the mass I should partake of the strength of the mass; I should be supported by the mass, and I should have the same incentives to endeavor with the mass of my fellowmen; it would be no particular burden, no particular deprivation; but here where universal suffrage is the rule, where that is the fundamental idea of the Government, to rule us out is to make us an exception, to brand us with the stigma of inferiority, and to invite to our heads the missiles of those about us; therefore, I want the franchise for the black man.

There are, however, other reasons, not derived from any consideration merely of our rights, but arising out of the conditions of the South, and of the country--considerations which have already been referred to by Mr. Phillips--considerations which must arrest the attention of statesmen. I believe that when the tall heads of this Rebellion shall have been swept down, as they will be swept down, when the Davises and Toombses and Stephenses, and others who are leading this rebellion shall have been blotted out, there will be this rank undergrowth of treason, to which reference has been made, growing up there, and interfering with, and thwarting the quiet operation of the Federal Government in those States. You will see those traitors, handing down, from sire to son, the same malignant spirit which they have manifested, and which they are now exhibiting, with malicious hearts, broad blades, and bloody hands in the field, against our sons and brothers. That spirit will still remain; and whoever sees the Federal Government extended over those Southern States will see that Government in a strange land, and not only in a strange land, but in an enemy's land. A post-master of the United States in the South will find himself surrounded by a hostile spirit; a collector in the Southern port will find himself surrounded by a hostile spirit; a United States marshal or United States judge will be surrounded there by a hostile element. The enmity will not die out in a year, will not die out in an age. The Federal Government will be looked upon in those States precisely as the Governments of Austria and France are looked upon in Italy at the present moment. They will endeavor to circumvent, they will endeavor to destroy, the peaceful operation of this Government. Now, where will you find the strength to counterbalance this spirit, if you do not find it in the Negroes of the South? They are your friends, and have always been your friends. They were your friends even when the Government did not regard them as such. They comprehended the genius of this war before you did. It is a significant fact, it is a marvellous fact, it seems almost to imply a direct interposition of Providence, that this war, which began in the interest of slavery on both sides, bids fair to end in the interest of liberty on both sides. [Applause.] It was begun, I say, in the interest of slavery on both sides. The South was fighting to take slavery out of the Union, and the North fighting to keep it in the Union; the South fighting to get it beyond the limits of the United States Consitituion, and the North fighting to retain it within those limits; the South fighting for new guarantees, and the North fighting for the old guarantees;-- both despising the Negro, both insulting the Negro. Yet, the Negro, apparently endowed with wisdom from on high, saw more clearly the end from the beginning than we did. When Seward said the status of no man in the country would be changed by the war, the Negro did not believe him. [Applause.] When our generals sent their underlings in shoulder-straps to hunt the flying Negro back from our lines into the jaws of slavery, from which he had escaped, the Negroes thought that a mistake had been made, and that the intentions of the Government had not been rightly understood by our officers in shoulder-straps, and they continued to come into our lines, threading their way through bogs and fens, over briers and thorns, fording streams, swimming rivers, bringing us tidings as to the safe path to march, and pointing out the dangers that threatened us. They are our only friends in the South, and we should be true to them in this their trial hour, and see to it that they have the elective franchise.

I know that we are inferior to you in some things--virtually inferior. We walk about among you like dwarfs among giants. Our heads are scarcely seen above the great sea of humanity. The Germans are superior to us; the Irish are superior to us; the Yankees are superior to us [Laughter]; they can do what we cannot, that is, what we have not hitherto been allowed to do. But while I make this admission, I utterly deny, that we are originally, or naturally, or practically, or in any way, or in any important sense, inferior to anybody on this globe. [Loud applause.] This charge of inferiority is an old dodge. It has been made available for oppression on many occasions. It is only about six centuries since the blue-eyed and fair-haired Anglo-Saxons were considered inferior by the haughty Normans, who once trampled upon them. If you read the history of the Norman Conquest, you will find that this proud Anglo-Saxon was once looked upon as of coarser clay than his Norman master, and might be found in the highways and byways of old England laboring with a brass collar on his neck, and the name of the master marked upon it. *You* were down then! [Laughter and applause.] You are up now. I am glad you are up, and I want you to be glad to help us up also. [Applause.]

The story of our inferiority is an old dodge, as I have said; for wherever men oppress their fellows, wherever they enslave them, they will endeavor to find the needed apology for such enslavement and oppression in the character of the people oppressed and enslaved. When we wanted, a few years ago, a slice of Mexico, it was hinted that the Mexicans were an inferior race, that the old Castilian blood had become so weak that it would scarcely run down hill, and that Mexico needed the long, strong and beneficent arm of the Anglo-Saxon care extended over it. We said that it was necessary to its salvation, and a part of the "manifest destiny" of this Republic, to extend our arm over that dilapidated government. So, too, when Russia wanted to take possession of a part of the Ottoman Empire, the Turks were "an inferior race." So, too, when England wants to set the heel of her power more firmly in the quivering heart of old Ireland, the Celts are an "inferior race." So, too, the Negro, when he is to be robbed of any right which is justly his, is an "inferior man." It is said that we are ignorant; I admit it. Be if we know enough to be hung, we know enough to vote. If the Negro knows enough to pay taxes to support the government, he knows enough to vote; taxation and representation should go together. If he knows enough to shoulder a musket and fight for the flag, fight for the government, he knows enough to vote. If he knows as much when he is sober as an Irishman knows when drunk, he knows enough to vote, on good American principles. [Laughter and applause.]

But I was saying that you needed a counterpoise in the persons of the slaves to the enmity that would exist at the South after the Rebellion is put down. I hold that the American people are bound, not only in self defence, to extend this right to the freedmen of the South, but they are bound by their love of country, and by all their regard for the future safety of those Southern States, to do this--to do it as a measure essential to the preservation of peace there. But I will now dwell upon this. I put it to the American sense of honor. The honor of a nation is an important thing. It is said in the Scriptures, "What doth it profit a man if he gain the whole world, and lose his own soul?" It may be said, also, What doth it profit a nation if it gain the whole world, but lose its honor? I hold that the American government has taken upon itself a solemn obligation of honor, to see that this war--let it be long or let it be short, let it cost much or let it cost little--that this war shall not cease until every freedman at the South has the right to vote. [Applause.] It has bound itself to it. What have you asked the black men of the South, the black men of the whole country, to do? Why, you have asked them to incur the deadly enmity of their masters, in order to befriend you and to befriend this Government. You have asked us to call down, not only upon ourselves, but upon our children's children, the deadly hate of the entire Southern people. You have called upon us to turn our backs upon our masters, to abandon their cause and espouse yours; to turn against the South and in favor of the North; to shoot down the Confederacy and uphold the flag--the American flag. You have called upon us to expose ourselves to all the subtle machinations of their malignity for all time. And now, what do you propose to do when you come

to make peace? To reward your enemies, and trample in the
dust your friends? Do you intend to sacrifice the very men
who have come to the rescue of your banner in the South,
and incurred the lasting displeasure of their masters thereby?
Do you intend to sacrifice them and reward your enemies?
Do you mean to give your enemies the right to vote, and
take it away from your friends? Is that wise policy? Is that
honorable? Could American honor withstand such a blow?
I do not believe you will do it. I think you will see to it that
we have the right to vote. There is something too mean in
looking upon the Negro, when you are in trouble, as a citizen, and when you are free from trouble, as an alien. When
this nation was in trouble, in its early struggles, it looked
upon the Negro as a citizen. In 1776 he was a citizen. At the
time of the formation of the Constitution the Negro had the
right to vote in eleven States out of the old thirteen. In your
trouble you have made us citizens. In 1812 Gen. Jackson addressed us as citizens--"fellow-citizens." He wanted us to
fight. We were citizens then! And now, when you come to
frame a conscription bill, the Negro is a citizen again. He has
been a citizen just three times in the history of this government, and it has always been in time of trouble. In time of
trouble we are citizens. Shall we be citizens in war, and
aliens in peace? Would that be just?

I ask my friends who are apologizing for not insisting
upon this right, where can the black man look, in this country, for the assertion of his right, if he may not look to the
Massachusetts Anti-Slavery Society? Where under the
whole heavens can he look for sympathy, in asserting this
right, if he may not look to this platform? Have you lifted us
up to a certain height to see that we are men, and then are
any disposed to leave us there, without seeing that we are put
in possession of all our rights? We look naturally to this
platform for the assertion of all our rights, and for this one
especially. I understand the anti-slavery societies of this
country to be based on two principles,--first, the freedom of
the blacks of this country; and, second, the elevation of them.
Let me not be misunderstood here. I am not asking for sympathy at the hands of abolitionists, sympathy at the hands of
any. I think the American people are disposed often to be

generous rather than just. I look over this country at the present time, and I see Educational Societies, Sanitary Commissions, Freedmen's Associations, and the like,--all very good: but in regard to the colored people there is always more that is benevolent, I perceive, than just, manifested towards us. What I ask for the Negro is not benevolence, not pity, not sympathy, but simply *justice.* [Applause.] The American people have always been anxious to know what they shall do with us. Gen. Banks was distressed with solicitude as to what he should do with the Negro. Everybody has asked the question, and they learned to ask it early of the abolitionists, "What shall we do with the Negro?" I have had but one answer from the beginning. Do nothing with us! Your doing with us has already played the mischief with us. Do nothing with us! If the apples will not remain on the tree of their own strength, if they are worm-eaten at the core, if they are early ripe and disposed to fall, let them fall! I am not for tying or fastening them on the tree in any way, except by nature's plan, and if they will not stay there, let them fall. And if the Negro cannot stand on his own legs, let him fall alone! If you see him on his way to school, let him alone, don't disturb him! If you see him going to the dinner-table at a hotel, let him go! If you see him going to the ballot-box, let him alone, don't disturb him! [Applause.] If you see him going into a work-shop, just let him alone,--your interference is doing him a positive injury. Gen. Banks' "preparation" is of a piece with this attempt to prop up the Negro. Let him fall if he cannot stand alone! If the Negro cannot live by the line of eternal justice, so beautifully pictured to you in the illustration used by Mr. Phillips, the fault will not be yours, it will be his who made the Negro, and established that line for his government. [Applause.] Let him live or die by that. If you will only untie his hands, and give him a chance, I think he will live. He will work as readily for himself as the white man. A great many delusions have been swept away by this war. One was, that the Negro would not work; he has proved his ability to work. Another was, that the Negro would not fight; that he possessed only the most sheepish attributes of humanity; was a perfect lamb, or an "Uncle Tom;" disposed to take off his coat whenever required, fold his hands, and be whipped by anybody who wanted to whip him. But the war has proved that there is a great deal of human nature in the Negro, and that "he will fight," as Mr. Quincy, our President, said, in earlier days than these, "when there is a reasonable probability of his whipping anybody."

1866
RECONSTRUCTION

The assembling of the Second Session of the Thirty-ninth Congress may very properly be made the occasion of a few earnest words on the already much-worn topic of reconstruction.

Seldom has any legislative body been the subject of a solicitude more intense, or of aspirations more sincere and ardent. There are the best of reasons for this profound interest. Questions of vast moment, left undecided by the last session of Congress, must be manfully grappled with by this. No political skirmishing will avail. The occasion demands statesmanship.

Whether the tremendous war so heroically fought and so victoriously ended shall pass into history a miserable failure, barren of permanent results,--a scandalous and shocking waste of blood and treasure,--a strife for empire, as Earl Russell characterized it, of no value to liberty or civilization,--an attempt to re-establish a Union by force, which must be the merest mockery of a Union,--an effort to bring under Federal authority states into which no loyal man from the North may safely enter, and to bring men into the national councils who deliberate with daggers and vote with revolvers, and who do not even conceal their deadly hate of the country that conquered them; or whether, on the other hand, we shall, as the rightful reward of victory over treason, have a solid nation, entirely delivered from all contradictions and social antagonisms, based upon loyalty, liberty, and equality, must be determined one way or the other by the present session of Congress. The last session really did nothing which can be considered final as to these questions. The Civil Rights Bill and the Freedman's Bureau Bill and the proposed constitutional amendments, with the amendment already adopted and recognized as the law of the land, do not reach the difficulty, and cannot, unless the whole structure of the government is changed from a government by States to something like a despotic central government, with power to control even the municipal regulations of States, and to make them conform to its own despotic will. While there remains such an idea as the right of each State to control its own local affairs,--an idea, by the way, more deeply rooted in the minds of men of all sections of the country than perhaps any one other political idea,--no general assertion of human rights can be of any practical value. To change the character of the government at this point is neither possible nor desirable. All that is necessary to be done is to make the government consistent with itself, and render the rights of the States compatible with the sacred rights of human nature.

The arm of the Federal government is long, but it is far too short to protect the rights of individuals in the interior of distant States. They must have the power to protect themselves, or they will go unprotected, spite of all the laws the Federal government can put upon the national statute-book.

Slavery, like all other great systems of wrong, founded in the depths of human selfishness, and existing for ages, has not neglected its own conservation. It has steadily exerted an influence upon all around it favorable to its own continuance. And to-day it is so strong that it could exist, not only without law, but even against law. Custom, manners, morals, religion, are all on its side everywhere in the South; and when you add the ignorance and servility of the ex-slave to the intelligence and accustomed authority of the master, you have the conditions, not out of which slavery will again grow, but under which it is impossible for the Federal government to wholly destroy it, unless the Federal government be armed with despotic power, to blot out State authority, and to station a Federal officer at every cross-road. This, of course, cannot be done, and ought not even if it could. The true way and the easiest way is to make our government entirely consistent with itself, and give to every loyal citizen the elective franchise,--a right and power which will be ever present, and will form a wall of fire for his protection.

One of the invaluable compensations of the late Rebellion

is the highly instructive disclosure it made of the true source
of danger to republican government. Whatever may be tol-
reated in monarchial and despotic governments, no republic
is safe that tolerates a privileged class, or denies to any of its
citizens equal rights and equal means to maintain them.
What was theory before the war has been made fact by the
war.

There is cause to be thankful even for the rebellion. It is
an impressive teacher, though a stern and terrible one. In
both characters it has come to us, and it was perhaps needed
in both. It is an instructor never a day before its time, for it
comes only when all other means of progress and enlightenment have failed. Whether the oppressed and despairing
bondman, no longer able to repress his deep yearnings for
manhood, or the tyrant, in his pride and impatience, takes
initiative, and strikes the blow for a firmer hold and a longer
lease of oppression, the result is the same,--society is instructed or may be.

Such are the limitations of the common mind, and so
thoroughly engrossing are the cares of common life, that
only the few among men can discern through the glitter and
dazzle of present prosperity the dark outlines of approaching
disasters, even though they may have come up to our very
gates, and are already within striking distance. The yawning
cam and corroded bolt conceal their defects from the mariner
until the storm calls all hands to the pumps. Prophets indeed, were abundant before the war; but who cares for
prophets while their predictions remain unfulfilled, and the
calamities of which they tell are masked behind a blinding
blaze of national prosperity?

It is asked, said Henry Clay, on a memorable occasion,
Will slavery never come to an end? That question, said he,
was asked fifty years ago, and it has been answered by fifty
years of unprecedented prosperity. Spite of the eloquence of
the earnest Abolitionists,--poured out against slavery during
thirty years,--even they must confess, that, in all the probabilities of the case, that system of barbarism would have continued its horrors far beyond the limits of the nineteenth century but for the Rebellion, and perhaps only have disappeared at least in a fiery conflict, even more fierce and bloody

that that which has now been suppressed.

It is no disparagement to truth, that it can only prevail where reason prevails. War begins where reason ends. The thing worse than rebellion is the thing that causes rebellion. What that thing is, we have been taught to our cost. It remains now to be seen whether we have the needed courage to have that cause entirely removed from the Republic. At any rate, to this grand work of national regeneration and entire purification Congress must now address itself, with full purpose that the work shall this time be thoroughly done. The deadly upas, root and branch, leaf and fibre, body and sap, must be utterly destroyed. The country is evidently not in a condition to listen patiently to pleas for postponement, however plausible, nor will it permit the responsibility to be shifted to other shoulders. Authority and power are here commensurate with the duty imposed. There are no cloud-flung shadows to obscure the way. Truth shines with brighter light and intenser heat at every moment, and a country torn and rent and bleeding implores relief from its distress and agony.

If time was at first needed, Congress has now had time. All the requisite materials from which to form an intelligent judgment are now before it. Whether its members look at the origin, the progress, the termination of the war, or at the mockery of a peace now existing, they will find only one unbroken chain of argument in favor of a radical policy of reconstruction. For the omissions of the last session, some excuses may be allowed. A treacherous President stood in the way; and it can be easily seen how reluctant good men might be to admit an apostasy which involved so much of baseness and ingratitude. It was natural that they should seek to save him by bending to him even when he leaned to the side of error. But all is changed now. Congress knows now that it must go on without his aid, and even against his machinations. The advantage of the present session over the last is immense. Where that investigated, this has the facts. Where that walked by faith, this may walk by sight. Where that halted, this must go forward, and where that failed, this must succeed, giving the country whole measures where that gave us half-measures, merely as a means of saving the elections in a few doubtful districts. That Congress saw what was right, but distrusted the enlightenment of the loyal masses; but what was forborne in distrust of the people must now be done with a full knowledge that the people expect and require it. The members go to Washington fresh from the inspiring presence of the people. In every considerable public meeting, and in almost every conceivable way, whether at court-house, school-house, or cross-roads, in doors and out, the subject has been discussed, and the people have emphatically pronounced in favor of a radical policy. Listening to the doctrines of expediency and compromise with pity, impatience, and disgust, they have everywhere broken into demonstrations of the wildest enthusiasm when a brave word has been spoken in favor of equal rights and impartial suffrage. Radicalism, so far from being odious, is now the popular passport to power. The men most bitterly charged with it go to Congress with the largest majorities, while the timid and doubtful are sent by lean majorities, or else left at home. The strange controversy between the President and Congress, at one time so threatening, is disposed of by the people. The high reconstructive powers which he so confidently, ostentatiously, and haughtily claimed, have been disallowed, denounced, and utterly repudiated; while those claimed by Congress have been confirmed.

Of the spirit and magnitude of the canvass nothing need be said. The appeal was to the people, and the verdict was worthy of the tribunal. Upon an occasion of his own selection, with the advice and approval of his astute Secretary, soon after the members of Congress had returned to their constituents, the President quitted the executive mansion, sandwiched himself between two recognized heroes,--men whom the whole country delighted to honor,--and, with all the advantage which such company could give him, stumped the country from the Atlantic to the Mississippi, advocating everywhere his policy as against that of Congress. It was a strange sight, and perhaps the most disgraceful exhibition ever made by any President; but, as no evil is entirely unmixed, good has come of this, as from many others. Ambitious, unscrupulous, energetic, indefatigable, voluble, and plausible,--a political gladiator, ready for a "set-to" in any crowd,--he is beaten in his own chosen field, and stands to-day before the country as a convicted usurper, a political criminal, guilty of a bold and persistent attempt to possess himself of the legislative powers solemnly secured to Congress by the Constitution. No vindication could be more complete, no condemnation could be more absolute and humiliating. Unless reopened by the sword, as recklessly threatened in some circles, this question is now closed for all time.

Without attempting to settle here the metaphysical and somewhat theological questions (about which so much has already been said and written), whether once in the Union,--agreeably to the formula, once in grace always in grace,--it is obvious to common sense that the rebellious States stand to-day, in point of law, precisely where they stood when, ex-hausted, beaten, conquered, they fell powerless at the feet of Federal authority. Their State governments were over-thrown, and the lives and property of the leaders of the Re-bellion were forfeited. In reconstructing the institutions of these shattered and overthrown States, Congress should be-gin with a clean slate, and make clean work of it. Let there be no hesitation. It would be a cowardly deference to a defeated and treacherous President, if any account were made of the illegitimate, one-sided, sham governments hurried into existence for a malign purpose in the absence of Congress. These pretended governments, which were never submitted to the people, and from participation in which four millions of the loyal people were excluded by Presidential order, should now be treated according to their true governments, in the formation of which loyal men, black and white, shall participate.

It is not, however, within the scope of this paper to point out the precise steps to be taken, and the means to be em-ployed. The people are less concerned about these than the grand end to be attained. They demand such a reconstruction as shall put an end to the present anarchical state of things in the late rebellious States,--where frightful murders and wholesale massacres are perpetrated in the very presence of Federal soldiers. This horrible business they require shall cease. They want a reconstruction such as will protect loyal

men, black and white, in their persons and property; such a
one as will cause Northern industry, Northern capital, and
Northern civilization to flow into the South, and make a
man from New England as much at home in Carolina as
elsewhere in the Republic. No Chinese wall can now be tolerated. The South must be opened to the light of law and
liberty, and this session of Congress is relied upon to accomplish this important work.

The plain, common-sense way of doing this work, as intimated at the beginning, is simply to establish in the South
one law, one government, one administration of justice, one
condition to the exercise of the elective franchise, for men of
all races and colors alike. This great measure is sought as
earnestly by loyal white men as by loyal blacks, and is needed
alike by both. Let sound political prescience but take the place
of an unreasoning prejudice, and this will be done.

Men denounce the negro for his prominence in this discussion; but it is no fault of his that in peace as in war, that in
conquering Rebel armies as in reconstructing the rebellious
States, the right of the negro is the true solution of our national troubles. The stern logic of events, which goes directly
to the point, disdaining all concern for the color or features
of men, has determined the interests of the country as identical with and inseparable from those of the negro.

The policy that emancipated and armed the negro--now
seen to have been wise and proper by the dullest--was not
certainly more sternly demanded than is now the policy of
enfranchisement. If with the negro was success in war, and
without him failure, so in peace it will be found that the nation must fall or flourish with the negro.

Fortunately, the Constitution of the United States knows
no distinction between citizens on account of color. Neither
does it know any difference between a citizen of a State and a
citizen of the United States. Citizenship evidently includes
all the rights of citizens, whether State or national. If the
Constitution knows none, it is clearly no part of the duty of a
Republican Congress now to institute one. The mistake of
the last session was the attempt to do this very thing, by a
renunciation of its power to secure political rights to any
class of citizens, with the obvious purpose to allow the

rebellious States to disfranchise, if they should see fit, their colored citizens. This unfortunate blunder must now be retrieved, and the emasculated citizenship given to the Negro supplanted by that contemplated in the Constitution of the United States, which declares that the citizens of each State shall enjoy all the rights and immunities of citizens of the several States,--so that a legal voter in any State shall be a legal voter in all the States.

SELECT
CHRONOLOGY

SELECT CHRONOLOGY

The following is a selection of events affecting Blacks which occurred during the Civil War. Certain other important events are included as benchmarks.

1860
November
6/Election of Abraham Lincoln

December
14/Georgia issues a call for a convention to deliberate on a Southern Confederacy

20/Secession of South Carolina

22/South Carolina appoints a commission to supervise the disposal of federal property

1861
January
Following the example of South Carolina, Deep South states proceed to seize federal, civil and military property

9/Mississippi secedes

10/Florida secedes

11/Alabama secedes

19/Georgia secedes

21/The New York legislature pledges support to the Union; other free states take similar action.

26/Louisiana secedes

29/Kansas admitted to the Union

February
1/Texas secedes

4/Convention held in Montgomery, Alabama by seceded states

8/Confederate Constitution adopted by Convention

9/Jefferson Davis of Mississippi elected president of Confederacy

18/Davis inaugurated

March
4/Inauguration of Abraham Lincoln, as sixteenth President of the United States

April
12/Fort Sumter is fired upon

13/Surrender of federal garrison at Fort Sumter

15/President Lincoln announces that an insurrection is in progress and calls on loyal states to supply troops

19/Lincoln orders blockade of Confederate ports

Frederick Douglass cancels projected trip to Haiti and calls for recruitment of Black troops. Writes *Nemesis.*

May
22/Gen. Butler arrives at Fort Monroe, Virginia as commandant

24/Butler refuses to surrender three slaves who had sought refuge in his command. This is beginning of "contraband" movement.

30/Secretary of War Camernon authorizes Butler to retain fugitives, to set them to work, and to maintain records of their service.

July
21/Battle of First Bull Run

22/U.S. House of Representatives passes the Crittenden Resolution, affirming that the war was being fought to preserve the Union and not to interfere with slavery.

25/U.S. Senate approves Crittenden Resolution, on motion of Andrew Johnson of Tennessee, later to be governor of Tennessee and Vice-President and President of the United States.

August
14/Gen. John Charles Fremont declares "martial law" in St. Louis, which is Confederate in sentiment

16/Lincoln declares Confederate states to be in a state of insurrection.

30/Gen. Fremont proclaims confiscation of rebel's property and emancipation of their slaves. The order causes wide protest and is disavowed by Lincoln.

October
Frederick Douglass writes approvingly of Fremont's proclamation, "Fremont is the right man in the right place," and criticizes Lincoln's response.

2/Gen. Fremont relieved of command

November
1/Gen. McClellan replaces aging Gen. Winfield Scott as Union Commander

7/Battle of Port Royal Sound (South Carolina). Union occupation of the area begins, serving as a base for the blockade of Charleston.

28/Union authorities at Port Royal ordered to use slaves remaining in the area to harvest crops and to work on installations.

December
5/Petitions introduced in U.S. Congress requesting abolition of slavery, particularly among slaveholders in the Confederacy.

1862
January
15/Gen. Thomas Sherman writes to the War Department requesting that teachers be sent to Port Royal to teach slaves left on plantations now in Union hands. On initiative of Secretary of the Treasury Chase, a young Harvard law graduate, Edward L. Pierce, is invited to submit a plan, thus beginning the Port Royal Experiment.

February
4/The Virginia House of Delegates debates the enrolling of free Blacks in the Confederate Army. No action is taken.

23/The Military Department of the Gulf is created and Gen. Butler named chief. He leaves for New Orleans

March
9/Battle of *Monitor* and *Merrimack* (Virginia) at Hampton Roads, Virginia

April
3/U.S. Senate votes to abolish slavery in District of Columbia by a vote of 29 - 14

7/Battle of Shiloh

U.S. House of Representatives appoints committee on emancipation and colonization of Blacks.

Treaty for strengthening the suppression of the Atlantic Slave Trade concluded at Washington between the U.S. and

Great Britain; exchange of ratifications in London, May 20; proclaimed June 7, 1862.

11/U.S. House votes to abolish slavery in the District of Columbia by a vote of 93 - 39

May
1/Gen. Butler's "rule" in New Orleans begins

8/Confederate Evacuation of Norfolk

9/Gen. Hunter's Emancipation Proclamation in Department of the South (Georgia, Florida, South Carolina). Hunter authorized the arming of able-bodied Blacks.

13/Robert Small delivers Confederate gunboat *Planter* from Charleston to Union fleet.

19/Lincoln disavows Hunter's order

June
5/Lincoln signs bill recognizing Haiti and Liberia

19/Lincoln signs law prohibiting slavery in U.S. territories

July
17/Lincoln signs Confiscation Act which authorizes him to utilize Blacks in suppression of the rebellion and to seek a colonization site in the tropics for Blacks freed in consequence of such activity

22/Lincoln reads first draft of Emancipation Proclamation to cabinet

August
11/Gen. Grant orders the utilization of services of all fugitive slaves behind his lines (Corinth, Mississippi)

14/Lincoln meets delegation of free Blacks; he advocates colonization of Blacks in Central America

21/Jefferson Davis pronounces Union Generals Hunter and Phelps outlaws because they wish to recruit slaves for the Union Army

Gen. Phelps resigns because his project was disavowed by Washington

22/Gen. Butler calls upon free men of color to rally to the Union (New Orleans)

29-30/Battle of Second Bull Run

September
16/In a letter replying to Postmaster Montgomery Blair, Frederick Douglass rejects the government's proposal to colonize free Blacks in Central America

22/Lincoln announces his intention to declare emancipation of all slaves in states still in rebellion on January 1, 1863

27/Regiment of free Blacks, "Chasseurs d'Afrique," mustered in New Orleans

October
10/Jefferson Davis asks Virginia to draft 4500 Blacks to work on fortifications of Richmond

December
18/South Carolina provides for recruiting Blacks to work in construction of defences

23/Jefferson Davis issues proclamation declaring that Gen. Butler's soldiers be considered "robbers and criminals, deserving death"; this is interpreted by Confederate troops as justifying the massacre of Black Union soldiers

1863
January
1/Lincoln issues Emancipation Proclamation

12/Jefferson Davis' proclamation of 23 December, 1862, approved by Resolution of the Confederate Congress

20/Secretary of War Stanton authorizes Governor Andrews of Massachusetts to recruit Black troops

February
9/Recruiting of Fifty-Fourth Regiment of Massachusetts Volunteers begun

26/Cherokee Indian National Council repeals its secession, adheres to the Union and abolishes slavery

March
3/Lincoln signs Draft Act

21/Frederick Douglass issues broadside, *Men of Color, To Arms.* Subsequently he recruits troops, including his sons Charles and Lewis.

26/Lincoln writes to Gov. Andrew Johnson of Tennessee that the Black population "is the great available and yet unavailed...force for restoring the Union."

April
2/"Bread Riot" in Richmond disturbs Confederate government

20/State of West Virginia proclaimed

May
26-27/Battle of Fort Hudson (Louisiana)

28/Fifty-Fourth Massachusetss Volunteers leave Boston for Department of the South

June
7/Battle of Milliken's Bend (Louisiana)

July
1-3/Battle of Gettysburg

4/Surrender at Vicksburg

8/Surrender of Fort Hudson

11/First Assault on Fort Wagner (Charleston, SC)

13/Draft riots in New York City

18/Second Assault on Fort Wagner; heavy losses in Fifty-Fourth Massachussetts Volunteers and death of Col. Robert Gould Shaw

??/First meeting of Frederick Douglass with Lincoln (date uncertain)

30/In response to Confederate atrocities against Black Union soldiers, Lincoln announces "the Government will give the same protection to all its soldiers"

August
Frederick Douglass terminates the publication of *Douglass' Monthly* to devote more time to recruiting Black soldiers. The promise of a commission to him is not honored

December
8/Lincoln issues Proclamation of Amnesty and Reconstruction, its conditions contingent on taking oath of loyalty to the Union

1864
February
20/Battle of Olustee (Florida)

24/U.S. Congress votes to compensate Union slaveholders whose slaves serve in the army. After service the slaves would be free. The same act also makes Blacks subject to the draft.

March
9/U.S. Grant named lieutenant-general and the next day takes command of Union Armies

18/Constitution ending slavery ratified in Arkansas

April
8/U.S. Senate passes Thirteenth Amendment with a vote of 38 - 6

13/Massacre at Fort Pillow (Kentucky)

18/Battle of Poison Springs (Arkansas)

June
15/U.S. House votes on Thirteenth Amendment (96 - 66), but falls short of required two-thirds majority

July
8/Lincoln announces support of Thirteenth Amendment

August
10/Frederick Douglass' second meeting with Lincoln

14-18/Action of Deep Bottom, Virginia

September
2/Sherman occupies Atlanta

5/Louisiana voters ratify state constitution abolishing slavery

6/Maryland voters ratify state constitution abolishing slavery

7/Sherman orders evacuation of Atlanta

12/Gen. Lee writes Jefferson Davis that Blacks should be used in support services in the Confederate Army

National Convention of Colored Men (144 delegates from 18 states) meets at Syracuse, New York, under presidency of

Frederick Douglass to discuss forthcoming election. The chief goals desired were complete abolition of slavery and "impartial" suffrage

29-30/Battle of Chaffin's Farm, Virginia

October
13/Maryland ratifies state constitution, providing for the abolition of slavery

November
7/Jefferson Davis proposes that the Confederacy purchase slaves for army support work, freeing them on discharge

8/Lincoln re-elected

16/Sherman leaves Atlanta and begins March to the Sea

18/Jefferson Davis orders the employment of Blacks to build obstructions to Sherman's march

30/Battle of Honey Hill, SC

December
6/In Annual Message to U.S. Congress Lincoln asks for reconsideration of Thirteenth Amendment

1865

January
6/Debate begun on the Thirteenth Amendment in the House of Representatives

31/House passes Thirteenth Amendment by required majority (119 - 56). Robert E. Lee named General-in-Chief of the Confederate armies

February
1/Illinois ratifies Thirteenth Amendment

3/Hampton Roads Conference: meeting of Lincoln with three Confederate Commissioners. The meeting was unproductive

March
4/Second Inauguration of Lincoln

5-7/Battle of Hatcher's Run, Virginia

13/Confederate Congress approves recruitment of Black soldiers; signed promptly by Jefferson Davis. Some troops were enlisted under this act.

April
2/Confederate government abandons Richmond

3/Union troops occupy Richmond

4/Lincoln visits Richmond; sees Black Union soldiers

9/Lee surrenders to Grant at Appomattox

12/Surrender of Mobile

14/Lincoln shot

U.S. flag raised over Fort Sumter

15/Death of Lincoln: Andrew Johnson succeeds as President

19/Funeral of President Lincoln

May
10/Capture of Jefferson Davis

12/Gen. O.O. Howard named to head the Freedman's Bureau

23-24/Grand Armies pass in review in Washington

29/President Johnson declares a general amnesty, allowing

for a few exceptions who could, however, expect clemency

December
18/Thirteenth Amendment declared ratified after approval by twenty-seven states. (Delaware, Kentucky, New Jersey and Mississippi reject the amendment.)

BIBLIOGRAPHY

BIBLIOGRAPHY

SOURCES

William Wells Brown. *The Negro in the American Rebellion*. Boston: Lee and Shepard, 1867; Repr. New York: The Citadel Press, 1971. Introduction and annotations by William Edward Farrison.

Frederick Douglass Archives, Library of Congress.

The Journal of Charlotte L. Forten, edited by Ray Allen Billington. New York: Dryden, 1953; Collier, 1961.

John Mercer Langston. *From the Virginia Plantation to the National Capitol*. Hartford, Conn.: American Pub. Co., 1894; Repr. New York: Kraus, 1969.

Frank A. Rollin (Francis Anne Rollin). *Life and Public Services of Martin E. Delany*. Boston: Lee and Shepard, 1868; 1883. Repr. New York: Arno, 1969.

Susie King Taylor. *Reminiscences of My Life in Camp*. Boston: The Author, 1902; Repr. New York: Arno, 1960.

Joseph T. Wilson. *The Black Phalanx*. Hartford, Conn.: American Pub. Co., 1890; Repr. New York: Arno, 1968.

George W. Williams. *A History of Negro Troops in the War of the Rebellion: 1861–1865*. New York: Harper, 1888; Repr. New York: Kraus 1969.

STUDIES

Henry Steele Commager. *The Blue and the Gray*. New York: The Fairfax Press, 1982 (orig. 1950).

Dudley Taylor Cornish, *The Sable Arm: Negro Troops in the Union Army, 1861–1865*, New York: Longmans, Green and Co., 1956; Repr. University Press of Kansas, 1987.

W.E.B. Du Bois. *Black Reconstruction in America*. New York: Harcourt Brace and Co., 1935.

William Edward Farrison. *William Wells Brown: Author and Reformer*. Chicago: University of Chicago Press, 1969.

John Hope Franklin. *The Emancipation Proclamation*. Garden City, New York: Doubleday, 1963.

_____. *George Washington Williams*. Chicago: University of Chicago Press, 1985.

_____. *The Militant South: 1800-1861*. Cambridge: Harvard University Press, 1956; Boston: Beacon Press, 1964.

E.B. Long. *The Civil War Day by Day*. Garden City, New York: Doubleday, 1971.

James M. McPherson. *The Negro's Civil War*. New York: Vintage Books, 1965.

Benjamin Quarles. *Black Abolitionists*. New York: Oxford University Press, 1969.

_____. *Frederick Douglass*. Washington, D.C.: Associated Publishers, 1948; Repr. New York: Atheneum, 1969.

_____. *The Negro in the Civil War*. Boston: Little, Brown, 1953.

Willie Lee Rose. *Rehearsal for Reconstruction: The Port Royal Experiment*. New York: Vintage Books, 1964.

Bell Irvin Wiley. *Southern Negroes: 1861-1865*. New Haven, Conn.: Yale University Press, 1938.